Macedonio Fernández

Macedonio Fernández

Between Literature, Philosophy, and the Avant-Garde

Edited by

Federico Fridman

BLOOMSBURY ACADEMIC
NEW YORK • LONDON • OXFORD • NEW DELHI • SYDNEY

BLOOMSBURY ACADEMIC
Bloomsbury Publishing Inc
1385 Broadway, New York, NY 10018, USA
50 Bedford Square, London, WC1B 3DP, UK
29 Earlsfort Terrace, Dublin 2, Ireland

BLOOMSBURY, BLOOMSBURY ACADEMIC and the Diana logo are trademarks of Bloomsbury Publishing Plc

First published in the United States of America 2022
This paperback edition published 2023

Copyright © Federico Fridman, 2022
Each chapter © of Contributors

For legal purposes the Acknowledgments on pp. ix–x constitute an extension of this copyright page.

Cover design: Eleanor Rose
Cover illustration: Arquicaricatura of Macedonio Fernández by Dardo Salguero Dela-Hatty, 1924. Courtesy Museo de San José

All rights reserved. No part of this publication may be reproduced or transmitted in any form or by any means, electronic or mechanical, including photocopying, recording, or any information storage or retrieval system, without prior permission in writing from the publishers.

Bloomsbury Publishing Inc does not have any control over, or responsibility for, any third-party websites referred to or in this book. All internet addresses given in this book were correct at the time of going to press. The author and publisher regret any inconvenience caused if addresses have changed or sites have ceased to exist, but can accept no responsibility for any such changes.

A catalog record for this book is available from the Library of Congress.

Names: Fridman, Federico, editor.
Title: Macedonio Fernández: between literature, philosophy, and the avant-garde / edited by Federico Fridman.
Description: New York: Bloomsbury Academic, 2022. | Includes bibliographical references and index.
Identifiers: LCCN 2021023832 (print) | LCCN 2021023833 (ebook) | ISBN 9781501384226 (hardback) | ISBN 9781501384233 (epub) | ISBN 9781501384240 (pdf) | ISBN 9781501384257
Subjects: LCSH: Fernández, Macedonio, 1874-1952–Criticism and interpretation. | LCGFT: Literary criticism.
Classification: LCC PQ7797.F312 Z76 2022 (print) | LCC PQ7797.F312 (ebook) | DDC 863/.62–dc23/eng/20211005
LC record available at https://lccn.loc.gov/2021023832
LC ebook record available at https://lccn.loc.gov/2021023833

ISBN: HB: 978-1-5013-8422-6
PB: 978-1-5013-8426-4
ePDF: 978-1-5013-8424-0
eBook: 978-1-5013-8423-3

Typeset by Integra Software Services Pvt. Ltd.

To find out more about our authors and books visit www.bloomsbury.com and sign up for our newsletters.

No creo que la Metafísica sea el placer directo de una explicación: es un trabajo que tiene el placer reflejo de una perspectiva de poder; es un poder lo que se busca; un poder directo del amor; que éste pueda ser causa inmediata.

(I do not believe Metaphysics to be the direct pleasure of an explanation: it is an effort that has the reflex pleasure of a perspective of power; power is what one is looking for; the direct power of love; that this could be an immediate cause).
                    Macedonio Fernández

Contents

Acknowledgments   ix
List of Abbreviations   xi

Introduction   *Federico Fridman*   1

Part 1   Life and Literature at the Edge

1. Jorge Luis Borges and Macedonio Fernández: History of a Literary Friendship   *Mónica Bueno*   23
2. Heroes without Selves: Macedonio Fernández and a New Ethics of the Heroic   *Todd S. Garth*   43
3. Consuelo-Eterna, Macedonio's Erotic and Metaphysical Passion   *Ana Camblong*   61
4. Macedonio Fernández's Neighborhood Metaphysics: *Belarte*, the Fool of Buenos Aires, and the Evidential Siesta   *Gonzalo S. Aguirre*   81

Part 2   Philosophy, Affects, and Politics

5. Macedonio Fernández: The First Egocide in the Río de la Plata   *Diego Vecchio*   101
6. A Metaphysics That Only Begins: On Macedonio's Writing Passion   *Julio Prieto*   121
7. Songs Without a Self: Macedonio's Anarchist Aesthetics   *Luis Othoniel Rosa*   141
8. The Thought of Macedonio Fernández: A Dictionary   *Daniel Attala*   157

Part 3   Metaphysics on the Move

9. Notes on Macedonio in a Diary   *Ricardo Piglia*   181
10. What Is Believing?   *Horacio González*   189
11. No hay proa sin popa   *Liliana Weinberg*   195

Notes on Contributors 205
Bibliography 209
Index 225

Acknowledgments

The collective nature of an edited collection always depends on combining the authors' effort, time, energy, and their passion to converge together in a single book. In this case, however, the sense of a collective project that introduces essays on Macedonio Fernández, who advocated for collective and creative appropriations of his own work, achieves a fundamental meaning dwelling at the heart of Macedonio's thought. Therefore, I would like to thank the contributors for entrusting me their work and allowing me to articulate their texts illuminating communicating vessels among them. I would like to especially thank Julio Prieto for reading drafts of the Introduction and providing me with crucial feedback, and Todd Garth for reviewing translations from both Macedonio's texts and the English version of essays originally written in Spanish. I would also like to express my gratitude to Sean Manning, who translated several chapters for this book, and to Amy Martin, Assistant Acquisitions Editor at Bloomsbury, who assisted me in navigating the production and publication process. Their relentless work and support at every stage was critical in assembling this book. I also want to acknowledge the Museum of San José in Uruguay for allowing me to use Dardo Salguero Dela Hanty's drawing, *Arquicaricatura* (Archicaricature) *of Macedonia Fernández* (1924) for the book cover, and in particular Julia Sierra from the museum for aiding me to receive their authorization.

Thanks are also due to the University of Michigan, Ann Arbor, and the Department of Romance Languages and Literatures for being a welcoming environment during times of uncertainty and during the last stage of editing this book. I would also like to express my immense gratitude to my former institution Oberlin College. In 2018, I received a grant from Oberlin to fund translations for the book, which allowed me to invite prominent scholars whose work could not have otherwise been made available in English. Finally, I would like to remember that the kernel of this project started to germinate in a seminar we organized titled "Macedonio Fernández's Metaphysics: An Affect Theory" at the American Comparative Literature Association's 2017 conference held at Utrecht University. Specialists from the USA, Latin America, and Europe gathered for a three-day roundtable to engage in dialogue and collaboration to further develop their critical engagement with the writings of Macedonio.

The book embodies the intensity of the conversations that began at the ACLA conference, and seeks to configure a network of specialists and new readers of Macedonio Fernández's work.

"Notes on Macedonio in a Diary" by Ricardo Piglia is translated by Sean Manning and included with permission. © Herederos de Ricardo Piglia, c/o Schavelzon Graham Agencia Literaria, www.schavelzongraham.com.

Abbreviations

Frequently cited works by Macedonio Fernández are referred to using the following abbreviations. The editions listed below follow the original title and chronological order in which they were published for the first time.

NTV: *No toda es vigilia la de los ojos abiertos* (Not All Wakefulness Is with Open Eyes), Buenos Aires: Manuel Gleizer, 1928.

PR: *Papeles de recienvenido* (The Newcomer Papers), Buenos Aires: Editorial Proa, 1930.

UNC: *Una novela que comienza* (A Novel that Begins), Santiago de Chile: Ercilla, 1940.

PRC: *Papeles de Recienvenido y continuación de la nada* (The Newcomer Papers and the Continuation of Nothingness), Buenos Aires: Editorial Losada, 1944.

MNE: *Museo de la novela de la Eterna (Primera novela buena)* (*The Museum of Eterna's Novel (The First Good Novel)*), Obieta, A. (ed.), Buenos Aires: CEAL, 1967.

CTN: *Cuadernos de todo y nada* (*Notebooks of Everything and Nothing*), Obieta, A. (ed.) Buenos Aires: Corregidor, 1972.

T: *Teorías, Obras completas* (*Complete Works*), vol. 3, Obieta, A. (ed.), Buenos Aires: Corregidor, 1974.

ABA: *Adriana Buenos Aires (última novela mala)* (*Adriana Buenos Aires (The Last Bad Novel)*), *Obras completas*, vol. 5, Obieta, A. (ed.), Buenos Aires: Corregidor, 1974.

E: *Epistolario* (Epistolary), *Obras completas*, vol. 2, Borinsky, A. (ed.), Buenos Aires: Corregidor, 1976.

PA: *Papeles antiguos* (Old Papers), *Obras completas*, vol. 1, Obieta, A. (ed.), Buenos Aires: Corregidor, 1981.

R: *Relato (cuentos, poemas y misceláneas)* (Story (short stories, poems and miscellaneous), *Obras completas*, vol. 7, Obieta, A. (ed.), Buenos Aires: Corregidor, 1987.

Introduction

Federico Fridman

On March 24, 1921, Macedonio Fernández left his room at a boarding house in the Balvanera neighborhood of downtown Buenos Aires and headed for *Dársena Norte*, the north dock where the passenger ships arrived. After seven years in Europe, an old friend and his family were returning home. Maybe he took the tram or the metro to *El Bajo*, the city's shore along the Río de la Plata. Buenos Aires had changed drastically during the last few years. The incessant flow of immigrants from Europe and a booming economy had raised a modern, dynamic, and cosmopolitan city in the pampas. Nevertheless, one would like to imagine that to reach the river, Fernández, or Macedonio as he is commonly known, decided to walk through the heart of the city, among the Government House and other state buildings, and the various cultural, religious, and financial institutions still standing there to this day. His writing and the movement of the characters that dwell inside it embrace a particular way of roaming the city, skipping social and cultural conventions to elude capture by the state apparatus and reveal its distorted foundation.[1]

What path might Macedonio have taken that day? Did he stop off briefly at a bar in the working-/middle-class and immigrant neighborhood where he had recently chosen to live? Or, did he visit a coffee shop on busy Florida Street, where maybe he encountered a former colleague or a friend from one of the upper-bourgeoisie and patrician families, whom he knew very well and with whom he had family ties and personal connections? Did he walk through Congress Square to laugh at the colossal statue commemorating the first National Assemblies?

---

[1] It is impossible to pinpoint the exact moment when his first name began to overshadow his last. One would presume that at some point his commonplace *criollo* family name was insufficient for transmitting the singularity of his persona. In Hispanic criticism and the Spanish-speaking academic world he is known as Macedonio, and the authors included in this book refer to him using either one or the other. For all bibliographic references, see Fernández.

Did the statue of Mariano Moreno situated in a small adjacent square remind him of his claim that these monuments only served to convey the tragic stories, bloody battles, and sad affections on which the country had been founded?[2] And after his friend's ship reached the port, did he spend time with him and his family at their house in the Palermo neighborhood, perhaps staying for light refreshments? It is impossible to trace Macedonio's exact route that special day, but the same is also true for all the days before and all those thereafter.

The scarce information regarding Macedonio's life has rendered reassembling a complete biography an impossible task.[3] He cultivated an anonymous existence and expressed, with acute wittiness and irony, his disdain for public recognition. He freed himself from social obligations and formalities. He often forgot invitations to attend public events or sent a written apology to be read aloud in his absence, although he might have been there sitting in a corner.[4] In his texts, this fading presence becomes paradoxically visible through an experimental form of writing intended to dislocate the conventional idea that the author is the origin of the enunciation, undermining a representational form of thought wherein fiction is distinct from reality.

The anecdotes about Macedonio recounted by others sketched the contours of his elusive figure and fostered his mythological representation.[5] One of the passengers whom Macedonio went to receive that day, a young Jorge Luis Borges, remembers him waiting alone at the dock:

---

[2] Mariano Moreno (1778–1811), an intellectual and a political leader of Argentina's independence movement, advocated for a radical revolution of the southern colonies to sever ties with Spain. In 1811, Moreno died in obscure circumstances while traveling for a diplomatic mission to Europe and was buried at sea (see Goldman, *Mariano Moreno*). Macedonio despised statues because they communicated sad affections and static experiences. In *PR*, he claims: "Aborrezco las estatuas: casi siempre son hombres con sobretodo griego, o amplia levita de mármol. [...] son intolerables, y todo para que un hombre esté allí asegurándonos con su mano y su boca que nos va a decir cosas elocuentes y no se le oye en todo el día" (I abhor statues: they are almost always men donning a Greek overcoat, or oversized marble frock-coat. [...] they are insufferable, and all so that a man can stand there persuading us with his hand and mouth that he will soon utter eloquent things, and yet nothing is heard from him all day) (1989, 13). All translations are mine, unless otherwise indicated.

[3] See Abós, *Macedonio Fernández. La biografía imposible* (The Impossible Biography). Nevertheless, we should consider that every biography is a partial glimpse of a person's life journey. The difficulty of reassembling an individual's biography does not mean this challenge could be overcome merely by piecing together the fragments of a life as if doing so would project a complete image of an individual history. In Macedonio's case, as we shall later see, this attempt has faced even more difficult obstacles.

[4] In the prologue for a new edition of Macedonio's book *PRC* in 1944, Ramón Gómez de la Serna mentions how Macedonio frequently avoided public events and the humorous interventions he staged to do so (7–46).

[5] See Obieta, *Hablan de Macedonio Fernández*.

Perhaps, the most important event when I came back [to Buenos Aires] was meeting Macedonio Fernández. Of all the people whom I have met in my life, nobody made such a deep and lasting impression on me as he did. When we disembarked at the *Dársena Norte*, he was there waiting for us, with his tiny figure and his black derby, and ultimately, I would inherit his friendship from my father.[6]

Borges has been particularly decisive in shaping the myth projected by his friend and mentor.[7] The two first met at the *tertulias* his father, Jorge Guillermo Borges, organized at the family's home when Borges was just a boy, and they remained in contact throughout the family trip to Europe, when the young literary-minded Borges had already published essays, poems, short stories, and several translations.[8]

The performative power of literature and its ability to transform politics seem to have been the initial interests that drew them together and cultivated their intellectual affinities.[9] Although Borges would eventually distance himself from the idea of literature's performativity, he always remembered the strong impact Macedonio's personality had had on him and praised him as his great teacher. At Macedonio's funeral in 1952, he delivered the following tribute: "In those years I imitated him to the point of transcription, to the point of devout and passionate plagiarism. I felt: Macedonio *is* metaphysics, Macedonio *is* literature. Those who preceded him may shine in history, but they were drafts of Macedonio, imperfect and preliminary versions. Not to imitate that canon would have been incredibly

---

[6] "Quizás el mayor acontecimiento de mi regreso fue Macedonio Fernández. De toda la gente que he conocido en mi vida [...] nadie me ha dejado una impresión tan profunda y duradera como Macedonio. Cuando desembarcamos en la Dársena Norte estaba esperándonos con su figura diminuta y su bombín negro, y terminé heredando de mi padre su amistad" (*Autobiografía*, 70).

[7] Todd S. Garth has studied this topic in particular in his article "Confused Oratory," 350-70.

[8] Macedonio met Jorge Guillermo Borges (the writer's father) while both of them were in law school. After their graduation Macedonio embarked with two other friends, Julio Molina y Vedia and Arturo Múscari, on a ship going up the Paraná River to Paraguay. Their plan was to found an anarchist utopian community. Allegedly, the plan failed due to the inclemency of the jungle, but Macedonio and his friends never denied their participation in this project and contributed to spreading the legend of their journey. See Abós, *Macedonio*, 39-51.

[9] See C. García, *Correspondencia*, 31. At the beginning of the 1920s, Macedonio conceived a conspiracy to become the president of Argentina; his intimate circle of friends actually considered this a possibility and spread the idea. This presidential scheme may have initially sought to achieve only a marginal effect (its actual range and circumstances still being a point of contention among critics), but the machination was a caricature that served to criticize the social and political system. See González, *Filosofía de la conspiración*; Piglia *Crítica y ficción*; and *Teoría del complot*; Prieto, *Desencuadernados*, 61-73; and *De la sombrología*, 61-7, 93-7. In his anthology *Macedonio Fernández* (1961), Borges says that the group's project also consisted of collectively writing a fantastic novel set in Buenos Aires, titled "The Man Who Will be President" (18).

negligent."[10] However, time and time again Borges referred to him as a thinker who could not translate his oratorial geniality into written intelligibility.[11]

The encounter between Macedonio and Borges in 1921 coincided with another event in his life that has also been pivotal in constructing the Macedonian myth. A few months earlier, Macedonio's wife, Elena de Obieta, unexpectedly died from a botched abdominal surgery, an experience he captured and immortalized in his acclaimed eulogy "Elena Bellamuerte" (Elena Beautiful Death).[12] Macedonio had been a well-established lawyer for twenty-five years, never feeling much enthusiasm for the profession, and when she died, he resigned and left his four children with their extended family. Although he maintained a close relationship with them, he adopted a nomadic lifestyle, moving from one place to another, almost never leaving the city and staying in the suburbs for short periods of time.

The convergence of his relationship with Borges and the death of Elena resulted in the dual origin that set in motion the myth of Macedonio: the metaphysician and genius thinker who, after losing his wife, withdrew from public circles and focused his attention on writing his poetry and his ruminations on the immortality of the soul, carelessly leaving his notes, papers, and manuscripts strewn behind him as he moved from one address to another.[13] Only at the insistence of friends did he decide to publish fragments from his poems and essays, and after Macedonio's death in 1952, it was his son, Adolfo de Obieta, who undertook the task of editing his father's handwriting and manuscripts, assigning them dates of composition, and publishing the bulk of his work.[14]

---

[10] "[...] Yo por aquellos años lo imité, hasta la transcripción, hasta el apasionado y devoto plagio. Yo sentía: Macedonio es la metafísica, es la literatura. Quienes lo precedieron pueden resplandecer en la historia, pero eran borradores de Macedonio, versiones imperfectas y previas. No imitar ese canon hubiera sido una negligencia increíble[...]" ("Macedonio Fernández," *Sur*, 146).

[11] Beatriz Sarlo has analyzed Borges's strategic aesthetic and ideological maneuverings to transform a marginal writer at the time such as Macedonio into the center of his system of thought ("Vanguardia y criollismo," 127–71). See also Camblong, "De Macedonio a Borges," 35–60; and G. García, "Duelo imposible," 69–94; Garth, "Confused Oratory;" Bueno, *Macedonio*; Prieto, *Desencuadernados* and "La inquietante extrañeza de la autoría," 475–504.

[12] See Fernández, *Relato. Cuentos, poemas y misceláneas*, 99–103.

[13] In this sense, Borges writes: "Macedonio gave not the least value to his written word; upon changing lodgings, he did not take with him the literary and metaphysical manuscripts that had piled up on the table and that filled trunks and cabinets. Much was lost that way, perhaps irrevocably [...]" (*Macedonio*, 15). Garth adds: "Adolfo de Obieta also often mentioned his father's lack of initiative to publish and his tendency to lose or discard his own writings; [...] But to dismiss the necessity of publishing one's words is not the same as disdaining one's writing" ("Confused Oratory," 366).

[14] For a chronological analysis of Macedonio's production, see N. Salvador, "Cronología," in *MNE* (1993, 341–61); and C. García, *Correspondencia, 1922-1939-* 261–96. For a meticulous analysis of the multiple changes that Macedonio and/or his son might have introduced in the new editions of previous texts, see C. García, "Arqueología."

During the 1920s, Borges actively participated in the formation of avant-garde literary groups, introducing Macedonio to these circles and publishing his work in their journals, while assuming a leading role in staging an intervention in the cultural scene. The new generation of writers—Oliverio Girondo, Raúl González Tuñón, and Leopoldo Marechal, among others—challenged the previous generation of intellectuals and their cultural institutions, which were influenced by Leopoldo Lugones and his *modernista* aesthetic.[15] Consequently, they created new journals for their work: *Prisma* (1921), *Inicial* (1923), *Proa* (1922), *Martin Fierro* (1924), and *Oral* (1925). Macedonio became an assiduous contributor. They promoted him as a mythical figure whom they believed could oppose Lugones. Macedonio's thinking, which he preferred to communicate through subterranean and hermetic oral narratives within a closed circle of friends, strengthened the young writers' imagination and inspired their plans to subvert the intellectual elite from the periphery of the cultural milieu.[16]

Nevertheless, for scholars, Macedonio's relationship with these groups is still a controversial topic that will perhaps only be resolved once his book notes are finally published, his letters currently in private collections are made available to the public, and rigorous research is conducted to retrieve the traces of his trajectory. On the one hand, in Macedonio's texts we can analyze the meaningful dialogues he established with the avant-gardes and his ongoing conversations with Borges that call into question the idea that the mentor/disciple binary only entails an unequivocal influence of the former over the latter.[17] Furthermore, an

---

[15] For an analysis of avant-garde groups in this context, see Barletta, *Boedo y Florida*; Masiello, *Lenguaje e ideología*; Sarlo, *Borges, un escritor en las orillas* and "Vanguardia y criollismo," 39–69; Gilman, "Florida y Boedo," 44–62; Montaldo, "El origen de la historia," 24–9; and Muñoz, "Macedonio Fernández y las vanguardias estéticas."

[16] Prieto has pointed out the ex-centric position that Macedonio occupied in this cultural milieu. He claims that his writings, "embody a discursive mode more faithful to the avant-garde 'spirit,' regarding his criticism of the literary tradition, than the critique of his contemporary rioplatenses, and relatively unfaithful to their local demonstrations and manifests, which wave, as a group, the flag of avant-gardism and move it toward a 'moderate' direction" (*Desencuadernados*, 25). Garth also claims: "Macedonio's poetics in many ways coincide much more closely with the principle of the historical avant-garde in Europe, at least when viewed retrospectively. That kinship with European movements is a result of Macedonio's faith in the relationship between art and daily life more than an adherence to aesthetic programs" (*The Self*, 48).

[17] In this sense, it interesting to consider Macedonio's own words: "Por culpa de la juventud artística de Buenos Aires, que conocí hace cuatro años, estoy abismado en un problema de estética. Me desvalijaron por aquel entonces con tanta prolijidad e inmenso provecho de mi estética pasatista que hasta la fecha no he podido recuperar una ignorancia igual" (The artistic youth of Buenos Aires, whom I met four years ago, should be blamed for my immersion in an aesthetic problem. They robbed me at that time with such neatness and immense profit from my pasatist aesthetic that until today I have not been able to recover an equal ignorance) (in R. Gómez de la Serna, "Macedonio Fernández," 172). Also see Prieto, *Desencuadernados*, 109–50; "La inquietante extrañeza;" and *De la sombrología*, 32–5.

examination of the cultural and literary journals edited by the young writers shows an intense fusion between Macedonio's thinking and the aesthetic project of the avant-gardes during the 1920s. However, on the other hand, his relationship with these groups has often been oversimplified to argue that the young writers served as his catalyst to become a literary writer, although there was in fact a bitter dispute in 1928 between the circles around Borges and Macedonio regarding the problematic continuities between the literary and intellectual production of both writers.[18]

The authors included in this book represent both of the positions schematically presented above. However, they all agree that the creation of Macedonio as a mythical figure has involved a reduction of the many origins and sources of his complex life journey and creative process, and that this myth has tended to preclude an in-depth analysis of his writings. Each chapter pulls back a portion of the veil that has kept his texts in the shadows, enabling new light to shine upon them. As a whole, they coalesce, drafting road maps that lead into the depths of Macedonio's work, expounding the meticulously articulated lines of thought that ramify throughout his philosophy, metaphysics, ethics, and aesthetic. This book has been conceived as both a companion for readers who would venture into Macedonio's writings for the first time and as an invitation for specialists to revisit his work through new perspectives. With this in mind, each chapter provides extensive background and bibliographical references, as well as English translations of Macedonio's original texts, allowing them to be read independently or following the book's structure down the multiple avenues of analysis the authors have paved.

The book comprises eleven chapters, organized into three Parts. The first Part, "Life and Literature at the Edge," presents chapters by Mónica Bueno, Todd S. Garth, Ana Camblong, and Gonzalo S. Aguirre. In these chapters, the authors intertwine various aspects of Macedonio's life and location in Buenos Aires, including his position in its cultural and social milieu and his relationship with Borges, particularly with regard to central ideas in their thought. They reveal the groundwork on which Macedonio developed his writing and demonstrate the centrality that the city and its people (*porteños*) occupied in his oeuvre. In an effort to demystify his figure and recuperate his writings, the authors trace the

---

[18] See Attala, "De la metafísica de la afección al personaje," 107–22. C. García explains that Guillermo de Torre (Borges's brother-in-law) initiated this controversy with his article "Buenos Aires, literatura" in *La Gaceta Literaria* (Madrid) in which he addresses Macedonio's writing style in a disdainful manner. Marechal, who had become a close friend of Macedonio, then wrote "Recriminó a De Torre," which is a radical defense of his friend. He suggests to De Torre that he should look closer to his own inner circle to understand the deep influence that Macedonio as a "spiritual father" has on the new generations of writers, tacitly implying that Borges was one of the authors who was more receptive to this influence ("Borges y Macedonio, un incidente de 1928," 59–66).

extent to which his personal and intellectual relationships, his way of being in the city, or his visions of an alternative future are inscribed in his texts. They also examine the prolific link his metaphysical reflections forge in his philosophical and literary works between his space and those who inhabit it.

The second Part, "Philosophy, Affects, and Politics," assembles essays dedicated to Macedonio's call for the radical overhaul of Western philosophical tradition and his assailing of two of its fundamental pillars: the Cartesian subject and Kant's moral philosophy. Authors Diego Vecchio, Julio Prieto, Luis Othoniel Rosa, and Daniel Attala examine the critical dialogues that Macedonio established with the history of philosophy, while tracing resonances between his work and a genealogy of thinkers that includes Spinoza, Schopenhauer, Kierkegaard, Nietzsche, Benjamin, and others. In addition, they analyze points of convergence or divergence between his thought and intellectual trends during the first decades of the twentieth century, and articulate contemporary theory to illuminate how his theories and metaphysics anticipated main questions that have arisen in recent debates. Moreover, this Part invites us to consider how Macedonio's work might polish new lenses through which to engage with literary and political theory, cultural studies, and philosophy, and especially, how his ethics and political thought can assist us in questioning our present and historical conditions.

The final Part, "Metaphysics on the Move," includes essays by Ricardo Piglia, Horacio González, and Liliana Weinberg. Macedonio's aesthetic and philosophical project urges future readers and new writers to appropriate and reshape his ideas, theoretical principles, and artistic techniques to lend continuity to a never-ending process of reading and rewriting. In particular, Piglia and González have furthered and intensified this project in their own literary and intellectual production. While Piglia's work has been integral to rearticulating the literary canon to include Macedonio, extending his reception beyond the Argentinean context, González's scholarship has offered interdisciplinary studies on Macedonio that integrate the complexity of his philosophical thought with his aesthetic project and positioning in his historical context.[19] Weinberg's research

---

[19] Piglia's scholarly work on Macedonio can be found in *Teoría del complot* and *Crítica y ficción*, while his literary production is permeated by Macedonio's thought. For instance, Macedonio's fundamental literary tropes are the clear source of inspiration for his acclaimed novel *La ciudad ausente* (1992) (*The Absent City* (2000)). In 2000, Piglia also co-edited the *Diccionario de La novela de Macedonio Fernández*. Horacio González published multiple articles on Macedonio Fernández, and his interdisciplinary research on this author is collected in his book *El filósofo cesante* (1995). He also dedicated several articles and books to Macedonio's contemporaries such as Roberto Arlt and Ezequiel Martínez Estrada; see *Arlt, Política y locura* (1996) and *Restos pameanos* (1999).

on fundamental Latin American essayists has also been crucial in rebuilding not only the constellation of Macedonio's contemporary authors in the region, but also in restoring the singularities and multiple, complex dimensions of this literary genre, especially in the Latin American context. She reveals this perspective to be key in analyzing the theoretical and aesthetic operations that Macedonio developed, and how they were creatively amplified by the avant-gardes.[20]

The present book comprehends a historical arch of Macedonio's intellectual and literary production that begins at the end of the nineteenth century when a young Macedonio had already begun publishing articles that expressed the seeds of his incipient anarchist ideas.[21] Although he published only a few essays and poems during the first two decades of the following century, he continued to write his ruminations on metaphysics and delineate its principles. He had also already initiated his explorations into the structure of the psyche, which he would later elaborate in his theory of the selfless soul. These texts, along with others written between 1896 and 1950, were included in subsequent expanded editions of his first book *No toda es vigilia la de los ojos abiertos* (Not All Wakefulness Is with Open Eyes), which was originally published in 1928.[22] The philosophical essays in this monograph show how in his first published book Macedonio produces a collage that does not follow one unifying concept, but rather myriad theoretical arguments that also highlight literary elements not present in his previous work.[23]

---

[20] Weinberg's exhaustive and comprehensive research on Latin American essayists and writers can be found in *El ensayo en busca del sentido* (2001), *El ensayo, entre el paraíso y el infierno* (2004), *Literatura Latinoamericana: Descolonizar la imaginación* (2014), among several other of her books, articles, and essays.

[21] The first volume of Macedonio's *Obras completas*, *Papeles antiguos* (Old Papers) (1981) collects the essays he wrote and published between 1897 and 1907, which were edited and ordered by Obieta. In the essay "La desherencia" (The Disinheritance) (1887), Macedonio writes: "[C]reo que el socialismo responde muy satisfactoriamente a las pregunta económica del problema social ..." (I believe that socialism provides a satisfactory answer to the economic question of the social problem) (10). In 1925, however, he will rectify this position in an editorial note: "[E]n aquel tiempo yo era socialista y materialista, hoy soy anarquista spenceriano y místico" (At that time I was a socialist and materialist, I am today a Spencerian anarchist and mystic) (*PR*, 1989, 45). This affirmation has prompted another intense controversy among different scholars. Luis Othoniel Rosa has particularly tackled this issue in his book *Comienzos para una estética anarquista* (2016).

[22] The original complete title of Macedonio's first book is *No toda es vigilia la de los ojos abiertos: arreglo de papeles que dejó un personaje de novela creado por el arte, Deunamor, el No-Existente Caballero, el estudioso de su esperanza* (Not All Wakefulness Is with Open Eyes: An Arrangement of Papers Left by a Novelistic Character Created by Art, One-Love, the Nonexistent Gentleman, a Scholar of His Hope) (Gleizer, 1928).

[23] Attala has pointed out the inclusion of literary elements in Macedonio's metaphysical treatise and problematized this transition in his production (see "De la metafísica"). Raúl Scalabrini Ortiz, one of Macedonio close friends, defined *NTV* as an "esoteric bible of the porteño spirit" (*El hombre que está solo y espera* (1931), 123).

Macedonio's second book *Papeles de recienvenido* (The Newcomer Papers) (1930) presents a step forward in his quest for a form of written expression capable of setting his metaphysical premises in motion. The book, whose title comes from a short piece he wrote in 1923, compiles essays published during the 1920s in the journals *Martín Fierro* and *Proa*, which were edited by Borges and his circle of writers.[24] The epithet "newcomer" was applicable to Macedonio who, already in his forties at the time, was himself a late arrival in the literary and cultural scene. Furthermore, it paralleled the idea of the foreigner arriving in the city, particularly resonant with his historical context, leading him to transmute this term into a literary trope for the creation of an artistic and humorous character invested with metaphysical ontological status: the *Recienvenido* (Newcomer). His development in Macedonio's texts allowed the author to articulate philosophical ideas, jokes, and literary narratives as he cultivated his metaphysical reflections.

It is also quite possible that instead of a collection of previously published essays, Macedonio's intention was to release his first novel, which he often publicized as nearly concluded and pledged would be available in print in the near future. By the end of the 1920s, his magnum opus *Museo de la novela de la Eterna (Primera novela buena)* (*The Museum of Eterna's Novel (The First Good Novel)*) had already started to germinate in a short fragment he published in 1929.[25] However, the novel remained a work in progress. He continued writing it until his death in 1952, and it was published posthumously in 1967. It would later be translated into English, French, Italian, Portuguese, and German.[26]

---

[24] See Fernández, "El recien venido (fragmento)," *Proa*, no. 3 (July 1923): 3–4; and also Borges, "Macedonio Fernández—El Recién venido—inédito aún," included in the same issue, 2. In 1944, a new edition of *PR* was published, which also included *Continuación de la nada* (The Continuation of Nothingness) (Buenos Aires: Losada). Borinsky has analyzed continuities between *NTV* and *PR*, as she argues that in the latter book Macedonio sought to elaborate theoretical and aesthetics answers to the queries posed by his previous book; see "Correspondencia," 101–23.

[25] In *NTV*, Macedonio left traces that may be interpreted as strategic advertising for his forthcoming novel when he says: "Lee mi 'Conclusión'; y no te preocupe el enredo de personajes aquí: es en vista de futura obra" (Read my Conclusion and don't worry about the entanglement of characters here: it is foreshadowing a future work) (1990, 232). In 1929, he also published in the journal *Libra*, "Novela de la 'Eterna' y la Niña de dolor, la 'Dulce-Persona' de un amor que no fue sabido" (Eterna's Novel and the Suffering Girl, the "Sweet-Person" of an Unknown Love) (34–46), which would later be included in the prologues of *MNE*. In 1941, he published *Una novela que comienza* (A Novel that Begins) in Chile, which as Jo Anne Engelbert has claimed was a clear anticipation of *MNE*; see Fernández, *UNC* (Santiago de Chile: Ercilla, 1941); and Engelbert, "El proyecto narrativo de Macedonio" (Macedonio's narrative project) in *MNE* (1993), 373–91.

[26] See Fabio Rodríguez Amaya, *Museo del romanzo della Eterna* (Genova: Il Nuovo Melangolo, 1992); Jean-Claude Masson, *Musée du roman de l'Éternelle* (Gallimard, 1993); Margaret Schwartz, *The Museum of Eterna's Novel* (Rochester: Open Letter, 2010); Gênese Andrade, *Museu do romance da eterna* (São Paulo: Cosac Naify, 2010); Petra Strien-Bourmer, *Das Museum von Eternas Roman* (Berlin: AB Die Andere Bibliothek, 2014).

Fifty-six prologues precede the beginning of the story, each one functioning as an independent series that at some point intersects with another, driving readers into different corners from which they can contemplate the beginning of a novel constantly postponed. Twenty chapters, four closing sections, and one dedication round out a book that deserves a place among other renowned twentieth-century works. Macedonio's experimental novel parallels Joyce's *Ulysses* (1922), his writing techniques and composition of characters are comparable to Gombrowicz's *Ferdydurke* (1937), and his perception of new forms of power and domination at the beginning of the twentieth century evokes Kafka's most acute short stories.[27]

Macedonio's initial strategy was to release two novels simultaneously as if they were conjoined twins or two facets of the same aesthetic project: *MNE* (The First Good Novel) and *Adriana Buenos Aires (última novela mala)* (Adriana Buenos Aires (The Last Bad Novel)), which he first drafted around 1922 and continued to edit until 1938. But rather than being antithetical, the two novels should be considered and read as complementary. While *ABA* is written following the institutionalized paradigm of the romantic and realist novel, *MNE* methodically undermines the idea that this literary genre has the ability to capture the metaphysical mystery and cosmic emotion of life.[28]

The books summarized above, among other essays, short stories, poems, and letters, were included in the nine volumes of *Obras completas* (Complete works) published by Ediciones Corregidor since 1974, but the bulk of Macedonio's manuscripts and notes is still waiting to be unearthed, examined, and edited. It was Obieta who initiated this process in 1964, compiling and writing the prologue for *Papeles de Macedonio Fernández* (Macedonio's Papers). He then released the first edition of *MNE* in 1967 based on a text, according to him, written in 1947, and new editions of *PR* and *NTV* were published as well. Later on, he edited the volumes for Corregidor, and a second edition of *MNE* was published in 1975.[29]

---

[27] As odd as is it may seem, Gombrowicz and Macedonio did not meet in Buenos Aires while the Polish writer was there in exile from the beginning of World War II until 1963. But Piglia asserts it is more than likely that Macedonio read *Ferdydurke*, which Gombrowicz translated into Spanish with the assistance of the Cuban poet Virgilio Piñera and a small group of young writers and linguists, among them Adolfo de Obieta; see Piglia, "¿Existe la novela Argentina? Borges y Gombrowicz;" also see Balderston, "Rex Café," 29–37.

[28] *ABA* was finally published separately in 1974, but in one of *MNE*'s prologues, "Lo que nace y lo que muere" (What Is Born and What Dies) (267–8), Macedonio clearly mentions his intentions to publish the last bad novel and the first good novel together. In the first edition of *PRC* published in 1944, he also announced the forthcoming publication of both novels. See Jitrik, *La novela futura*, 49; Pérez Melgosa, "Macedonio Fernández's Narrative Pharmakon"; Attala, *Macedonio, lector del Quijote*, 127–34; and Prieto, "*Pro cosmética* (Pro cosmetic)" and *De la sombrología*, 133–45.

[29] Obieta also published *Macedonio: Memorias errantes* (Macedonio: Wandering Memories) (1999), and German García asserts that this text could be read as a cyphered dialogue between a son and the memories of his father. See *Macedonio Fernández, la escritura en objeto* (Literature as an object), 232.

In 1993, Obieta and Ana Camblong edited a new critical edition of *MNE*, which has become the main source of reference for scholars.[30] As the director of the series *Historia crítica de la literatura argentina* (2006) (A Historical Critique of Argentinean literature), Noé Jitrik dedicated the entirety of volume eight to Macedonio, which was edited by Roberto Ferro. The more than six hundred pages of this massive volume show its dimensions and ambition to restitute Macedonio's rightful place among a fundamental genealogy of writers. It is important to note that the only other author in the series to receive similar attention was Domingo F. Sarmiento: the nineteenth-century intellectual, founding father, and president of Argentina (1868–74).[31]

Also deserving of mention here are some of the pioneers who introduced Macedonio's work to the North American academic world: Alicia Borinsky, Jo Anne Engelbert, and Naomi Lindstrom. In 1971, Borinsky published the first article to rebuild Macedonio's transatlantic network as she traces, edits, and compiles his exchange of letters with Spanish writer Ramón Gómez de La Serna. In 1972, she released an article in which she further develops her doctoral dissertation and her analysis of Macedonio's theory of the novel.[32] Engelbert furthered this first breakthrough in 1978 when she published *Macedonio Fernandez and the Spanish American New Novel*, and later in 1984 with *Macedonio: Selected Writings in Translation*, which was the first anthology to translate and publish his texts.[33] Lindstrom's book *Macedonio Fernández* (1981) confirmed scholars' increasing interest in his work, and her study of his theories, philosophy, and literature through the lens of deconstruction opened and signaled a new fertile territory for literary criticism to explore.[34]

---

[30] See Fernández, *MNE*, Nanterre: ALLCA XX, (1993). I would like to mention here Ana Camblong's lifework devoted to the rigorous study of Macedonio's oeuvre. Her books and multiple articles, among them, *Macedonio. Retórica y política de los discursos paradójicos* (2002) and *Ensayos macedonianos* (2006), have become canonical references.

[31] See Jitrik, ed., *Historia crítica de la literatura argentina*, vol. 4. Contributors include: Julio Premat, Germán García, J. Prieto, M. Bueno, Marisa A. Muñoz, Raúl O. Cadús, Isabel Stratta, Alicia Borinsky, Ana Camblong, Gonzalo Aguilar, C. García.

[32] See Borinsky, "Correspondencia de Macedonio Fernández a Gómez de La Serna" (1970); *Humorística, novelística y obra abierta en Macedonio Fernández* (diss, 1971); and "Macedonio: su proyecto novelístico" (1972). In 1987, Borinsky published the influential book *Macedonio Fernández y la teoría crítica: una evaluación* (1987), and in 2007, she compiled and edited Macedonio's letters for the second volume of his complete works, *Epistolario*, published by Corregidor.

[33] Engelbert also collaborated with the piece "El proyecto narrativo de Macedonio" for the critical edition of *MNE* (1993) edited by Camblong and Obieta.

[34] Lindstrom also published multiple articles on Macedonio and his experimental writing, among them: "Macedonio Fernandez: Strategies against Readerly Sloth," (1977) and "Macedonio Fernández y su reinvención del discurso metafísico" (1985).

Nevertheless, it was not until 2010 that Margaret Schwartz assumed the courageous task of translating *MNE*, a translation praised by specialists. In 2022, seventy years after Macedonio's death, his copyright will enter the public domain and we can expect to soon see more translations of his texts. This event coincides with renewed interest in his work as new generations of scholars have started to explore its connections with fields beyond Latin American studies such as visual studies and contemporary arts. The essays included in this book seek to support this process by facilitating Macedonio's rediscovery.

In the opening chapter, "Jorge Luis Borges and Macedonio Fernández: History of a Literary Friendship," Mónica Bueno recovers Macedonio's dissertation *De las personas* (On Personhood) (1897) to search for the principles of his notion of person, which she reveals as crucial for understanding not only his creative process and conception of artistic characters, but also his attitude regarding Borges's remarks on the geniality of his thought and oratory.[35] Bueno examines their relationship and the problematic continuities between their work as she addresses to what extent Macedonio's subsumed influence persisted as a vague trail or a distant voice in Borges's texts. She also explains how Borges's gestures toward Macedonio were a reflection of the nature and dynamic of their ludic dialogues, as they both elaborated their notions of literature, author, character, and intellectual property. Through an analysis of the figure of the Newcomer in *PR*, the literary devices in *MNE* inducing readers to become characters within the story, Borges's texts in which we can sense the presence of his mentor's voice, as well as Borges's own testimonies, Bueno argues that Macedonio embraced the idea of becoming himself a fictional character.

In "Heroes without Selves: Macedonio Fernández and a New Ethics of the Heroic," Todd S. Garth explores Macedonio's notion of heroism in light of his aesthetic and philosophical project, which posits a radical critique of the autonomous individual. He proves that Macedonio, in contrast to Borges whose search for the heroic implied a gaze toward the past, provoked a fundamental torsion of traditional definitions of the hero. Following the work of postmodern theorists Zygmunt Bauman and Nomy Arpaly, Garth develops lines of analysis to comprehend the multiple facets of Macedonio's definition of the heroic. He claims that the heroic reveals itself in Macedonio's literature, particularly in *ABA*, *PR*, and *MNE*, where he galvanizes his central ideas on ethics. But rather than a philosophical concept, Garth explains that, for Macedonio, ethics should provide

---

[35] For Fernández's dissertation, see Muñoz, "Macedonio Fernández: su tesis inédita *De las personas*."

us with practical guidelines that can be applied in everyday life. On the other hand, he also shows how Macedonio projected his visions of heroism toward the future, by drawing attention to an uncanny and disturbing dimension of the heroic in his thought: in order to accomplish a heroic mission, the individual must recognize the potential for its own human monstrosity; only by acknowledging its true self could it be dissolved, and give birth to the ethical act.

In "Consuelo-Eterna: Macedonio's Erotic and Metaphysical Passion," Ana Camblong dismantles one of the central ideas that has long consolidated Macedonio's mythical figure: that after his wife's death, Macedonio became a melancholic and ascetic writer who withdrew from social and public circles, and that it was her everlasting and mournful absence that inspired him to write *MNE*.[36] Camblong shows that this thesis is not properly founded and through a semiotic examination of his essays and novel, she reveals the influence in his texts of Consuelo Bosch, another enigmatic woman who was his secret lover and the muse that Camblong argues moved him to write his experimental novel.[37] She also revisits Macedonio's life journey to reflect on an apparent aporia lying at the foundation of his system of thought. Macedonio assigned the highest metaphysical value to the emotion of passion but, at the same time, he embraced its pragmatic consideration and expressed an intense appreciation of the practical experiences that passion should involve.

Macedonio's particular way of inhabiting Buenos Aires is the point of departure for Gonzalo S. Aguirre's "Macedonio Fernández's Neighborhood Metaphysics: *Belarte*, the Fool of Buenos Aires, and the Evidential Siesta." In his essay, Aguirre examines how the conceptual character "el Bobo de Buenos Aires" (the Fool of Buenos Aires), which Macedonio introduces in subsequent editions of *PR*, conveys the ethos of his city and becomes an operative agent who enacts the principles found in his theories on metaphysics, aesthetics, and humor. Aguirre traces the seeds of these principles in early essays included in *NTV* and in *Teorias* (Theories) and their crystallization through Macedonio's artistic and humoristic techniques. He also highlights the "evidential siesta," a daily practice Macedonio thought could incite a commotion within the individual's

---

[36] This article was first published in Spanish in the journal *Nadia lo inquietante en la cultura* (6), Rosario, 2003, 13–24, and then in Camblong's book *Ensayos macedonianos* (2006): 185–205.
[37] Also see Attala, "El amor secreto de Macedonio," in *La Nación* (Buenos Aires), February 2, 2010. His relationship with Consuelo's patrician family—he was also a close friend of her brother Ricardo—also proves how problematic it can be to circumscribe his work exclusively within the frame and experience of the avant-garde groups that formed and organized in Argentina during the 1920s. Robert Wells addresses this topic in his article "Macedonio Fernández at the Front of the Rearguard."

senses that would lead to their release from a web of apperceptions. Aguirre clarifies, however, that for Macedonio such liberation would rely on the courage of people to overcome their fears, extricate their affects from outside influence, and develop a pure vision, which would efface previous forms of power and knowledge, and any moral categorical imperative that invests affects with a singular origin, value, and finality.

While Aguirre shows how Macedonio steadily pushed aside Kant's philosophy, the second Part, "Philosophy, Affects, and Politics," opens with Diego Vecchio's essay "Macedonio Fernández: The First Egocide in the Río de la Plata," which confronts the notion of the Cartesian subject. Vecchio explores Macedonio's radical critique of the idea of the subject present in his theory of literature and the writing techniques he developed to dislocate the consciousness of the reader, pointing out the metaphysical implications of his aesthetic project, which seeks to restore a pure vision of the phenomenological world as it was prior to the distinctions between subjects and objects. But rather than a regression to an archaic and (pre)conceptual perception, Vecchio explains that this perspective restitutes an immanent field of phenomena. It creates a plane on which all entities are continuously reconfigured as they affect each other without composing a closed system or drawing rigidified correlations. Moreover, Vecchio asserts that in order to dissolve these impure perceptions, Macedonio was convinced that we must obliterate the ego, which drives individuals to organize, structure, and classify the world. Through this lens he examines Descartes's meditations, identifies constitutive literary elements at the root of the idea of the subject-ego, and traces the writing strategies Macedonio designed to activate these elements and provoke this concept's implosion.

On the ruinous edifice of Western philosophy left by Macedonio's thought, in the following chapter, "A Metaphysics that Only Begins: On Macedonio's Writing Passion," Julio Prieto reconstructs the alternative genealogy in which his work should be inscribed. He situates Macedonio among prominent intellectual trends active during the first decades of the twentieth century and establishes dialogues with a philosophical tradition that includes thinkers such as Kierkegaard and Schopenhauer. As he considers in tandem Kierkegaard's and Macedonio's idiosyncratic styles of philosophy, he explains that Macedonio searched for a form of expression capable of calling affections into action and conveying their quasi-corporeal dimension. Prieto also perceives resonances with Spinoza's philosophy, pointing out the centrality of affect in Macedonio's metaphysics, and traces their ramifications in contemporary affect theory. From this angle, he analyzes how Macedonio articulated three main lines of inquiry around the key notion of passion: metaphysics, ethics, and aesthetics. Prieto proposes that Macedonio and Spinoza concur in their decisive search for a mystical outcome, a secular *via mystica* of understanding that could eradicate suffering and improve life, directly establishing a political dimension in their metaphysics and ethics.

Luis Othoniel Rosa directs his attention specifically to Macedonio's political thought and the anarchist principles that sustain it. In "Songs without a Self: Macedonio's Anarchist Aesthetics," he sharpens Macedonio's ideas into spearheads with which to posit a critical and historical ontology of our present. But first, Othoniel returns to the twentieth century to establish a counterpoint between Macedonio's ideas on the reproduction of information and Walter Benjamin's critiques of the effects of technological developments on the work of art.[38] He claims that Macedonio's notion of intellectual property, which rejects the uniqueness of the work of art, upholds that it cannot be attributed to a singular author. Consequently, it advocates for collective and creative appropriations of any form of cultural and artistic expression, foreshadowing strategies of resistance in our current informational revolution. Othoniel contends that recent developments in technology, which have multiplied the virtual social platforms that enable the flow of information, whether fake or not, at unprecedented speeds could be used by any political force that has the power to dominate it. However, by analyzing Macedonio's essays and *MNE* as an assemblage of enunciations in which readers have the potential to become characters in the plot as well as writers and storytellers, Othoniel provides continuity to this communal experience and underlines his argument that modern literature can still catalyze an emancipatory project.

Daniel Attala's "The Thought of Macedonio Fernández: A Dictionary" is a critical tool for understanding Macedonio's philosophical and aesthetic project. This essay should be regarded as a mobile lighthouse, illuminating key concepts for readers as they navigate Macedonio's neologisms or argumentative structures that can at times encircle certain voids of meaning. In Macedonio's view, any attempt to free individuals from a web of apperceptions through extensive philosophical arguments would only be detrimental as it submerges them in an intricate rhetoric still entrenched in that same apperceptive web. Attala explains that, contrary to this, Macedonio sought to reach the greatest degree of precision possible, even against the nature of things and rules, by introducing literary

---

[38] See Benjamin, "The Work of Art in the Age of Mechanical Reproduction" (1935).

devices into his philosophical texts (and philosophical devices into his literature) to develop his philosophy of affections through his writing. This essay offers an essential selection of Macedonio's lexicon, clarifying the position and value that each notion holds in his system of thought and tracing the sources used to elaborate them. Furthermore, Attala introduces a previously unpublished text in which Macedonio elaborates on the notion of Passion, a conceptual thread that runs throughout all chapters of this book.

In the third Part, "Metaphysics on the Move," Ricardo Piglia's essay "Notes on Macedonio in a Diary" presents a series of seemingly unrelated entries in a personal diary, which collectively orient readers as they enter Macedonio's work, conveying a cadence that is in tune with his fragmentary writing.[39] In the essay, we first hear the voice of a professor delivering a lecture on anarchism who unexpectedly mentions a peculiar anecdote about Macedonio's performance as an attorney in Posadas, Misiones.[40] The conversation with one of his students then continues outside of the classroom, and following their voices into the hallways of the National University of La Plata, or it could be in the hallways of any other public institution, we can see the curious and attentive student heeding his professor's advice to look for a copy of *Una novela que comienza* (A Novel That Begins) at the university's library, which has handwritten notes from Macedonio himself. During the train ride home, as he considers the implication of his find, his ideas drift and converge, plunging us in Macedonio's own thoughts. The notes address various of the central topics in his oeuvre: the relevance of oral language, the poetics of plagiarism, the multiple facets of an artist's self-portrait, the lover's melancholy as a metaphysical quest, and the process of writing as inherently a process of thinking in plain sight.

In "What Is Believing?" Horacio González reflects on Macedonio's text "Una imposibilidad de creer" (An Impossibility of Believing) (1949), one of his last metaphysical essays, which was published in the journal *Davar* edited by the Jewish community in Buenos Aires. The essay revolves around a terrible event: a father drowning at sea while trying to save his son, who also perishes beneath

---

[39] "Notas sobre Macedonio en un diario" was included in Piglia's book *Formas breves* (Anagrama, 2000).
[40] Macedonio was appointed as an attorney in Posadas (1908–13), the small capital city of Misiones in the northeast of Argentina. Even though there is not much information about his abilities, which would be interesting to study considering his ethical-juridical stance, the perspective of another famous writer locates him in this setting. In 1912, Horacio Quiroga, who had accepted a position as a judge while he was already living in the region, sent a letter to his close friend Lugones and mentions his peculiar random encounter with Macedonio. Quiroga writes: "El fiscal es hombre cuasi de letras—Macedonio Fernández—que me inquietó, al conocerlo, con un juicio sobre Rodó: / -Es, todo él, una página de Emerson" (The attorney is a quasi-man of letters—Macedonio Fernández—who concerned me when I first met him with his view on Rodó: / He is, all of him, a page out of Emerson) (Visca, "Del epistolario de Horacio Quiroga," 53).

the waves.[41] The biblical references in the text, used to address the unimaginable thought that the father might have let his own child drown, were certainly easy to identify for the journal's audience.[42] We can also imagine the deep reverberations of his words if we consider that at the time the atrocities committed in the concentration and extermination camps were already well known around the world. Such immense and irremediable loss would only generate sad affections. Nonetheless, González shows how Macedonio creates an instant of a profound reconciliation in which the father and his son are given the chance to resignify the circumstances that led to the breakdown of their physical bond. He explains the metaphysical premises that sustain Macedonio's argument, but he also points out that it requires a necessary leap toward a transcendental dialogue that could restitute the truth of their relationship.

In "No hay proa sin popa" (There Is No Bow without the Stern), Liliana Weinberg closes the book by returning to the beginning and to Macedonio's relationship with the Borges-led group of avant-garde writers and artists associated with the literary journal *Proa* (Bow). Weinberg focuses on Macedonio's contributions and explores how, rather than importing artistic techniques from the European avant-gardes and inserting them into a different cultural matrix, both Borges and Macedonio sought to carry out a literary refoundation, centered in Argentina yet capable of provoking a creative intervention in the worldwide context of the avant-gardes. As Macedonio infused his texts with wordplay, humorous *criollo* expressions, and complex literary operations that articulated his metaphysical principles, the group incorporated these literary and philosophical devices as central pillars of their own cultural and literary program. Weinberg also examines Borges's references to Macedonio throughout the journal and Dardo Salguero's "Arquicaricatura" (Archicaricature), in which, she argues, the Uruguayan artist not only illustrates the dynamic of Macedonio's relationship with the group and the contours of their avant-garde program, but also the mechanics of his writing.

While reading the chapters of this book, as the editor of this collective work, I believe there is a serious question that we must ask ourselves: How is it possible in our own era in the twenty-first century to assimilate the work of an early twentieth-century author who immersed himself in deep metaphysical meditation and was reluctant to accept the progress of modern societies? In this sense, it may be interesting to first consider William James's opening remarks

---

[41] See Fernández, "Una imposibilidad de creer," in *NTV* (1990), 381–3.
[42] See Attala's "The Thought of Macedonio Fernández" in this book, 171–2.

as he began his series of lectures in 1908, which particularly resonate with Macedonio's metaphysical essays in *NTV*. James said: "Fortunately, our age seems to be growing philosophical again—still in the ashes live the wonted fires."[43] It would not be fair to judge the fortune of the resurgence of philosophical and metaphysical inquiries in the twentieth century by how these became swept up in the wave of mystification that, gaslighted by tremendous historical forces, led to the idolatry of nationalism and fascist ideology. These are the same forces that Macedonio heard knocking at his door in Buenos Aires, and if their echoes are continuing into our present day, they should give us cause to tremble.

Macedonio did not tremble and if it was not a bonfire visible to the cultural capitals of the world that he ignited in his remote Atlantic south, he certainly lit a candle and gathered his friends around it, sharing *mate*, reflections, and stories and playing music on his guitar. And during the thin silence between notes, broken only by the sound of his fingers moving and subtly pressing the chords, he imagined an aesthetic and philosophical project that proposed an alternative future. Standing in opposition to the technological world that scientific knowledge and rationalism predicted to be the inexorable march of progress driving modern societies to enter the first decades of the century at full throttle, confident they had subjugated the forces of nature, that the natural environments and resources needed for the expansion of the global trading system had been classified and controlled not only by the international order but also by the rigid categories that humans forced upon the species, Macedonio asked one simple and witty question: What if it does not work?

In *PR*, Macedonio conceives a list of curiosities useful for restoring his oblique perspective on modern societies. He defines them as "aquenó" (maybe not) and explains that their existence and function is preceded by a skeptical expectation. Among them, he enumerates the following: "indestructible objects; gas lighters; the automatic pen; the ink pencil; [...] infallible remedies; [...] parachutes; [...] the safety features on revolvers, penknives and elevators; [...] antidotes and the assurance that each one is innocuous; survival rates; [...] the 'balance of power' and the system of 'checks and balances,'" and so forth.[44] The list of "aquenó"

---

[43] James, *A Pluralistic Universe*. Macedonio claimed that he had an epistolary exchange with William James between 1906 and 1911, and he quotes one of these letters in *NTV* (1990, 237), but T. Garth has pointed out that it has not been possible to corroborate the existence of such letters; see Garth, 2005, 198, note 2.

[44] "los irrompibles; [...] los encendedores a nafta; la lapicera automática; [...] el lápiz de tinta; [...] los remedios infalibles; [...] los paracaídas; [...] los seguros de revólveres, navajas y ascensores; [...] los antídotos y el seguro de inofensibilidad de cada específico; los plazos de sobrevivencia; [...] el 'equilibrio de poderes' y el sistema de 'frenos y contrapesos'" (*PR* (1989), 114–15).

reflects Macedonio's strong interest in the new dynamic of the free market, its advertising techniques, and how new technological developments in mass media put into circulation narratives that conflated news and advertisements into a single package for the customer's consumption. As if skimming a newspaper in which the ads for an innovative new product are superimposed over reports of crimes, accidents, miracle cures, or political developments, Macedonio articulates a list of devices that prompts us to think the unthinkable.

In the face of Buenos Aires's exponential growth and the new urbanism applied in the planning of its magnificent boulevards and avenues, Macedonio perceived, for instance, the negative consequences for the people's well-being. Indeed, the city's modernization resulted in the segregation of immigrant workers, who were forced to crowd together in boarding houses in relegated neighborhoods, pushed the incipient urban and suburban proletariat to the outskirts of the city, and limited the majority of the population to rental housing for the rest of their lives. In 1939, in a letter sent to his cousin, Gabriel del Mazo, a civil engineer who worked on the organization of the city's mass transit, Macedonio states that urbanism will bring about "the incineration of cities" because, due to the demographic hyper-concentrations, commercialism, and consumerism that big cities foster, these spaces have transformed into unaffordable monsters.[45]

Nevertheless, the vastness of the pampas still closely surrounded the city. One only needs to search for historical photos of Retiro Railway Station to see the majestic British architecture of the public building rising out of the plains like a submarine in the middle of the ocean. This disjuncture between the rural countryside and the capital city, a constitutive dichotomy of the Argentine nation-state building process, which sparked a series of civil wars during the nineteenth century, emerges in Macedonio's utopia of the *ciudad-campo* (country-city), but reformulated as a positive and inclusive collective social network. He imagined a modern urban and rural self-sufficient commune in which each worker would have his/her own house, and each family would have cultivable land on which plant and harvest in proximity to natural resources that would not be privately exploited. Macedonio believed that this urban/rural setting would deter wars and social unrest, minimize social inequalities and the size of the state, prevent the spread of disease, and reduce "unproductive" commerce.[46]

---

[45] See Fernández, *Epistolario*, 1991, 153–4; and Garth, *The Self*, 175–84.
[46] See Fernández, *Teorías*, 1990, 115–19.

The proposal here is not to elevate Macedonio's thinking to a meta-historical narrative, and even less to invest him with the power of clairvoyance, which would restitute the mythological qualities of which we seek here to divest him. Our aim is to understand the origins and circumstances that shaped his thinking and capture its recurrence in our present in order to rediscover the singularities of our own time. Thus, this book should serve as a platform from which to launch new studies into Macedonio's work and the implications of his thought in current debates, not only in the field of Latin American studies but also in the English-speaking world and beyond. Consequently, it is crucial that we delve deeper into his oeuvre, translating it and unearthing those texts still waiting to be discovered and published. *Macedonio Fernández: Between Literature, Philosophy, and the Avant-Garde* encourages new readers, as well as scholars, to continue entering into Macedonio's collective assemblage of enunciation, which he thought would guide us toward the realization that we all share the same deep concern for a common destiny; perhaps, there is still time to rewrite it, maybe not.

Part One

Life and Literature at the Edge

1

Jorge Luis Borges and Macedonio Fernández: History of a Literary Friendship

Mónica Bueno

> *But in this singular world of singularities, these 'sworn friends of solitude' are conjurers; they are even called to be conjurers by one of the heralds, the one who says I but is not necessarily the first, though he is one of the first in our twentieth century to speak this community without community.*
>
> Jacques Derrida. *The Politics of Friendship.*

Introduction

An author's name embodies the name of his/her literature. It designates both an individual and a textual existence. In the Argentine literary tradition, however, the name "Macedonio Fernández" calls for another name: "Jorge Luis Borges," and this name evokes the literary avant-garde scene in Buenos Aires during the 1920s. In this case, the names of these two writers also designate a mentor/disciple relationship with problematic axes of continuity and evolution that Borges subsumed and further developed through his writing. Consequently, the name of his mentor remains as a vague trail, a distant influence on his literary and intellectual production. Macedonio became something of a fictional character or, as Manuel Gálvez defined it, a "nonexistent gentleman."[1]

---

[1] The affirmation of Manuel Gálvez, the Argentine realist writer, in his monumental cultural autobiography underlines the relationship between the author's name and his social figure. It is a matter of writing about known writers, not about literature. He says: "Although my work is panoramic, I did not propose to talk about every writer, only about those of whom I have personal memories. Therefore, certain omissions are not due to ill will. Because of this, while I dedicate some pages to individuals of no literary importance and with whom I interacted often and who were picturesque, I do not say anything about others of authentic value and with whom I had no friendship. This would be the case, for example, of Macedonio Fernández, whom I have never seen and whose books I have not read, perhaps because I have never had them in my hands" (8). Unless otherwise indicated, all translations are mine.

For a long time, Macedonio's literature has been overshadowed by the myth that Borges built and conjured out of the former's oral expression rather than his writing.[2] He admirably created the public image of his friend/mentor, but Macedonio laughed at such tributes. He emerged in the public literary scene of Buenos Aires thanks to his relationship with the group of young writers whom Borges met on his return from Europe in 1921. However, Macedonio had written and published since the turn of the century and had connections and dialogues with prominent intellectuals. Still, Borges talked and wrote frequently about Macedonio, about his singular figure and his exceptional attributes, and invoked him against the intellectual figure of Leopoldo Lugones who structured the cultural milieu at the time.[3]

Borges attempted to commit intellectual parricide by using the mask of another father, Macedonio, that Borges himself had crafted, although there existed a certain relational distance between him and the myth he projected.[4] In this sense, he writes:

> I inherited from my father the friendship and worship of Macedonio. Around 1921 we returned from Europe after a long stay. The bookstores in Geneva and a certain generous oral lifestyle that I had discovered in Madrid were very much needed at the beginning. I forgot that nostalgia when I met, or recovered, Macedonio.[5]

---

[2] This has been one of the most controversial topics for specialists on both authors. Todd Garth, for instance, has addressed the lines of analyses that I further develop in "Confused Oratory," 350–70, and in "An Avant-garde Apart," included in *The Self of the City*, 48–88. Also see Camblong and Obieta, "Primera conversación"; González, *El filósofo cesante*, 173–4; and Prieto, *Desencuadernados*, 122–4.

[3] During the 1920s, a young generation of writers, Borges among them, provoked a deep rupture in cultural history as they sought to problematize the place of literature. The "new" was the key category demarcating the line of confrontation between the young generation of writers and the previous one, but such innovation was more a slogan than an achievement of their work. The word "new" is repeated in the texts of the young writers, we may say, more like the announcement of a program to be made than as a concretion. From the texts of the young Borges published in Spain ("Al margen de una moderna estética") to the manifesto of Oliverio Girondo or to the proclamations of the controversial Elias Castelnuovo ("New forms of art or new forms of life but, anyway, new forms"), the category of the new will be a *sine qua non* condition of the debate in the literary scene. This controversy created a network of relationships that is established not only between the two recognized groups of young writers: Florida and Boedo, but also with the canonized names of the past and with tradition. Macedonio Fernández and Leopoldo Lugones were born the same year, with a difference of days, but they are the two-sided sign that hybridizes continuities and divergences.

[4] In this sense, Garth and Heather Dubnick analyze the conception of Borges's story, "Tlön, Uqbar, Orbis Tertius," through his relationship with Macedonio. They argue that Macedonio's presence actually emerges in this text as an inspirational paternal figure whose influence drives the author to subvert it and, ultimately, erase it. See "Uninvited Inversions," 157–70.

[5] "Yo heredé de mi padre la amistad y el culto de Macedonio. Hacia 1921 regresamos de Europa después de una estadía de muchos años. Las librerías de Ginebra y cierto generoso estilo de vida oral que yo había descubierto en Madrid me hacían mucha falta al principio. Olvidé esa nostalgia cuando conocí, o recuperé, a Macedonio" ("Macedonio Fernández," (1975), 53).

Nevertheless, as mentioned before, Macedonio found Borges's praise of him amusing. In an autobiographical text that precedes the story "Cirugía psíquica de extirpación" (Psychic Surgery of Extirpation) published in the journal *Sur* in 1941, he creates kaleidoscopic images of his evanescent and fictitious ego. He writes:

> I was born in Buenos Aires and in a very 1874 year. Not right away, but yes, soon after, I began to be invoked by Jorge Luis Borges, with so little shyness in his praise that as a result of the terrible risk he ran with this vehemence, I began to be the author of the best that he had produced. I was a de facto talent, by overpowering him, by usurping his work.[6]

He deconstructed the typical master/disciple relationship, while playing with the positions of their names and with the notion of intellectual property.

Macedonio, like Samuel Beckett or Michel Foucault, ruminated: What does it matter who speaks or who writes? Or, even better: Does anybody actually care who is speaking and writing? Macedonio always created fictions of himself and, joking about the place his friend had given to him, he embraced the idea of becoming a fictional character, which he thought was one of the highest achievements for any form of artistic expression. Borges acknowledged Macedonio's complicity and in his own work decoded and transcribed fundamental premises of his mentor's thought. And as he built and propagated the mythical figure of his friend, they both elaborated their concepts of literature, author, and fictional character.

On Characters and Authors

On May 22, 1897, the lawyer Macedonio Fernández presented his doctoral thesis entitled *De las personas* (On Personhood) at the University of Buenos Aires. In the Introduction, Macedonio justifies the subject of his research with the following words:

> Many reasons invited me to choose the theoretical and positive study of Law and Social Sciences in spite of the insurmountable obstacles stemming from my obvious insipience, and behind which the vast problem enviously conceals its own solution; so great are they that from the very beginning they have limited my pretensions to only the conquest of a bit of light for my spirit, without any hope

---

[6] "Nací porteño y en un año muy 1874. No entonces enseguida, pero sí apenas después, ya empecé a ser citado por Jorge Luis Borges, con tan poca timidez de encomios que por el terrible riesgo que se expuso con esta vehemencia comencé a ser yo el autor de lo mejor que él había producido. Fui un talento de facto, por arrollamiento, por usurpación de la obra de él" (*PRC* (2007), 9).

of increasing [the light] of those more interned in the legal world who have been able to appreciate up close the demands of a solution, and yet these [demands] were so attractive that, even with everything planned, they drove me to release my tenuous sail out into such a hazy sea in search of such a dubious shore.

The first of these [reasons] has undoubtedly been a driving force rather than a motive: the irresistible fascination that arduous problems, symbolized within concepts of inexhaustible content such as the notion of <u>subject</u>, exert on a speculative mind, but the most persuasive [reason] for one who is preparing to devote his life to the defense of the <u>spirit</u> of Argentine legislation ...[7]

In consonance with his later fictions and theories, the thesis reveals one of the central pillars of Macedonio's thought: the question of the self, which structures all of his work, constitutes it, and guided his literary and life experiments, which he practiced every day as he described them in his personal diary.[8]

In *Papeles de recienvenido* (The Newcomer Papers) (1930), Macedonio specifically addresses the question of the self as he writes a sort of autobiography. Rather than presenting an account of his life's journey, he offers several fragments of biographies that overlap, communicate, and contradict each other. This multiplicity of life trajectories subverts the rules of the genre and mocks its proper definition. Macedonio writes: "Everything that the autobiographer affirms of himself is what he was not and wanted to be."[9] Fiction is the underlying

---

[7] The underlining is included in the original text: "Muchas razones me invitaban a escoger el estudio teórico y positivo del sujeto del Derecho y Ciencias Sociales a pesar de los obstáculos insuperables por mi manifiesta insipiencia, tras los cuales el vasto problema oculta envidiosamente su propia solución; tan grandes éstos que han limitado desde el principio mis pretensiones a solo la conquista de un poco de luz para mi espíritu, sin esperanza de aumentar la de que los que más internados en el mundo jurídico, han podido apreciar de cerca las exigencias de una solución y sin embargo tan atrayentes aquellas, que aun todo previsto me decidieron a soltar mi tenue vela en un mar tan nebuloso en busca de tan dudosa ribera. / La primera de éstas ha sido sin duda móvil más que motivo, la fascinación irresistible para una mente especulativa que ejercen los problemas arduos simbolizados en conceptos de un contenido inagotable como el de <u>sujeto</u>, pero la más persuasiva para quien se dispone a consagrar su vida a la defensa del <u>espíritu</u> de la legislación argentina" ("De las personas," 6). I would like to express here my gratitude, remembrance, and admiration to the "father of the father," as Ricardo Piglia defined him, Adolfo de Obieta, who gave me a transcription of the manuscript, which he produced on his old typewriter.

[8] Ana Camblong's research has been particularly concerned with the analysis of Macedonio's annotations about experiments on himself. Camblong distinguishes two figures in these exercises: the mystic and the pragmatic. "The mystic executes and rehearses his experiences of *intellectual exaltation* and the pragmatist asserts that with effort even the impossible becomes possible. On the other hand, it must be noted that these 'mystical experiments' have practical consequences, as William James suggests; that is, they transform life, create a different conversation, make art, encourage humor and involve love" ("Primera conversación," 159).

[9] "Todo lo que afirma de sí el autobiografiado es lo que no fue y quiso ser" (*PRC*, 29). In 1930, the first edition of *Papeles de recienvenido* was published through Borges's intervention because Macedonio was never interested in publishing it. The book has a peculiar structure: it is composed of letters, toasts, speeches, and chapters, but without any continuity between them. Macedonio created this text as a disordered movement that only allowed for a fragmentary reading. The inorganic unity that characterizes it creates the feeling that it is an incomplete text, which allowed Macedonio to add texts and modify its title in the 1944 edition: *PRC*.

foundational principle of every biography. Thus, in his essay he depicts five poses of *a fotografiarse* (what we would now call "taking selfies"), each one presenting a different image of himself. By using the first-person singular in this essay, Macedonio seems to announce his entry into a literary realm. And as he creates an innocent character who has no experience living in the city, ignores local customs and urban rites, and roams around Buenos Aires, but who is released from social conventions, he may have drawn a fine line between this subject and himself.

In the figure of this character, the *Recienvenido* (Newcomer), who later in the essay becomes *El Bobo de Buenos Aires* (The Fool of Buenos Aires), also converged Macedonio's critical perspectives on the modern state, its juridical apparatus, and on the legal status of the person. Furthermore, he aimed to expose the absurdity that he saw in the legal code. Macedonio conceived this character as a literary device that escapes and cannot be recaptured by social constrictions and legal norms, which he thought regulated an individual's social interactions. In the essay, Macedonio explores how to undermine the state and its juridical structure through a literary lens.[10]

Macedonio created an absurd character that represents the less-valued features of a human being: ignorance, stupidity, and incongruity. Nevertheless, as if he himself were this fictional character, he claimed that absurdity was the best way to define our collective life, and in his own life he cultivated a sort of nonexistent presence. Adolfo de Obieta, Macedonio's son, writes: "I believe that my father has been the most natural and sincerely 'different' person I have ever met."[11] What distinguished his singular way of being was his evanescence, his attempts to administrate a modest economy of his human existence and to project himself as a fictional character who only manifested his presence through subtle gestures, while his actual existence was constantly fading away and moving toward nonexistence. According to Obieta's depiction of his father's unique perspective on the world and on himself, "he felt that humanity was suffocated by unnecessary

---

[10] I am bearing in mind here Giorgio Agamben's essay *What Is an Apparatus?* In this essay, he defines a device as having the ability to "capture, guide, determine, intercept, model and ensure the gestures, behaviors, opinions and discourses of living beings." According to Agamben, the notion of the individual modern subject is constituted as the result of an intersection between living beings and devices. Facing this apparatus of capture, he proposes to develop "counter devices" that can restore what has been separated and divided in order to be classified ("O que é um dispositivo," 9–16). Macedonio conceives of the *Recienvenido* as a literary device that can carry out this counterattack and, as we shall see, he designed several different devices for this purpose according to the nature of the capturing apparatus he sought to undermine.

[11] "Creo que mi padre ha sido la persona más natural y sinceramente 'diferente' que habré conocido" ("Introduction" in Museo de la novela de la Eterna (1993)).

things or by experiences that were lived senselessly, by twisted rules and deities that agonized, and by innumerable absences of necessary things and true faith."[12]

Since Aristotle, the link between fictional character and actual person has been a starting point for the creative process of a literary figure. In his *Poetics*, Aristotle writes: "[though] the subject of the imitation, who suggested the type, be inconsistent, still he must be consistently inconsistent."[13] Edward M. Forster posits the following question: "[I]n what senses do the nations of fiction differ from those of the earth?" and concludes that from an empirical point of view, a person and a fictional character have nothing in common.[14] However, there may be a relationship between the two based on similarity and identification, because a fictional character is constituted as a synecdoche and as the ethopoeia of a person. On the other hand, Jean-Philippe Miraux asserts that the character is an irreplaceable textual category in the novel and identifies its three basic functions: "a typological marker, a textual organizer, and an entity invested [with meaning]."[15]

As the fictional character stands in a fictional realm, it reaffirms the fictional plane on which the story is told, but it also retains a strong mimetic power. Nonetheless, as Barthes points out about Sade, there is a kind of literature that antagonizes with this form of representation: "[b]eing a writer and not a realistic author, Sade always chooses the discourse over the referent; he always sides with *semiosis* rather than *mimesis*: what he 'represents' is constantly being deformed by the meaning, and it is on the level of the meaning, not the referent, that we should read him."[16] Macedonio's literature should be inscribed in this genealogy. For instance, in *Museo de la Novela de la Eterna* (*The Museum of Eterna's Novel*) (1967) the mimetic condition of its characters emerges on the text's surface, but they extend beyond the novel's plot and escape from it. This disruptive power destabilizes the text's border and erodes the notion of mimesis. As these characters participate in disconnected scenes, engage in dialogues with each other, as well as with an author and a reader who are also characters in the novel, they undermine the possibility of articulating a linear temporality or a specific narrational order.

---

[12] "Sentía a la humanidad asfixiada entre innúmeras cosas innecesarias o sobrevividas, y reglas retorcidas y deidades agónicas, e innumerable ausencia de cosas necesarias y fe verdadera" ("Introduction" in Museo de la novela de la Eterna (1993)).
[13] *Poetics*, 55.
[14] Forster, *Aspects of the Novel*, 51.
[15] Miraux, *El personaje*, 10.
[16] See Barthes, *Sade*, 37.

It is interesting to consider that Macedonio anticipated Barthes's idea that the writer is a modern character. In *MNE*, the author as a character has a proper role in the story and circulates through the spaces that he himself configures.[17] This transmutation of the "I" from a first-person singular voice narrating a story to a fictional character that participates in it is akin to the magical transition that Macedonio experienced when he realized that he had become a literary author once Borges had started to define him as such. This passage or transmutation allowed him to discover that characters (either novelistic or dramatic) and authors could become elements of the work of art if they are used for the sole purpose of making the reader a character. He thought that in this way literature could expose the unnecessary constrictions of our social existence, release us from the burden of our previous forms of knowledge and from our own determination to continue bearing the weight of the world on our shoulders.

As Noé Jitrik has pointed out, in his literature the character itself expresses and organizes his theory of the novel.[18] Macedonio called them "people of art" and assigned them a specific task: "to make the Reader a 'character,' incessantly attacking the certainty of his/her existence, through procedures that attempt to induce 'characters' to perform as 'people' in order to, by way of a counterattack, make the Reader a character."[19] The characters that dwell in his novel enjoy relative autonomy from both the text and from the author who conceives them. Macedonio gives them allegoric names such as "Quizagenio" (Maybe-Genius) or "Deunamor el no existente caballero" (One-Love the Nonexistent Gentleman) to highlight their essential features and to distinguish them from any other concrete human existence. Nonetheless, as they overflowed the novel's limits and escaped into the city of Buenos Aires, they found a liminal space in which the reader would join them, and in which their allegoric names would click with the reader's affections.[20]

---

[17] Barthes, *The Rustle of Language*, 49.
[18] Jitrik, "La novela futura," 170.
[19] "... hacer 'personaje' al Lector, atentando incesantemente a su certeza de existencia, por procedimientos que tratan de hacer desempeñarse como 'personas' a 'personajes'" (*Teorías* (1974), 248).
[20] Germán García recollects several anecdotes of Macedonio's performances playing with the idea of he himself becoming a character. For instance, Federico García Pedrido tells García what happened when he met him for the first time in 1948, through a mutual friend, who had set an appointment at Macedonio's apartment in the Palermo neighborhood. Pedrido says that even though they arrived on time and Macedonio was already there, he made them wait longer and longer, as he always did every time he had an appointment. Pedrido depicts their unusual first encounter: "there was a curtain reaching the floor (on one side [of the living room]) and you could hear him dragging his feet, and it seemed as if he was going to appear but he did not, instead he moved away" ("Desvivirse de Macedonio Fernández," in *Hablan de Macedonio*, 40).

Macedonio intensified the tension between life and fiction, and imagined that *MNE*, "the first good novel," as he defined it, would demolish the genre of the realistic novel, which for him could only consummate bad novels. He believed that this literary genre not only impoverished the experience of life, but also the opportunity for individuals to experience art. However, life paradoxically arises within his novel's pages as the characters themselves appeal to both the author and the reader to help them become alive. For Macedonio there was an intrinsic continuity between life and literature, but he believed that in order to dwell in them and to be able to fathom each dimension, it was necessary to create and experiment with different devices.[21]

In *MNE*, Macedonio presents himself in the following manner: "This is what I imagine here: non-death; also the artistic work involved in the transformation of the self, routing the stability of each person in his [or her] self."[22] His ultimate goal was to provoke a sensorial commotion inside his readers that would induce them to become characters in the story. For this reason, Macedonio defined fictional characters as "persons of art" as opposed to "persons of life." The writer invented the persons of art for the novel, although, as mentioned before, Macedonio maintained a distant relationship with the mask of the author and rejected the social prestige bestowed upon this figure. In order to achieve his objective, he believed that the author should no longer be considered the demiurge of the story, but rather just another character and, as the readers also became characters within the novel, they would abandon their position as passive recipients of the literary text to be protagonists of their own story.

For this reason, Macedonio claimed that he needed a specific type of reader: the *Lector Salteado* (Reader Who Skips Around), who would be able to articulate the novel's fragments. He thought that these readers would be captivated by the story and as they gradually transformed into participatory characters, they would perceive the continuum that links their life and literature.

---

[21] Let us remember his "Diario de vida e ideas" (Diary of Life and Ideas) written throughout his life. Macedonio's journal seems to accommodate the peculiar game that exists between his life and his work because the text does not wield the singularity of a life but is instead only an excuse for experimentation because it seeks to obtain some formalization: from life to the idea. His diary describes the exercises he undertook intending to show that the perception of things is always a distortion of both the subject and the object. In this sense, he writes: "El libro del saber propio y ajeno de un individuo podría llamarse este, pues poco se hablará de mi vida, y seré muy severo conmigo mismo en cuanto afirme como saber de cierto" (This book could be titled the book about an individual's knowledge of oneself and of the other, since little will be said about my life, and I will be severe with myself as soon as I claim any certainty to know [something]) (96).

[22] "[S]oy el imaginador de una cosa: la no muerte; y la trabajo artísticamente por la trocación del yo, la derrota de la estabilidad de cada uno en su yo" (32). English translation by Margaret Schwartz, 28.

Macedonio's aesthetic utopia creates and revolves around this enigmatic figure: a reader who should let themselves be carried away by his writing's acrobatic leaps and who can inhabit in the novel's gaps. In *MNE*, he writes:

> To the reader who skips around, however, I accommodate myself. You read my entire novel without knowing it, because I scattered the telling of the whole novel before I started, and so you turned into an unknowing orderly reader. With me, the reader who skips around is most likely to read in an orderly fashion.
>
> I wanted to distract you, not correct you, because contrary to appearances you are a wise reader, since you practice inter-reading, which makes the most forceful impression, in keeping with my theory that characters and event that are only insinuated or skillfully truncated are the most memorable.
>
> I dedicate my novel to you, Skip-Around Reader; you, in turn, should be grateful to me for a new sensation: reading in order. On the other hand, the orderly reader will experience a new way of skipping: the orderly reading of a skipping-around author.[23]

Similarly, Borges's literature is a theory and practice of reading that reproduces the irreverent gesture of the *Lector Salteado*. As Borges articulated his own genealogy and literary tradition, he projected his well-known and recurrent metaphor of an infinite library that holds the books he used to compose these constellations, which seem to be secretly connected according to the location of these books in the universal library.

In his texts, Borges introduced the names of authors, historical events, ideas, and concepts, which could allude either to actual references, sources, and meanings, or suggest veiled continuities and elusive resonances, the matrix of his fictions. Therefore, Borges's maneuvering implied a double dislocation of books and authors. He first rearranged the universal library and developed a new catalogue based on his own readings. Then, as if he were Diogenes with his lantern, he established analogies where there were none and identified differences where historical analyses had pointed out similarities. Macedonio situated himself beyond the figure of the author; however, if we accept Borges's

---

[23] "Al lector salteado me acojo. He aquí que leíste toda mi novela sin saberlo, te tornaste lector seguido e insabido al contártelo todo dispersamente y antes de la novela. El lector salteado es el más expuesto conmigo a leer seguido. / Quise distraerte, no quise corregirte, porque al contrario eres el lector sabio, pues que practicas el entreleer que es lo que más fuerte impresión labra, conforme a mi teoría de que los personajes y los sucesos sólo insinuados, hábilmente truncos, son los que más quedan en la emoción y en la memoria. / Te dedico mi novela, Lector Salteado; me agradecerás una sensación nueva: el leer seguido. Al contrario, el lector seguido tendrá la sensación de una nueva manera de saltear: la de seguir al autor que salta" (*MNE* (1993), 273). English translation by Schwartz, 119.

mythical representation of his friend, we can perceive traces in the formation process of this literary character that prove their common ways of understanding the meaning of literature and, more importantly, points of convergence in their metaphysical reflections on the question of the self.

Borges: *Lector Salteado* of Macedonio

On June 23, 1974, Borges published a short text in the newspaper *La Opinión* commemorating the centenary of Macedonio's birth. In this note, "Testimony of Borges," which was transcribed by Tomás Eloy Martínez, he reiterates similar characteristics and personal features that during the last fifty years he had attributed to his friend. Again and again, he elevates Macedonio to the status of a genius due to his pure presence and his oral narratives, but not for his writing. He says: "If as a writer he was mediocre because he used confusing and difficult to read language, as a man he was exceptional."[24] Borges drew a line between the man and the writer, placing Macedonio's readers in an awkward position. Because Borges fostered a process of collective entropy regarding Macedonio's work, we have lost the genius, and all that remains are his unexceptional texts. This was not the first time he voiced this idea. However, he had also said: "[…] I imitated him to the point of transcription, to the point of devout and passionate plagiarism. I felt: Macedonio *is* metaphysics, Macedonio *is* literature."[25] So, what exactly did Borges plagiarize from his work if he thought he was a bad writer?[26]

Borges's assessment of Macedonio's writing consequently includes him within a profuse saga of Argentinean authors who wrote badly (a genealogy that could be traced back to Domingo F. Sarmiento) and who developed an obscure writing style. As Barthes has pointed out, every author writes using their language in its own present conditions and showing its own nature at the time. Designing literary devices against the power of the state or against notions such as genre, author, narrator, reader, characters, space, or time was not the only thing Macedonio did. He also invented new conditions for the language in which he wrote and

---

[24] In "Testimonio de Borges," he says: "Si como escritor era mediocre porque empleaba un lenguaje confuso y de difícil lectura, como hombre era genial" (11).
[25] "[…] lo imité, hasta la transcripción, hasta el apasionado y devoto plagio. Yo sentía: Macedonio es la metafísica, es la literatura" (*Borges en Sur* (1999), 146).
[26] Garth (2005; 2008), Prieto (2002, 122–4; 2005), and Bueno (2001, 19) have also addressed this question regarding Borges's self-promotion strategy whereby he incorporated Macedonio's poetics while blurring his writings.

invested it with properties that provoke distant resonances. He invented a sort of baroque *criollismo* or a baroque *criollo* that transformed his contemporary language. This fictionalization of a form of enunciation that did not actually exist at his time also signaled his quest for a utopian form of expression. In this sense, Daniel Attala points out: "As paradoxical as it may seem, this author's bad writing is the result of a desire for perfection. A perfection, however, that is not measured according to its compliance with a law [of grammar/style] but rather for having repealed or, at the very least, suspended all law."[27]

In his prologue to the new edition of his 1923 *Fervor de Buenos Aires* included in *Obras completas* in 1969, Borges asserts: "I have mitigated its baroque excess, limited its rough [edges], crossed out sentimentality and vagueness."[28] Would it be the same baroque excess that he claimed characterized Macedonio's literature? Although in the prologue he admits that when he was young he aimed to be like him, he refused to republish three books that corresponded to this stage of his early production. In one of these books, *Inquisiciones* (Inquisitions) (1925), specifically in the essay "La nadería de la personalidad" ("The Nothingness of Personality") (1922), we can detect strong similarities between Borges's conceptual way of writing and Macedonio's style, as well as between their argumentative structures demonstrating the precariousness of the notion of the individual ego. Borges seems to follow his mentor's guidance, opening his essay with following statement:

> Intention.
> I want to tear down the exceptional preeminence that is now generally awarded to the self: a task whose realization incites within me a concrete certainty, and not the caprice of carrying out an ideological ambush or a frivolous intellectual prank.[29]

While for Macedonio the nothingness of the self or, in his own words, the *almismo ayoico* (selfless soul) was a precondition for a pure perception of the world, Borges embarks on a similar quest to achieve this same mode of perceiving the self.

For the centenary of Macedonio's birth in 1974, Borges also published a note in *La Nación* in which he expanded the ideas he had introduced in *La Opinión*.

---

[27] Attala, "Macedonio y el orden," 119.
[28] "He mitigado sus excesos barrocos, he limado asperezas, he tachado sensiblerías y vaguedades" (Borges, *OC*, 1974, 13).
[29] "Intencionario / Quiero abatir la excepcional preeminencia que hoy suele adjudicarse al yo: empeño a cuya realización me espolea una certidumbre firmísima, y no el capricho de ejecutar una zalagarda ideológica o atolondrada travesura del intelecto" (Borges, *Inquisiciones*, 93).

In this case, however, even though the portrayal of his friend bolsters certain features already mentioned, he sheds light on new nuances of Macedonio's personality. He says: "He was an Argentine lawyer, a tenuous gray gentleman, who lived in the neighborhood of Balvanera and who had surrendered, a unique [case] in his century perhaps, to the curious occupation of thinking."[30] Whereas in the note for *La Opinión* Borges had praised Macedonio's oratory as one of his exceptional features, in *La Nación* he recognizes that it was his thinking that made him a genius. Furthermore, he even aligns his thinking with the Greeks: "Some six hundred years before Christ, in a time of oracles and myths, the Greeks set about thinking; a history of the Greek pre-Socratic could include Macedonio."[31] This affirmation is revealing because it suggests that Macedonio's thinking was not only experimental, but also evocative of a foundational and inaugural event.

Following Michel Foucault in *The Hermeneutics of the Subject*, it is possible to argue that Borges was right when he included Macedonio as part of a genealogy of great thinkers that began in Ancient Greece. In the first lecture of his seminar, Foucault explains that for the Greeks the principle of "know yourself" also implied the "care of the self."[32] He also points out that this principle, which the Greeks called *epimeleia heautou*, was comprised of three different levels: "an attitude towards the self, others, and the world."[33] This "care of the self" implies turning our vision inward and, while we are submerging ourselves in meditation on our thought, we are also directing our attitude toward others and the world. Foucault adds: "The *epimeleia* also always designates a number of actions exercised on the self by the self, actions by which one takes responsibility for oneself and by which one changes, purifies, transforms, and transfigures oneself."[34] Macedonio's experiments and daily practices centered precisely on how to configure a process of *subjectivation* that, folding inward into an individual existence and perception, could release the self from any form of constriction and, at the same time, liberate others and the world.

---

[30] "Era un abogado argentino, un tenue señor gris, que vivía en el barrio de Balvanera y que se había entregado, único en su siglo tal vez, a la curiosa ocupación de pensar" (Borges, *Textos recobrados*, 178).

[31] "Unos seiscientos años antes de Cristo, en un tiempo de oráculos y de mitos, los griegos se pusieron a pensar; una historia de los presocráticos griegos podría incluir a Macedonio" (Borges, *Textos recobrados*, 179).

[32] Foucault, *The Hermeneutics*, 4–5.

[33] Foucault, *The Hermeneutics*, 10–11.

[34] Foucault, *The Hermeneutics*, 11.

This practice on oneself to transform one's relation with the world can be traced to a letter that Macedonio mailed to his aunt Angela del Mazo: "I think and I always want to think. I want to know at once if the reality that surrounds us has the key to explain it or [if it] is totally impenetrable."³⁵ Borges also alluded to this decision in Macedonio's thinking, which for him was a way of life, in the following anecdote: "One Saturday he told us that if he could understand himself in the countryside, in the middle of the plains [pampas], perhaps he would understand the universe, but he was not sure that this revelation would be communicable in words."³⁶ How would it be possible to write about this form of thinking? Attala once again suggests an answer: "His would be *bad writing* because he is a *thinker*, a [way of] being that comes not from a particular external order, but from a certain immanent and autonomous disorder."³⁷ Macedonio rehearsed how to think out loud or, in other words, in plain sight. His writing encompasses this quest and his ethic of writing, which assumes the limitations of a language for accomplishing such a mission, provoking radical linguistic torsions and producing new inflections in words to supersede these limits.

Voices of a Metaphysical Conversation

For Borges, Macedonio was a thinker: he embodied the act of thinking. So, how did he position himself with respect to his friend/mentor? In "Una versión de Borges" (A Version of Borges), he asserts: "Chance (such is the name that our inevitable ignorance gives to the inevitable fabric of effects and causes) has been generous with me. It says that I am a great writer. I appreciate this curious opinion, but I do not share it [...] I am not a thinker."³⁸ Throughout his life and work, Borges meticulously assembled a system of fictitious doubles and alterities of himself, and created dialogues between an I and an Other, but an Other who, in turn, is the same; dialogues that evoke his own specular conversations with Macedonio.

---

[35] "Pienso y siempre quiero pensar. Quiero saber de una vez si la realidad que nos rodea tiene una llave de explicación o es totalmente impenetrable" (*Epistolario* (1991), 238).
[36] "Un sábado nos dijo que si él pudiera entenderse en el campo, en plena llanura, quizá entendiera el universo, pero que no estaba seguro que esa revelación fuera comunicable en palabras" (Borges, *Textos recobrados*, 178).
[37] Attala, "Macedonio y el orden," 116.
[38] "El azar (tal es el nombre que nuestra inevitable ignorancia da al tejido inevitable de efectos y de causas) ha sido generoso conmigo. Dice que soy un gran escritor. Agradezco esa curiosa opinión, pero no la comparto ... No soy un pensador" (Borges, *Textos recobrados*, 173).

As Borges developed these dialogues projecting kaleidoscopic images, the faces of the two writers seem to overlap, collapse, and cancel each other out. However, Borges could not stop looking for the Other: the maker, the metaphysician, the storyteller, and the thinker who was incapable of translating his voice into written words. He said: "The effectiveness of his [Macedonio's] reflections lay in the intonation with which he said them. It is a pity that these intonations cannot be translated into the written word."[39] Would it not then be more appropriate to consider that neither of them could actually transcribe Macedonio's voice into written words? However, Borges introduced in his own work the central pillars of Macedonio's theory of art and metaphysics, for instance, when he makes himself a narrator and character in his short stories.

In his prologue for *La invención de Morel* (*The Invention of Morel*) (1940), Borges claimed that Bioy Casares's science fiction novel was based on a "reasoned imagination," which is an interesting concept to consider in light of the procedure he followed when implementing Macedonio's ideas in his writing. In this sense, it is also relevant to remember that he and Casares invented the fictitious writer Honorio Bustos Domecq, whose surnames originated with the authors themselves; Bustos was Borges's great-grandfather, and Domecq was an ancestor of Casares. For Borges, proper names became an object of his creative exercises: his own name, the name of his family, ancestors, and friends, as well as of the authors he admired, became the names of characters in his texts. One of the most interesting and well-known examples of how his writing performs the principles of Macedonio's theory of art is "Pierre Menard, autor del *Quijote*" ("Pierre Menard, Author of the *Quixote*") (1939), a short story that has led scholars to think about the status of the author and the condition of the literary text, while reflecting on the contingencies of human existence.

In his conversations with Macedonio, Borges found evidence of the exceptionality that characterized him, which according to Borges, as mentioned before, was impossible to recover. Nonetheless, through his persistent reconstruction of these conversations, he drew up perfect scenes for his friend/mentor. Borges's essay "Diálogo sobre un diálogo" ("Dialogue about a Dialogue") (1961) crystallizes this meeting between the two writers, an encounter that occurs in a pure present, as Borges elaborates a metaphysical reflection on the immortality of the soul, and the two writers' voices reverberate. He writes:

---

[39] "La eficacia de sus reflexiones estaba en la entonación con que las decía. Es lástima que esas entonaciones no puedan traducirse a la letra escrita" (*Textos recobrados*, 173).

A- Absorbed in our discussion of immortality, we had let night fall without lighting the lamp, and we couldn't see each other's faces. With an offhandedness or gentleness more convincing than passion would have been, Macedonio Fernandez's voice said once more that the soul is immortal.[40]

In "La noche de los dones" ("The Night of the Gifts") (1971), he also seems to return to this scene when a dialogue about metaphysics triggers an old man's memories of Juan Moreiras's death that he then shares with his interlocutors.[41] At the end of his narration, he says: "After so many years, I'm not sure anymore whether I remember the man that was actually there that night or whether it's the man I was to see so many times afterward around the slaughterhouses."[42] Remembrance and memory, repetition and time, constitute both of Borges' essays, which bring back distant voices from the past and reenact them in the pure present of the text.

In his essays and fictions, Borges frequently introduces dialogues as key rhetorical devices to further develop his arguments and plots. During the early stages of his work, as he conceived a new *criollo* aesthetic and outlined the principles of his metaphysics, he also began developing his conversational strategy. In "El tamaño de mi esperanza" (The Extent of My Hope) (1926), for instance, he asks for "a conversational *criollismo* of God and of the world," a plea that condenses and anticipates two maneuvers that he will later carry out.[43] First, it signals the future development of his writings, which will be characterized by the tension between his own Argentine language and location and the possibility of conveying a universal experience. Second, his words encompass a dialogue between literature and philosophy that will also be an essential feature of his work. Nonetheless, when Borges asserted that Macedonio's geniality stemmed from his conversational skills he tended to foster a condescending perception of his mentor's writing.

---

[40] "A- Distraídos en razonar la inmortalidad, habíamos dejado que anocheciera sin encender la lámpara. No nos veíamos las caras. Con una indiferencia y una dulzura más convincentes que el fervor, la voz de Macedonio Fernández me repetía que el alma es inmortal" (Borges, *OC*, 1974, 784).

[41] See Borges, *El libro de arena*. Juan Moreira was a gaucho who worked for politicians as their bodyguard and was assassinated by the police c.1870. The Argentinean writer Eduardo Gutiérrez, after reading this police news, wrote a novel about him, which the newspaper *Diario La Patria Argentina* published as a booklet between November 1879 and January 1880. The novel was an immediate success and, at the same time, marked the beginning of a popular myth, created, written, and rewritten in several different formats, including, pantomime, theater, prose, and film until the present day. This genealogy of varying narratives is known as "moreirismo," and even Borges participated it. His short story "La noche de los dones" should be inscribed within this tradition.

[42] "Pasado el tiempo, ya no sé si me acuerdo del hombre de esa noche o del que vería tantas veces después en el picadero" (Borges, *OC*, 1974, 784).

[43] "Un criollismo conversador del Dios y del mundo" (Borges, *Inquisiciones*, 11).

In his fictions, Macedonio also strategically introduces dialogues. In *MNE*, everybody speaks: author, reader, and characters. In the novel, he configures a framework in which what is possible or impossible is always at stake, and between these two options, the author's voice can be heard reflecting on the process of writing the novel or inviting the reader to perceive with him their mutual participation in the emerging plot. These fictional dialogues, a consistent strategy throughout the text, produce a pure existence in the process of reading the novel, which, paradoxically, also reaffirms their inexistence.

Horacio González has pointed out the specific relevance of these conversations in Macedonio's literature and how they function:

> The Macedonian conversation then relies on a double demand. On the one hand, the nullification of the speaking subject in the conversational act. And then the conversation as a playful act, whose consequence is irony and where the speakers are absent. Borges recounts how Macedonio uses a technique that consists in saying things in a derisory and carefree way, which leads to (wishing) that they be disregarded. Once this purpose is fulfilled, those same things, said in an elementary or impoverished fashion, may remain in the mouth of another interlocutor who enunciates them with the approval and praise of Macedonio himself.[44]

He also identifies three main features of these dialogues: a democratization of enunciations, the practice of irony, and a permanent tension that arises from metaphysical questions, which he claims constitute Macedonio's literary style and the foundation for his fictions. In a similar vein, Ana Camblong has suggested that in *MNE* conversation during "a genuine encounter lacks façades, yet it inaugurates a fictional world that disregards the *other world*; we now find the fictional condition that sustains the semiosis of the amorous dialogue to be confirmed."[45] The Macedonian conversation dwells in a space between the novel and life, and reveals an ethical and metaphysical strategy to convey the status and condition of the "people of art" that inhabit the story.

The dialogues that Borges introduces in his stories—akin to Macedonio's dialogues with his actual interlocutors and through his writing with his readers—act as a liaison between life and fiction, and Borges's writing moves

---

[44] González, *El filósofo cesante*, 51.
[45] For Ana Camblong, the Macedonian conversation is constituted in a knowledge that opposes the stasis of common sense, false intellectualism: "With this mere knowledge, what does not banish the reading from whatever text circulates, the subjects placed into conversation achieve wonders: creation, humor, and enjoyment. Silence is present, accompanying and intervening; its presence is a paradoxical guarantee of the word" (*Macedonio. Retórica y política*, 51–2).

in both directions to bring elements from the real world into literary realm and introduce literary devices in the world. His story "Tlön, Uqbar, Orbis Tertius" (1940) could be read as a manifesto of this process of writing. The dialogues among its characters, their shared readings, and their friendship support the fictional plane on which the story is told, which could be simplistically defined as fantastic. However, it should also be considered that Borges's story delves deeper into a metaphysical exercise to fathom themes such as the inconstancy of the real world, the restitution of inexplicably lost objects, and the pure present of storytelling. He includes a footnote in the text that condenses and thematizes the force that propels his fiction: "Today, one of Tlön's religions contends, platonically, that a certain pain, a certain greenish-yellow color, a certain temperature, and a certain sound are all the same, single reality."[46]

Also, for Macedonio fiction was a means for metaphysical exploration and for individuals to sense their metaphysical existence. In Tlön, metaphysics is a branch of fantastic literature, a premise that constitutes the foundation of the aesthetic experience that Macedonio sought to achieve. Thus, it would be interesting to consider Borges's story as a tribute to his friend/mentor. Fictions are mental structures and states that create the world, and one's imagination is the substrate of fiction. "Tlön, Uqbar, Orbis Tertius" and *MNE* are both fictions created with remnants of the real world, with its ontological ruins, which undermines the consistency of our own actual ground and our own ontological status as subjects. In both texts, while the double fictional identity of their characters give us the possibility of choice, the authors develop an allegorical sense in the stories that uncovers an archaic vestige and transforms what has been lost into the source of a lesson, and the narration about this absence into a form of consolation.[47]

Borges and Macedonio sought to achieve a literary experience of a pure present and a metaphysical thought capable of transforming what is absent into an epiphany that could only be revealed by the process of reading fictions. They both shared a common definition of literature and proposed that readers should be, according to a young Borges, like conversationalists "of God and of the world." Nevertheless, these readers must be able to listen to the speech of literature, and in order to respond to its eternal calling, they should follow Macedonio's

---

[46] "En el día de hoy, una de las iglesias de Tlön sostiene platónicamente que tal dolor, que tal matiz verdoso del amarillo, que tal temperatura, que tal sonido, son la única realidad" (*OC*, 1974, 438).

[47] By contrast, Garth and Dubnick analyze Borges's story as a complex maneuvering to criticize Macedonio's idealism. See "Uninvited Inversions," 158.

advice: "you will read more like a slow approach approaching than like an arrival."[48] Jean-Luc Nancy's use of the French word *entendre*, which means both to listen and to understand, with regards to how an individual experiences the world, can shed more light on the converging thinking and aesthetic projects of Macedonio and Borges. For Nancy, *entendre* is a revelation of a secret resonance that allows the individual to develop an acute perception of something that is almost unnoticeable.[49]

Macedonio invited his readers to assume this attitude in order to hear the sound of a voice that emanates from the text and that always arrives as a reverberation. In Borges's literature, this resonance becomes a pure present in the fictional scene of the conversation. He was a seeker of the particular nuances of the voice, and a translator whose writing aimed to follow the form and dynamic of a voice. The primordial matter of several of his stories, in fact, relies on a trace left by listening, on previously heard stories, and on fictional dialogues. Furthermore, in the conversations that Borges and Macedonio introduce in their texts, there are two simultaneous tones that draw two different figures: the ironist and the metaphysician. While the ironist undermines previous forms of knowledge and beliefs, the metaphysician proposes to explore an experience that crosses the boundaries between actual life and the sense of nonexistence.

The same scene of his conversations with Macedonio that Borges often recalled, the attributes with which he invested a Macedonian character, in sum, his practice of reading as an intrinsically literary exercise, offer us the opportunity to participate in the aesthetic experience of an imaginary community, which only demands that we release ourselves from the burdens of our pre-given Self. In this manner, paradoxically, Macedonio is saved from Borges's solipsism in the reenactment of the conversation with his friend as he performs the core principles of Macedonio's metaphysics, such as altruism and passion put into play in the dynamic of their conversation.[50] His literature creates the illusion that we are present in their infinite conversation. Borges's words at Macedonio's funeral in 1952 illuminate the nature of their dialogue: "The Historians of Jewish

---

[48] "leerás más como un lento venir viniendo que como una llegada." See Fernández, *Teorías*, 133.
[49] See Nancy, *A la escucha*, 29.
[50] For Macedonio love and friendship are two forms of "la Altruística" (Altruistics). In *NTV* (1990), he states: "la traslación del yo es más heroica en el amor que en la amistad, pero el régimen altruístico entre iguales (no la piedad) es el mismo" (the transferal of the self is more heroic in love than in friendship, but the altruistic regime between equals (not piety) is the same) (335).

mysticism speak of a sort of teacher, the Zaddik, whose doctrine of the Law is less important than the fact that he himself is the Law. Something of the Zaddik was in Macedonio."[51] Borges's recurrent conversations with this mythical Macedonio demonstrate that not only should these texts be used in our search for the real Macedonio, but that we must also mutinously examine Macedonio's own writings in order to perceive how they inherently participated in his creation.

---

[51] "Los historiadores de la mística judía hablan de un tipo de maestro, el Zaddik, cuya doctrina de la Ley es menos importante que el hecho de que él mismo es la Ley. Algo de Zaddik hubo en Macedonio" (Borges, "Macedonio (1874–1952)," in *Borges en Sur*, 300).

2

Heroes without Selves: Macedonio Fernández and a New Ethics of the Heroic

Todd S. Garth

Given the evident centrality of the concept of the autonomous individual in popular notions of the heroic, and the importance of the related idea of individual genius as the seat of heroic action, examining Macedonio Fernández's writing in terms of the heroic would seem contradictory. Reconciling heroic discourse with the words of one of Latin America's foremost deniers of the existence of self and refuter of the role of consciousness and genius in individual identity sounds counterintuitive at best. However, if one takes into account the apparently unbridgeable gap between popular representations of the heroic in contemporary Western culture and the dismantling of the individual as a generator of meaning in postmodern intellectual thought, the potential of seeking out the heroic possibilities of Macedonio's narrative becomes more compelling. What would a philosophy of the heroic look like in the context of the negation of the self? Can one discern in Macedonio's words the makings of an anti-Cartesian, arguably anti-modernist, heroic? Might Macedonio point the way to an anarchist heroism, one not constrained by the structures of individual—state relations that, according to Luis Othoniel Rosa, define the complex of bourgeois discourses that Macedonio disavows?[1] How would Macedonio's heroes personify, as Daniel Attala puts it, an "ethics of Altruism and its hyperbole, Passion and Love"?[2] If there is such a thing as the postmodern hero, can Macedonio help us understand it?

Several theorists of postmodern morality and ethics, complemented by recent examinations of Macedonio's ideas, suggest he can. While a straightforward equivalency of ethical and moral discourses with heroic discourse would not address the question—ethics, morality, and heroism are not the same thing—it is

---

[1] See Othoniel Rosa, *Comienzos para una estética anarquista* (2016).
[2] See Attala, "Naturaleza y anti-Naturaleza," 260.

undeniable that heroic discourse must incorporate the problem of what is moral and ethical and must consider to what extent morality characterizes heroes. Or, to reverse the equation, inquiry into the nature of heroism clearly can have a weighty bearing on the parameters of ethical and moral discourses. Zygmunt Bauman's 1993 study of postmodern ethics is particularly helpful in this regard as it expressly addresses the idea of the "moral hero."[3] Similar, less comprehensive, studies of the nature of ethics in postmodern thought, such as Nomy Arpaly's concept of "unprincipled virtue," will also furnish guidelines as to how Macedonio can be regarded in terms of an alternative—and at moments as an explicit alternative—to traditional and contemporary heroic discourses.[4] Analyses of Macedonio's own philosophical referents, particularly his unstinting campaign against both pragmatists and moralists, exemplified by Hobbes and Kant, will lend support to this effort. A further ingredient to this study are the more generic nineteenth-century precedents in defining the heroic that Macedonio certainly knew, namely the writings of Thomas Carlyle and Ralph Waldo Emerson, writings upon which, this argument will maintain, Macedonio works conceptual inversions.

Essentially, this essay argues that an analysis of Macedonian ethics in light of postmodern theory and philosophical precedent helps lead us to a prototype of Macedonian heroism. But more importantly, the heroic reveals itself in some of the most characteristic moments of Macedonio's narrative—in *Adriana Buenos Aires*, in *Papeles de Recienvenido* (The Newcomer Papers), and in *Museo de la Novela de la Eterna* (*The Museum of Eterna's Novel*). These are precisely the moments in which Macedonio galvanizes his most fundamental ideas on ethics, not to philosophical precedents and abstractions, but to everyday life—in other words, to popular discourses. The expression of Macedonio's "almismo ayoico" (selfless soulism) in the everyday gives us a sense of how an anti-modernist, anti-bourgeois, and anti-Cartesian heroism operates beyond the confines of intellectual discourse.

A discussion of the heroic in Macedonio, however, would be inchoate without consideration of its direct counterweight, the heroic in Jorge Luis Borges. Concrete evidence demonstrates that Borges is at the nexus of the encounter between the heroic tradition, condensed in Carlyle and Emerson, and Macedonio's efforts to disembowel that tradition. Borges's obsession with the concept of hero, his quest to absorb the heroic into a post-realist cultural theater that Argentina would take part in, is amply documented.[5] The timing of the onset

---

[3] See Bauman, *Postmodern Ethics*.
[4] See Arpaly, *Unprincipled Virtue*.
[5] See, for example, Comas de Guembe, "Jorge Luis Borges: El sentido heroico de la vida," and Hernández, Juan José, "Borges y la espada justiciera."

of this obsession is worth noting. Borges translated Carlyle's *On Heroism, Hero-Worship and the Heroic in History* and Emerson's *Representative Men* in a joint volume in 1949, but one can very nearly pinpoint the genesis of his fascination to 1928, the year in which Borges published his first fully formed short story, "Hombres pelearon" (Men Fought). This story, only slightly altered and finally released under the title "Hombre de la esquina rosada" ("Pinkcorner Man"), is the anti-heroic narrative ballad that launched the series of vignettes similarly exploring anti-heroism under the rubric of *Historia universal de la infamia* (*A Universal History of Infamy*).[6] 1928 is the same year that saw a documented rift between Borges and his *porteño* mentor, a rift which was evidently temporary and whose causes scholars continue to speculate on, but which logically had philosophical as well as personal implications.[7] Without making any further speculations on the nature of this rift, this study will use Borges's stance on the heroic as a kind of illuminating mirror, suggesting that the modernist Borgesian heroic can serve as an antithesis to Macedonio's implicitly anti-modernist heroic, under the inference that Borges developed his version of the heroic both in conversation with and in contrast to Macedonio.

One convenient short-cut for delineating the heroic tradition that Emerson and Carlyle attempt to reconcile with both Western cultural history and nineteenth-century pragmatic thought is the model elaborated by Joseph Campbell, who, although never obtaining a doctorate, achieved notoriety for his concept of "monomyth"—an overarching paradigm of myth that Campbell proclaimed as universally human—and its corollary paradigm of the heroic.[8] The usefulness of Campbell's model is actually enhanced by its flaws, as his yardstick

---

[6] A relatively skeletal precursor to this story, titled "Leyenda policial," appeared in *Martin Fierro* (4.38, 1927), and "Hombres pelearon," very much as we know the story today, was included in 1928 in *El idioma de los argentinos* (151–4). The story next appeared in *Revista Multicolor de los Sábados*, the Saturday supplement of the popular daily *Critica*, on September 10, 1933 under the title "Hombres de la orilla" with authorial pseudonym "F. Bustos." Borges served as the editor of the *Revista Multicolor* through the entire run of the series which, with the following installment, was titled "Historia Universal de la Infamia." The story title "Hombre de la esquina rosada" was finally used for the version in the book that comprises this series. A number of sources demonstrate that Borges's obsession with the anti-hero, and particularly with the aggressive, morally ambiguous hero who knew how to fight, coincided with the crystallization of his particular conception of timeless contemporary myth. Among these are the fact that in *Idioma de los argentinos*, "Hombres pelearon" was paired with the meditation "Sentirse en muerte," which muses on a feeling of mythic timelessness, obviously in tune with Macedonio's analogous ideas. In unpublished notes dating from 1952 (see Red Avon notebook), Borges reinforces this association by describing the genesis of this story in a timeless oral legend that had circulated in an erstwhile working-class Buenos Aires neighborhood called "Tierra del Fuego." See also Montiveros de Mollo's 1995 analysis.

[7] See C. García, "*Vigilia*," 45–53.

[8] See Campbell, *The Hero*.

for heroism is so obviously imbued with the Western modernist reliance on the Cartesian autonomous individual. Campbell's primary cultural point of reference is James Joyce (his first publication was a concordance to *Finnegan's Wake*), and his primary heroic archetype is Daedalus, an individual hero "dedicated to the morals not of his time but of his art."[9] Although an imperfect analysis of myth and heroism as generically human cultural phenomena, Campbell's work is an excellent testament to the absorption of the heroic tradition into Western modernism, the very discourse that Borges so devotedly pursues and Macedonio so determinedly gainsays.

Among the most salient qualities of Campbell's heroic paradigm are: (1) the call to adventure under a supernatural guardianship that protects the hero from harm; (2) a journey into a primal "zone of magnified power," previously unexplored by mortals and bristling with unimagined challenges;[10] (3) the triumphant, transformative return back from the unknown; (4) the imbuing, by means of this adventure into and return from a transcendent dimension, of the divine into the human and the realization of humanity's divine potential;[11] and finally, (5) the self-sacrifice or self-annihilation that aims to save the world from the monstrous and that culminates in a rebirth.[12] This modernist heroic discourse, necessarily simplified here, has for both Borges and Macedonio profound implications for the possibility of a contemporary (for today's reader, postmodern), ethics.

Zygmunt Bauman argues that modernity's flawed paradigm of ethics is founded on an essential contradiction in Kantian thought. Kant's conception of duty, in which the self acts purely out of obligation towards the Other, relies on the belief in symmetry between self and Other—both self and Other are free subjects.[13] Morality is determined by universal standards of duty that apply equally to all subjects, to "I" and to "Thou." But Kant's duty in fact requires a fundamentally asymmetric relation between self and other, because the "moral hero," as Alastair McIntyre further develops the concept, can only measure himself by a unique yardstick—by standards that the Other cannot be expected to adhere to.[14] Habermas attempts to solve this problem by positing a symmetry among subjects that is prior to ontology—prior to the distinction between self

---

[9] See Campbell, *The Hero*, 18.
[10] See Campbell, *The Hero*, 57–73.
[11] See Campbell, *The Hero*, 188–212.
[12] See Campbell, *The Hero*, 77–82, and 90–3.
[13] Bauman, *Postmodern Ethics*, 49.
[14] Bauman, *Postmodern Ethics*, 51.

and Other. Regardless, Bauman asserts, the insistence on symmetry between self and Other precludes the application of duty by means of any overarching or generic *rule*, because the application of universal rules requires *asymmetric* relations between self and something greater, more purposeful, more expedient, than self.[15] Morality, Bauman concludes, is "endemically and irredeemably *non-rational.*" The moral call is "thoroughly personal"; the moral person is moral by his or her essence alone, although socially *with* others.[16] Morality is also prior to thought—while ethics is shaped through reason, morality is the function of solitary and self-sacrificing impulse. Macedonio's extended campaign against Kantian thought pertains here and has direct bearing on the possibility of heroism in the twentieth century and beyond. His solutions to the impasse identified by Bauman nearly a century after Macedonio first addressed similar problems make use of a stance similar to that of Emmanuel Lévinas, Bauman's primary reference for a postmodern morality.

In discussing Macedonio's implicit treatment of these problems, a logical place to start is with the notion of the hero-poet, promoted by Thomas Carlyle and taken up indirectly by Ralph Waldo Emerson. The central concept behind this figure is that of artistic integrity, which Carlyle elaborates in terms of personal sincerity and a resistance to all forms of self-promotion.[17] Carlyle's stance is fundamentally Kantian, based on the separation of inner feeling from public action and the reliance on personal duty to reconcile the two.[18] His poet-hero, personified by Shakespeare, demonstrates his artistic integrity—and thus the genuineness of his genius—by virtue of his artistic triumph without self-aggrandizement.[19] Emerson similarly disallows self-promotion of the heroic poet, but—logically, for a man who relied on public appearances to disseminate his ideas—qualifies individual genius as a conduit for collective spirit. The collective genius of a nation or a time is distilled in the individual poet, whose heroism is thus manifested.[20] Borges's preference for Emerson's version of this phenomenon is unsurprising. His quest to integrate a collective Argentine presence into the Western cultural tradition finds its primary vehicle precisely in the figure of the individual genius who personifies a nation's distinctive voice—one of the foremost candidates for that vehicle being Macedonio Fernández.

---

[15] Bauman, *Postmodern Ethics*, 54–5.
[16] Bauman, *Postmodern Ethics*, 160–1.
[17] See Childers, "Baroque Quixote," 439.
[18] See Childers, "Baroque Quixote," 441.
[19] See Carlyle, *On Heroes*, 96–7.
[20] See Emerson, *Representative Men*, 110.

Macedonio, however, offers an implicit retort to this set of problems by inverting the roles of poet and collective. He does this not just by constantly circling back to the reader's reception of *MNE*, insisting that the real creator of the novel is the reading public. He also accomplishes the inversion by making the novel itself the main protagonist of the narrative and placing the novel in the role of conquering hero—the characters of this fiction set out to save the city of Buenos Aires by "novelizing" it.

And yet Macedonio does not simply ignore the heroic individual wrought by centuries of cultural tradition and adapted by Borges to a modernist sensibility. In contrast to Borges's invented, equivocal, mythical, unstable, and arguably interchangeable heroes, Macedonio gives us heroic lacunae—figures who place themselves at the center of the narrative by virtue of being perpetually ungraspable, nonexistent, or absent. This is most obvious in Recienvenido (Newcomer), whose entire story relates his rendering himself ungraspable, both literally by the police and any public that happens to witness his acts, and figuratively by a readership that is taunted with language designed to frustrate apprehension.[21] In the chapter titled "El 'capítulo siguiente' de la autobiografía del Recienvenido" (The "Next Chapter" in Newcomer's Autobiography), for example, a large portion of the text is presented as from the pen of an editor, explicating both the unknown-ness and the absence of the author of this autobiography:

> Our author is truly anonymous; if it weren't that Shakespeare already has someone to confuse him with, it would be a pleasure to offer him up for the purpose. The reading of his works does not secure a basis by which to judge his talents as a writer; we are still ignorant as to whether he has had a birthday, whether he was upset at birth, whether he recovered from his illnesses or died each time; whether his life lasted to the end of his days or whether science managed to conclude it earlier ...[22]

The text continues in this vein for a very long paragraph until it meanders off into an account of a dinner hostess's indignation at the unknown author's grammatical slips while discoursing on the nature of holes in the tablecloth:

---

[21] See Macedonio *PRC*. Cívico-Lyons analyzes in detail Macedonio's technique of evoking humor through frustration in *Papeles de Recienvenido*, precisely by making the apprehension of representation and meaning impossible (see "El humor de Macedonio Fernández").

[22] "Nuestro autor es verdaderamente incógnito; si no fuera que Shakespeare tiene ya con quien se le confunda, sería una satisfacción ofrecérselo para ese propósito. La lectura de sus obras no nos procura base para juzgar sus talentos de escritor; ignoramos siempre si cumplía años, si nació disgustado, si mejoraba de las enfermedades o moría cada vez; si su vida se prolongó hasta el fin de sus días o pudo la ciencia hacerla concluir antes ..." (*PRC* (1989), 23).

... and then he looked all over, claiming that the most replenished of them could be found nowhere, which was, metaphysically speaking, indefensible; according to the most plausible and celebrated hypothesis, it must have unloosed itself from within and disappeared; for which he accepted no responsibility.[23]

Recienvenido not only repeatedly reinforces his own absence—or the impossibility of his own existence—he serves to reinforce the constant and perpetual effects of absence as a generalized phenomenon. In other words, Recienvenido heroically sacrifices himself to the metaphysical principle of absence and unknowability.

An important aspect of this self-sacrifice is Macedonio's persistent rejection of publishing and presenting himself as an author while simultaneously relying on the joint phenomena of public opinion and public consumption to maintain his fame as an unknown, unproductive and insignificant author. This is in direct contrast to Emerson's employment of tireless self-presentation on the lecture circuit in his efforts to illustrate exemplary individuals of Western civilization while simultaneously deprecating self-promotion in favor of the collective genius of that civilization as manifested in those individuals.[24] Inverting Emerson's model, Macedonio relies on public opinion and consumption to promote his individual fame but reveals that fame to be empty of anything meaningful to a supposed cultural or historical collective. The more renowned he (or his heroic absence in the form of Recienvenido) is as an author, the less "known" he becomes as a coherent individual, because fame is social, public, and therefore necessarily fragmented. He *must* be famous publicly to be unknown as a coherent self. And if both public fame and individual coherence depend entirely on absence and unknown-ness, then the integrity of Civilization itself is placed in doubt. The supposed heroic potential of Everyman—of a given people, age, or civilization—cannot be concentrated in the individual hero because that hero, by virtue of his fame, is fragmentary and elusive. If the potential of Everyman is instead to be found in the spiritual collective, that collective ends up affirming the nonexistence of the coherent hero and the existence of the incoherent one, suggesting that the collective itself must be fundamentally incoherent.

Macedonio's disparagement of Shakespeare emphasizes this last point. Carlyle and Emerson elect Shakespeare as the quintessential poet hero and England's (or

---

[23] " ... y luego remiraba todo alegando que el más surtido de ellos no estaba en ninguna parte, lo que metafísicamente era indefensible; según la hipótesis más plausible y festejable, debía haberse zafado por dentro de sí mismo y desaparecido; de lo que no se responsabilizaba" (*PRC* (1989), 23).

[24] See Elbert, "From Merlin to Faust," 116–20.

more accurately, the Anglophone world's) greatest treasure, specifically because they regard Shakespeare as the principal factor in the cohesion of English culture.[25] This is a model that endured throughout the nineteenth and twentieth centuries in Europe and the Americas; whether or not Carlyle was the genesis of that model, there is no question that he had an important role in consolidating and promulgating it. There is equally no doubt that Borges, while questioning the objectivity of national cultures and the autonomy of cultural icons, admitted and also promulgated the symbiosis between cultural icons and national cultural coherence. Borges's critical caveat was that icons were the product of myth and national culture the vehicles of myth; that caveat, however, served to facilitate a more subtle and complex idea of cultural coherence rather than to discard it. But for Macedonio, Shakespeare's status as a cultural icon—an arguably heroic figure—is only possible because he doesn't exist as a coherent entity, individual sensibility, or historical presence. His genius can exist precisely because he is nowhere in time, place, person, or nation. The nation, accordingly, must also be an incoherent fiction.

In *MNE*, Macedonio turns his attention to other such figures—both national heroes and Western cultural icons. His dismissal of the very idea of national heroes runs throughout the novel and is almost too obvious for comment here: his hatred of statues, his proposal to eradicate representative nomenclature from streets and plazas, and his belittling of Argentine cultural celebrities— even Camila O'Gorman doesn't escape.[26] Among the supposed immortals of the Western cultural tradition, in addition to Shakespeare, Macedonio singles out Goethe, Poe, Flaubert, Tolstoy, Zola, and Ibsen, as well as the sacred Spanish Golden Age quadrivium of Cervantes, Quevedo, Góngora, and Calderón, allowing, in select cases, for isolated moments of true art almost entirely smothered by the consecration of false art. This canon of false cultural icons, moreover, is owing precisely to the "existence of the public" that encourages "this recitative calamity" to suffocate art.[27]

More interesting, and less commented on, is Macedonio's effort to replace what he terms these "multitud de nulidades" (legion of nullities) consecrated by posterity as glorious artists and objects of cultural veneration, with constituents of everyday life and with metaphorical figures of an eternalized present.[28] Curiously, the fate of Shakespeare and other such poet heroes suffers

---

[25] See Emerson, *Representative Men*, 116–19, and Carlyle, *On Heroes*, 96–7.
[26] Fernández, *MNE* (1996), 195–203.
[27] *MNE* (1996), 44–5.
[28] *MNE* (1996), 44.

in Macedonio's work a transformation very similar to what Borges gives us. In the case of Beethoven, for example, Macedonio characterizes the supposed musical genius as merely a compiler and annotator of popular tradition: "Maybe everything we call music, starting from Bach, is just obsessive elaborations wrought on ditties and fragments of song that those other musicians and peoples left behind in vast number."[29] This is a passage that of course could have directly inspired Borges's ideas on cultural tradition, but Macedonio's implications are more radical than those of Borges: for Macdedonio, Beethoven *never existed* as an artist of individual identity or integrity; the romantic model of individual, heroic genius is simply wrong. The everyday people who dreamed up and sang bits and themes that the great composers contrived into compositions are the true hero artists. In this fashion Macedonio inverts the Emersonian model that Borges respects and perpetuates: rather than Emerson's poet-hero Shakespeare, "suffering the spirit of the hour to pass unobstructed through the mind," *MNE* gives us the collective mind of everyday life passing through the spirit of the hour, making the present moment eternal.[30] Macedonio's nonexistent, incoherent heroic voice attempts to eternalize Buenos Aires, to eternalize his readers as well as his characters, ridding them of the past and rendering them eternally present. This is an operation upon the everyday moment only possible in a dimension that is both incoherent and unreal—the dimension of the metaphorical novel. The heroic genius that accomplishes this operation can only be a nonexistent author with no objective individual autonomy, one completely subordinated to the novel itself.

Macedonio's outright rejection of poet heroes as autonomous beings and sensible and productive consciousnesses also pertains to the moral dimension of heroism and its relationship to the idea of autonomy. Contemporary philosophers make cogent arguments as to why the Kantian link of individual autonomy and moral acts is untenable and how the discarding of that link can lead to reformed conceptions of morality and to rethinking the connection between the ethical and the heroic. Bauman, in addition to explicating the essential asymmetry of moral relations that Kant requires to be symmetrical, also notes that the "command" relations between self and Other preclude the autonomy of moral decisions in anyone except the self and its own representations of knowledge:

---

[29] "Quizá todo lo que llamamos música desde Bach, son elaboraciones de obsesión pegada a los temitas y fragmentos de canto que en inmenso número dejaron aquellos músicos y pueblos" (*MNE* (1996), 53).
[30] *MNE* (1996), 10.

The Other is recast as my creation; acting on the best of impulses, I have stolen the Other's authority. It is now I who says *what* the command commands. I have become the Other's plenipotentiary, though I myself signed the power of attorney in the Other's name. "The Other for whom I am" is my own interpretation of that silent, provocative presence.[31]

Nomy Arpaly, approaching the question of moral agency through pragmatic discourse, also arrives at the conclusion that Kantian autonomy and its corollary of rational deliberation is not coherent with moral responsibility and decision making. Indeed, Arpaly expands this observation to all notions of "heroic autonomy" posited by philosophical tradition: Kant's duty, Nietzsche's superior free spirit, Aristotle's exceptional contemplative life, and—especially significant for Borges's approach to heroism—Spinoza's ideal of freedom.[32] Arpaly points out that autonomy and rationality, rather than being seen as exceptional, heroic qualities, are generally regarded as the norm. She offers numerous examples of why this contradiction reflects a more important reality—that moral action is dependent on neither autonomous consciousness nor deliberative thought.[33] Perhaps her most interesting and pertinent example is a literary one: Huck Finn, she observes, arrives at a moral assessment of slavery not through an autonomous consideration of laws, justice, and morality; on the contrary, he recognizes that his duty is to respect the laws governing an enslaved black man. Rather, Huck acts morally through compassion acquired experientially and emotionally, through his personal affection for the slave Jim, and not through reason.[34]

When it comes to the moral repercussions of autonomy, Recienvenido might be regarded as the preliminary study for Macedonio's most far-reaching challenge to the autonomous heroic paradigm, *MNE*'s Presidente. The defining characteristics of the Presidente are almost exactly inverse to the modernist heroic paradigm articulated by Joseph Campbell. Rather than venture forth on a lone journey, the Presidente sends forth a collective. Instead of traveling to an unknown dimension and returning triumphantly to the known world, this collective, the characters inhabiting "La Novela" (The Novel), ventures forth from an imaginary realm, vaguely delineated in abstract terms, into the brutal reality of Buenos Aires; while they return thinking they have succeeded in their mission, ultimately they are defeated. Rather than work a transformation on

---

[31] Bauman, *Postmodern Ethics*, 91.
[32] Arpaly, *Unprincipled Virtue*, 124. For a discussion of Borges's conception of self as influenced by Kantian, Hegelian, and Spinozian thought, see Faucher.
[33] Arpaly, *Unprincipled Virtue*, 76–8.
[34] Arpaly, *Unprincipled Virtue*, 93.

individual humans, imbuing them with god-like qualities that enable them to thrive in the mortal world, the Presidente's mission aims to transform the mortal world to make it more amenable to the otherworldly—that is, to fictionalize Buenos Aires. Finally, rather than save humanity from monstrosity, the Presidente opens the otherworldly territory of La Novela and its characters to human monstrosity—a monstrosity that is distinctly individual, intimate, secret, and erotically troubling in nature.

Initially, the Presidente sends his characters individually out of La Novela into the "real" world of Buenos Aires, charging them at first with seeking out real-world abstractions and bringing them into his fictional dimension:

> To Sweetperson: ... to seek out and bring back the "so very good thing," after which whoever snuffs out his life is only optimistic and happy having been determined to do as much beforehand as, being an optimist, whether this "so very good" thing is something in life or something in art, it is followed by silence like suicide.
>
> To Father: to seek and bring back the injury that would kill the unjust offender, whose error in a paroxysm of justified fury kills us out of desperation or leaves us miserable forever after ...
>
> To Maybegenius: fetch the secret that is told, but "in secret."
>
> To OneLove: bring back imperturbable hope, in unwiltable memory.
>
> To Simple: find the only reader of novels left who gets worked up when the novelist allows his veracity to be doubted or concedes that something in his narration might not be possible.[35]

But the Presidente faces two fundamental problems: (1) that the individuated characters, sent out as autonomous individuals, cannot act true to their natures and thus can't enact their heroic essences; and (2) that merely finding abstract qualities in the real world won't help save it. He is also hobbled by his own nature—a president, like an author, is by definition a commander and cannot be the source of a heroic unfolding of inner sincerity.

When this initial attempt to integrate the real with the unreal proves unsatisfactory, the Presidente tries again. At first, he and his characters celebrate

---

[35] "Dulce-Persona: ... que buscara y trajera lo 'tan bueno' que después de ello sólo es optimista y feliz quien extingue su vida y estuvo determinado a hacerlo así desde antes por lo mismo que era optimista, sea eso 'tan bueno' cosa de la vida o cosa del arte seguida en este caso del silencio como suicidio. / A Padre: buscar y traer la injuria que mataría al ofensor injusto y cuya falta en el paroxismo de justa ira, nos mata de desesperación o deja desdichados para todo el porvenir ... / A Quizagenio: recoger el secreto que se dice pero 'en secreto.' / A Deunamor: traer la espera imperturbable, en la memoria inmarchitable. / A Simple: encontrar el lector de novelas que todavía quede y que se atufa cuando el novelista consiente en que se dude de su veracidad o admite que algo de lo narrado puede no ser posible" (*MNE* (1996), 131–2).

the success of the revised heroic project to conquer and save the city of Buenos Aires. This second effort is accomplished by the inverse of the mythological (according to Campbell) triumphant return from an unreal or magical dimension in which the autonomous hero earns superior powers. Instead, the Presidente realizes that both the illness and the cure lie in collectives—the ailment being a function of "real" political collectives, the city's "... two bands into which the population had divided: Tenderizers and Histericizers."[36] The strategies of these two adversarial groups are noteworthy for being competing techniques of mimesis, arguably corresponding to Romanticism versus Kitsch, applied to political ends. The antidote of the Presidente's "Conquest" is to impose "recursos, ejercitados indistintamente por toda la compañía del Presidente ..." (strategems, exercised as a group by the whole of Presidente's company), everyday manifestations of Macedonio's "idealism" intended to transgress and frustrate, throughout the ordinary routines of the city's inhabitants, the very principle of mimesis.[37] In other words, the heroic campaign to conquer Buenos Aires transposes the unrepresentable principles of an unreal dimension on to the representative principles of a real one. A crucial ingredient to the campaign's success, however, is Eterna's specific role as the metaphorical bearer of inspirational light for an artist struggling to create.

The Presidente's realization that all his efforts have failed—that the city is "irremediably ugly"—owes apparently to the inherent absence of nature in human-made urban environments.[38] This surprisingly brief passage argues that contemplation neither of mystery nor of timeless daily life, with its "suggestion of time,"[39] are possible in the city. However, there are three other related problems associated with the failure of the Presidente's project: the built-in paradox of love and its consequent frustration; the necessary isolation of an author of any project, aesthetic or otherwise; and the inevitable end of the novel itself.

Meditation on nature of love is central to *MNE* as it is to all of Macedonio's writing, is infused throughout the text and, not surprisingly, gives rise to myriad ambiguities and contradictions. Two of those conflicts are pertinent here. The first

---

[36] "dos bandos en que se había dividido la población: Enternecientes e Hilarantes" (*MNE* (1996), 198).

[37] *MNE* (1996), 201–02. The specifics of this campaign are detailed by numerous critics, some of whom note the similarity between this passage of *MNE* and accounts of Macecdonio's own burlesque 1921 and 1927 campaigns for the Argentine presidency. See for example: G. García 23; Garth, *The Self*, 106–09; Prieto, *Desencuadernados*, 67, 79–80, 85–6.

[38] *MNE* (1996), 229. Macedonio brings up similar points in other texts, including *ABA*, but nowhere as emphatically as in his correspondence with his cousin, civil engineer Gabriel del Mazo (*Epistolario*, 153–4).

[39] *MNE* (1996), 230.

is the gulf between the Presidente's conception of love, which is contained in his vision of mystery; of life as unreal, timeless nonexistence, and Eterna's conception, which requires a time previous to love's existence and an acknowledgment of a time after life's conclusion. The Presidente's failure to "conquer Eterna's all-love," to convert her life into pure timeless passion, is analogous to the failure of the inhabitants of the Novel to permanently transform Buenos Aires into pure aesthetics—an impossibility given the manmade ugliness that *defines* the city.[40] Just as the city yearns for a beauty and a resolution of its tumult that its very nature precludes, so Eterna's inherent yearning for life—part of her nature as a novelistic character—precludes the full realization of love between her and the Presidente. The Presidente's heroic conquest of life by passion is forestalled by the implacable reality of his eternal heroic muse. (A similar impasse can be inferred in *MNE*'s complement, Macedonio's Last Bad Novel, *ABA*, in which its male protagonist, Eduardo de Alto, comes to affirm that a passion between him and the young Adriana is, effectively, an oxymoron.)

Bauman gives us a philosophical solution of sorts to this dilemma by distinguishing the merging of identities in collective emotion or collective morality from a togetherness that integrates apartness. Following Lévinas, Bauman argues that moral relationships are prior to ontology, prior to any synthesis of individuals into collectives, meaning that morality lies outside of any temporal or corporeal principles of ordering. Rather than being sought in primordial myth, morality is to be established in a transcendent present that results in a "face-to-face" relationship with self and Other, a togetherness between "faces" that acknowledge the separateness of each. This encounter confirms a relationship of self *for* Other rather than *with* Other, giving oneself over to the Other.[41] Culminating in something very similar to what Macedonio's writing gives as an alternative moral hero realized through passion, Bauman asserts that:

> ... as a moral person I am taking this responsibility as if it was not me who has taken it, as if the responsibility was not for taking or rejecting, as if it was there "already" and "always," as if it was mine without ever being taken by me. My responsibility, which constitutes, simultaneously, the Other as the Face and me as the moral self, is *unconditional*.[42]

---

[40] *MNE* (1996), 230–2.
[41] See Bauman, *Postmodern Ethics*, 70–4.
[42] See Bauman, *Postmodern Ethics*, 74.

The resonance of Bauman's ideas with Macedonio's voices of both author and Presidente lies in the rejection of an ordered ontology that privileges the "real," in the foregrounding of the affective and, as will be argued below, in the concomitance of togetherness with apartness.

The second conflict occasioned by love is less explicit in the text, but for that reason more troubling and even more intractable: the inescapable galvanizing of heroic passion to monstrous abuse. This is alluded to in Padre's (Father's) initial assignment, noted above, in the first chapter of the Novel (following *MNE*'s fifty-six prologues), of seeking a corrective to the perpetrator of "error in a paroxysm of justified fury." Later in the first chapter is a passage between Padre and his daughter, Dulce-Persona (Sweetperson), further exploring this problem. Dulce-Persona tells Padre that she has happened upon a portion of the Presidente's manuscript detailing the cause of the rift between them; Padre's daughter thus informs him of the specifics of his own creation. Padre's passionate anger in the wake of his daughter's "incredible carelessness" and his unwarranted suspicion of her harboring "certain passions" had determined him to administer a punishment that would make an example of her. Padre's own recollection of this moment merits reproducing here:

> Father recalls with horror the instant in which, it is true, he thought of tarnishing his daughter with a stain that nothing might erase. And he thinks: "fortunately I couldn't consummate an act that only desire, never hate, can commit."[43]

A father's unjust punishment of his daughter "in a paroxysm of justified fury," ultimately resulting in their separation, clearly involves pressing some sort of sexual act upon her. There is something monstrous about love, whether erotic or paternal—Macedonio implies a close association between the two.[44] Immediately following this passage, however, the chapter relates Dulce-Persona's "sensual and innocent curves" with the splendor of Buenos Aires, discoursing on the virtues of passion in inspiring the eternal limitless present.[45] Inverting the heroic tradition of defeating the monstrous by means of heroic passion, Macedonio asserts that the monstrous, secret and shameful dimensions of passion are inseparable from

---

[43] "Padre recuerda con horror el instante en que, es cierto, pensó dejar en su hija una mancha que nada pudiera borrar. Y piensa "felizmente no pude consumar lo que sólo el deseo y nunca el odio puede ejecutar" (*MNE* (1996), 134).

[44] This association—along with an explicit discussion of forcible incest as a fictional exploration of the problem of paternal love—is addressed in an unpublished 1928 letter from Macedonio to Ramón Gómez de la Serna. See Garth *The Self*, 136-7.

[45] *MNE* (1996), 135.

its virtues; heroic passion does not rescue us from monstrosity but instead gives us permission to own it. In terms Arpaly and Bauman might recognize, the priority over moral laws of affective relations and experience and of the Other's face—including the Other's erotic presence—opens us up to the possibility of a postmodern moral heroism.

Bauman, again following Lévinas, turns to the concept of "the caress" as addressing this aspect of moral passion.[46] The caress, on the one hand, is unequivocally erotic; on the other hand, it is a purely metaphorical phenomenon, an erotic love that is simultaneously general and particular, that simultaneously connects with the Other and establishes his or her apartness, "the gesture of one body reaching towards another; already, from the start, in its inner 'structure,' an act of *invasion*, let it just be tentative and exploratory."[47] This concept not only resonates with Macedonio's presentations of "innocent" erotic passion between characters, but also coincides with his calls for an eternal present and for the role of passion in eliminating both past and future. Because for Bauman the caress recognizes the "absolute alterity" of the Other, it exists in an ungraspable abyss of a future that "cannot possibly be found in the present" and is directed at an Other that is perpetually elusive and that exists in mystery, in a way that does not intend to possess.[48]

When, in the last chapters of *MNE*, the Presidente declares that the characters of the Novel must disband, in part because he and Eterna cannot reconcile their differing conceptions of love, Macedonio pointedly leaves open not only the possibility that readers will continue the novel, but that Eterna *could* find love. The obstacle of her passion with the Presidente is manifested in her refusal to accept any of his caresses: "to this day she refuses every caress that he invites or that he covets; she would be tireless and undiscriminating in caresses, but only loving and being loved without any perplexity whatsoever."[49] Having created Eterna, having commanded her, having posited her as an individuated ideal, the Presidente is proscribed from engaging her love. But one of his other characters, Quizagenio, is distinguished as "*the man with the greatest power of caring* that there is in the world."[50] Being the perfect and complete object of love, Eterna is

---

[46] See Bauman, *Postmodern Ethics*, 92–5.
[47] See Bauman, *Postmodern Ethics*, 93.
[48] See Bauman, *Postmodern Ethics*, 93–4.
[49] "le niega hasta hoy toda caricia que él le convida o que él le codicia; sería incansable e indiscerniente en cariacias, pero sólo amando y amada sin perplejidad alguna" (*MNE* (1996), 235).
[50] "*el hombre de mayor poder de cariño*" que hay en el mundo" (italics are in the original text, *MNE* (1996), 235).

unable to find passion of an individual, a state of affairs that makes her "the most miserable and the happiest" of characters.[51] But this does not preclude erotic love from ever reaching her.

The fundamental apartness of all of these arguably alternative heroic figures—Eterna, Dulce-Persona, the Presidente, Recienvenido, Eduardo de Alto, the author, the Novel, and Macedonio himself—brings us to a critical aspect of this attempt to articulate a postmodern heroic: the paradoxical nature of individuation. At the end of *MNE*, the fragility of these individual characters, once cast out from their imagined and authored community, is explicit.[52] The possibility of happiness for Eterna and the Presidente, whose very essence—their respective isolation in the absoluteness of Eterna's perfection and in the Presidente's unreality—make remote the possibility of contentment. An important implication of the final chapters is that the "command structure" of the novel, the asymmetry of its discourse and the imposition of that discourse upon readers and characters, renders impossible either fulfilling relationships or a productive community. This is arguably the aspect of Macedonio's philosophy that most troubled Borges. The implied hermeticism of the alternative hero, his or her possibility of completeness only in the dimensions of absence, unreality, dreaming, metaphor or affect essentially untouched by the objective world, cannot have been acceptable to him. This helps explain why Borges was so intent on Macedonio's mythic status—not only in order to consolidate him as a poet hero of the Argentine cultural dimension, but also to save him from being merely a wise old man living alone in boarding houses, cut off from the life of the city as well as the lifeblood of Argentine cultural discourse. Macedonio's response to this was to maintain not a mere absence, but a heroic state of artistic production in perpetual absence, ever elusive and unknown, in complete contrast to Emerson's self-presentation.

The paradigmatic opposite of Macedonio's self-dissolution in aesthetic exercise might be Beau Brummel's "abolition of any trace of subjectivity from his own person" as it is represented by Giorgio Agamben.[53] As a result of Brummel assuming the role of the ultimate flaneur-cum-exhibitionist, all outward appearance and no interior substance, all outward observation and no inward feeling, his individual identity vanished, but did so as a gesture integral to his comprehensive "commodification of the real." This stance resulted in the

---

[51] *MNE* (1996), 235.
[52] *MNE* (1996), 252.
[53] See Agamben, *Stanzas*, 53.

appropriation and objectification of unreality as well as reality for Brummel's private, individual aesthetic ends. Agamben's response to this phenomenon is a retort to the entire cultural and philosophical history of individuation. Individuation in community, he argues, begins with "indifference of the common and the proper, of the genus and the species, of the essential and the accidental."[54] "In-diference with respect to properties" (18.9) is what enables the coming of self into community. Macedonio might argue something similar, only going further and eliminating the possibility of self.

Macedonio's heroes—or his metaphorical alternative to the heroic—inhabit that zone in which the lone individual, eschewing any objectivity that might be commodified, any sense of self that might be exploited for an asymmetrical differentiation between I and Thou, self and Other. Inverting the heroic discourse of the mythic tradition that Borges still sought after, Macedonio give us metaphors for transforming the everyday into art, for inciting transcendent passion that admits the potential of the monstrous and thus can forestall it, for perpetuating poetry without laying claim to it or presenting oneself as its author, for sacrificing self to Other without commanding a recognition of self, for attempting to shape ideal—and idealistic—communities out of our fragile oneness.

---

[54] See Agamben, *The Coming Community*, 18.9.

3

Consuelo-Eterna, Macedonio's Erotic and Metaphysical Passion*

Ana Camblong

In feminine homage to Consuelo Bosch

A Corpus of Bodiless Passion

Passion occupies the highest position of value in Macedonio's think-writing; a romantic vestige that, with wide-ranging and unbiased freedom, merges Stoic propositions, Heraclitan aspects, Cynic viewpoints, baroque conceptism, pragmatic beliefs, avant-garde aesthetic judgments, Nietzschean influence, and so on and so forth in this eclectic convergence of elements taken from the most diverse sources to achieve such an extravagantly original mixture. A rare paradoxical alchemy that adamantly detests rationalism, empiricism, classes of Kantian Enlightenment, and the values from that project of modernity that splintered into so many sarcastic *isms*: moneyism, diplomaism, scientism, academicism, and herdism in all of its forms. In Passion (always capitalized for Macedonio), this complex universe finds its driving force, its true impetus, the invincible force of every cherished human enterprise as well as its guiding principle, the absolute power to which the preeminent acts of men and women in their epistemic, ethical, aesthetic, political, and general amorous searches respond: "A State, culture, art, science or book not conceived to serve Passion, either directly or indirectly, has no explanation."[1]

---

* Translated from the Spanish by Sean Manning.
[1] "Un Estado, cultura, arte, ciencia o libro no hechos para servir a la Pasión, directa o indirectamente, no tienen explicación" (*NTV* (1994), 230). Translator's note: All translations are mine. Translations of passages from *Museo de la Novela de la Eterna* were made in consultation with Margaret Schwartz's *The Museum of Eterna's Novel* (Rochester, Open Letter, 2010).

If Macedonio defines his own metaphysics as Absolute Idealism, we could then very well define Macedonio using Kaminsky's same characterization of Spinoza as an "Absolute Passionalist,"[2] especially because it fits and places him alongside another great solitary soul unwavering in his intellectual ethics, although the two differ in other philosophical aspects. Macedonio the thinker adopts an emphatic and "impassioned" stance that considers its tensions against the concept of Will put forth by Schopenhauer, his greatest teacher. In his early essays, annotations in his unpublished *Diary*, and other passages scattered throughout his works, we can locate evidence of Will's meddling and reflections on its impact, especially on everyday life. However, these traces lose their clarity once Passion begins to invade every field, govern every act, and articulate discourse through an intricate mesh connecting and embroiling each and every dimension of the human endeavor. Macedonio's temperament finds a more visceral intensity in Passion, more primal if you will, whose drive incorporates the vector of desire, the escape toward the Other, the intrinsic eudaemonic finality (Pleasure–Happiness) of the human animal's struggle for life. A comprehensive look at his philosophical universe confirms Passion to be the dominant global and interstitial principle, consuming his leisure, his caprices, his nonsense's infinite transformation, his anarchical decisions, outrageous projects, erratic trajectories, and the all-embracing child-world of art, love, thought, and humor. It is clear that Schopenhauer's Will, with its demands and forfeited paths, does not sympathize or agree either with Macedonio's discourse or with the life he led with singular persistence, against the grain of history, against sociocultural obligations and the canonical norms of his time, or of almost any time for that matter. There we will find Passion, not Will, which is almost always ridiculed by Macedonio's decisions.

> That Knowledge founders, it matters little; Passion lives true.[3]
>
> I follow Passion, which holds every certainty and whose dogma is: "Nothing diminishes me; only I am precious within the Being, only in me is there an I; not mine, but Hers, says the Lover; not mine, but His, says the Beloved."[4]
>
> Oh, Passion, never humble, always right![5]

Passion, therefore, solicits various argumentative precisions to justify such invulnerable power. One attribute possibly conspiring against its omnipresence

---

[2] See Kaminsky, *Spinoza: la política de las pasiones*, 16.
[3] "Que el Conocimiento se desconcierte, poco importa; la Pasión vive cierta" (*NTV* (1994), 325).
[4] "Yo sigo a la Pasión, que tiene toda certeza y cuyo dogma es: 'Nada me aminore; sólo yo soy preciosa en el Ser, sólo en mí hay un Yo; no el mío sino el de Ella, dice el Amante; no el mío sino el de Él, dice la Amada" (*NTV* (1994), 332).
[5] "¡Oh, Pasión nunca humilde, siempre cierta!" (*NTV* (1994), 333).

might be the impossibility of its representation, a condition, however, in which Macedonio identifies its strength, yet another confirmation of his sarcastic distrust of signs, perceptions, "empiric reality," and its verifiable materiality.

> Passion loses nothing by being unrepresentable, that is, not visualizable; it has no tactile or visual form; just as there is no tactile or visual form, there is also no form in images of Pleasure-Pain.[6]

It is difficult to talk about Passion. It is difficult to find the necessary discourse or language to truly represent it. Passion's ubiquity speaks through gestures, distance, smells, looks, the body, tones, laughter, and with the semiotic ductus of any act, including of course linguistics. Yet its dissipated, molar evanescence, forceful and elusive, decisive and wayfaring, establishes itself inside the very meaning of human interaction. In his essay *La idilio-tragedia* (The Idyll-Tragedy) (1922), concerning Passion, he writes:

> Passion is any total and perpetual substitution of living for oneself with "living-for-another." It is metaphysics, since it is the death of the Ego substituted with the ego-other.[7]

In addition to constituting a metaphysical category, the ego's transmutation into the "ego-other" is captured inside two further notions that act as synonyms, though with slight variations: *Almismo ayoico* (Selfless soul), associated with psychology, and *Altruística* (Altruistics), which is more suggestive of ethics. Nevertheless, it is important to clarify that these two designations are not absolutes, merely slants emphasizing a particular aspect, which does not at all complicate their inclusion in Passion's plenitude; they refer to manifestations of Passion within different states of Affection and Sensitivity. The following passages will allow me to develop the basis for such assertions:

> [and] for that reason I call the Being a selfless soul, because it is always complete in its states without demanding correspondence with supposed externalities or substances [...] Selfless, or without a self, because it is one, unique Sensitivity, and nothing can occur, be felt, that is not my own feeling.[8]

---

[6] "Nada pierde la Pasión con ser irrepresentable, es decir, no visualizable; no tiene versión táctil ni visual; así como no hay versión visual de lo táctil, no hay versión en imágenes del Placer-Dolor" (*NTV* (1994), 327).

[7] "Toda sustitución completa y constante del vivir para sí mismo por el 'vivir otro' es Pasión, es metafísica, pues es la muerte del Ego sustituido por el ego-otro" (Relato (1987, 147).

[8] "[y] llamo por eso al Ser un almismo ayoico, porque es siempre pleno en sus estados y sin demandar correlación con supuestas externalidades ni sustancias [...] Ayoico, o sin yo, porque es una, única la Sensibilidad, y nada puede ocurrir, sentirse, que no sea el sentir mío" (*NTV* (1994), 243).

> I use *Passion* to refer only to the order of Altruistics; [...] everything that is not a thirst for the transferal of the self, a mutual desire for one to be the other, a reverential happiness for another's personal being, holds no ethical or mystical interest, or better yet, is the Ugliness of Being and Art.[9]
>
> Passion is to live the life of another, with secondarity, almost nullity of one's own. It is without a doubt an emotional state, but it is also metaphysical to the extent that it breaks the link with a body: and if we are not linked to a body, we are not linked to anybody.[10]
>
> There are no ethics or aesthetics involved in asking for oneself and acting, intellectually or muscularly, for oneself. Only altruism is ethics and beauty. And it is happiness.[11]

The negation of the self is just as much a part of the Dream and the Mystic State as it is of the amorous Passion of a couple, a friendship, or a mother's care. One could condense this spectrum of Love's variants, but each instance possesses its own characteristics. Within the realm of Passion relative to the love-couple and friendship there is a sensorial and emotional convergence that makes no distinctions based on gender or sex; the body is reduced to sheer appearance, an existence immersed in its own contingent becoming and carried along by the passionate confusion of every boundary:

> To love the person apparently occupying another body and to know that person more than ourselves is the only Passion. Passion is friendship with or without gender disparity [...] the transferral of the self is more heroic in love than in friendship, but the altruistic system between equals (not pity) is the same.[12]

Macedonio's passionateness finds itself caught inside an inescapable aporia with the body; a dead-end street that is not avoided, but instead traveled and inhabited: the "paradoxical habitat" that is accepted as a starting point and a

---

[9] "*Pasión* llamo únicamente al orden de la Altruística; [...] todo lo que no es una sed de traslación del yo, un recíproco afán de ser uno el otro, la alegría admirativa por el ser personal de otro, no tiene interés ético ni místico, o mejor dicho, es lo Feo del Ser y del Arte" (*NTV* (1994), 334).

[10] "Pasión es vivir la vida de otro, con secundaridad, casi nulidad de la propia. Es sin duda un estado emocional, pero es también metafísico en cuanto anula la ligazón a un cuerpo: y si no estamos ligados a un cuerpo no lo estamos a ninguno" (*NTV* (1994), 335).

[11] "En el pedir para sí y en el obrar para sí intelectual o muscularmente, no hay ética ni hay estética. Sólo el altruismo es ética y es belleza. Y es felicidad" (*R* (1987), 163).

[12] "Amar la persona que aparencialmente hay en otro cuerpo y conocerla más que la nuestra, es la sola Pasión. La amistad con o sin disparidad de sexo es la Pasión [...] la traslación del yo es más heroica en el amor que en la amistad, pero el régimen altruístico entre iguales (no la piedad) es el mismo" (*NTV* (1994), 334–335).

result of the passionate event's inventions. The metaphysical state grants access to a field beyond immediacy, the leap into the void (of the body, of time and space) where the absolute encounter awaits, and to the lovers' *mise en abîme* of infinity, of the continuity of two, of discontinuities:

> Metaphysically speaking, Passion's great intellectualist contribution is accomplishing the complete realization of the my-body's revocability: not opting for a consciousness without a body, but for a consciousness that exchanges its my-body. [...] in *plenoamor* (total love) one lives on what happens psychically to an expressive figure that is not the my-body received at birth, it is the my-body of another (another who continues to be other).[13]

The aporetics of love exceed corporality while concentrating its transformation inside this extreme possibility of abandoning the my-body in order to become the other-body, without ceasing to be aware that it is another-body. The body exists and breathes using the demands of its senses inside this metaphysical universe built with eccentric conceptual structures that envelop it, elevate it, and subject it to a precarious state of dissipation. The potency of the intellect imagines complex artifacts to refute the burden of the "real," the siege of "materiality," the limits of this "human, all too human" condition, the unacceptable impact of death. And in this magnificent mechanism of erroneous transmutations, there dwells a disconcerted body, tormented by paradox. In the course of passion, the body imposes its evidence, but also sacrifices itself at the altar of Absolute Idealism. The Absolute devours its flesh, which remains there, without *absolutely* surrendering its material and desirous emergence.

To give an approximate idea of this basic aporia present throughout Macedonio's life and discourse, I would simply add the following: on one hand, we find texts that maintain a careful register of daily habits, food, hours slept, strategies for preserving good health, for treating the body hedonically, which include the manifestations and urgencies of sexual life. But, on the other hand, all the body's needs are an aggravation, a demand to be attended to as little as necessary, and sex in particular is an inconvenience that, to the extent possible, must be avoided or neutralized. Thus, in the aforementioned text on the Idyll-Tragedy, he states, "(I exclude sexual physiology completely, so foreign to art and to poetry or natural beauty; its only relation to Passion is as an obstacle, just

---

[13] "Metafísicamente, el gran aporte intelectualístico de la pasión es cumplir la íntegra realización de la revocabilidad del mi-cuerpo: no una opción por una conciencia sin cuerpo sino por una conciencia que cambia de mi-cuerpo. [...] en el plenoamor se vive de lo que acontece psíquicamente a otra figura expresiva que no es el mi-cuerpo congénito, es el mi-cuerpo de otro (y que sigue siendo otro)" (*NTV* (1994), 335).

another zoological appetite),"[14] while in a letter to Natalicio González, a later text from 1951, he emphatically insists, "And I call Passion only what belongs to Altruistics, and I do not attribute any value or meaning to our sexual animalities, foreign to everything Ethical and everything Artistic."[15] This is a problem that also appears in the occasional annotations throughout his notebooks; below are two such passages:

> There are those who possess greater artistic instinct than sexual instinct: the melodic and harmonic series is more sought after and pleasurable than the procreative series.[16]
>
> In the future the sexual organs and function will disappear. Man will be born in a laboratory. The world will then change dramatically. Sexuality is the scourge of civilization: it offers no pleasure and causes disease, neurosis, crime, secrecy, responsibility, distress and even marriage or bachelorhood for men and spinsterhood for women. (A man's bachelorhood is his happiness; a woman's spinsterhood is her shame.)[17]

In his ideological distinction between animality (physiological and sexual) and art (the sublime), passion holds firm over the entire *corpus*, which rejects the body; contrarily, the body remains equally demanding, petitioning and speaking for itself. The tensions of creation and procreation intertwine in incompatible struggles, while at the same time evoking a dimension of natural equilibrium that Macedonio constantly accepts and challenges. His prophetic words on reproductive technologies reveal the brilliant inspiration of the thinker who sees the future with too much foresight, which explains why he kept private his notes on what was unspeakable, unthinkable at that time. In this context, maternal love receives a substantial advantage: "Maternal passion is complete, but it does not possess the drama posed by the risks of animalization through physiological

---

[14] "(Excluyo totalmente el fisiologismo sexual tan ajeno al arte y a la poesía o belleza natural; sólo como obstáculo tiene algo que ver con la Pasión, es uno cualquiera de los apetitos zoológicos)" (*Relato* (1987), 146).

[15] "Y que llamo Pasión sólo a la altruística y no doy ningún valor ni sentido a nuestras animalidades sexuales, extrañas a todo lo Ético y a todo lo Artístico" (*Epistolario* (1976), 74).

[16] "Hay gente que tiene más instinto artístico que sexual: la serie melódica y armónica es más buscada y placentera que la procreadora" (*Todo y nada* (1995), 205).

[17] "En el porvenir van a desaparecer los órganos y la función sexual. El hombre nacerá en el laboratorio. Entonces va a cambiar extraordinariamente el mundo. La sexualidad en la civilización es la mayor calamidad: no da nunca placer y trae enfermedades, neurosis, crímenes, ocultaciones, responsabilidades, desasosiegos y hasta el casamiento y la soltería del hombre y la soltería de la mujer. (La solteronía del hombre es su felicidad, la soltería de la mujer es su desgracia.)" (*Todo y nada* (1995), 152).

sexuality."[18] Of course, babies are not brought by storks arriving from Paris, but this contradiction is of no importance because anyone, regardless of sex or age, is capable of practicing maternal love through the magic of Passion. Still, Macedonio locates this unparalleled love, deserving of admiration and envy, fully within the realm of the feminine. Conceptual comings and goings roll out passionate territories with flexible laxity in certain respects and with tenacious rigidity in others. We will revisit this quality of passion later.

Lastly, to bring this framework to a close, we must consider the implicatures of Passion with regards to life pierced by the arrow of time:

> Passion's splendid "Today" is diminished in finalities. Loving its today is the greatest tribute and service to the Future.[19]
>
> There is eternity for all of us, but only fully realized Passion can eternalize a moment, that is, memory triumphs over eternity, replacing it with *todoamor*'s (totalove's) instant of Passion, which occurs at any stage throughout the totality of time.[20]

Macedonio's eternity is established in "*todoamor*'s instant of Passion" in a fundamentally baroque metaphysical proposition that, like an irrefutable refrain, repeats the Quevedian certitude "Amor constante más allá de la Muerte" (Love constant beyond Death). His think-writing achieves the impossible: the abolition of time, and it does so with magnificent poems, with rigorous essays that attempt to explain the unexplainable, and with his monument to eternity, *Museo de la Novela de la Eterna* (*The Museum of Eterna's Novel*). Indeed, it is Passion, with its multifaceted impact, that sustained and drove Macedonio's original creative imagination until his death. Whoever loves from inside a body designed for death and with it formulates a non-death based on Passion placed inside another-body, reaches an invincible eternity. Regarding this, Kierkegaard would say: "This seems to be a paradox. But one need not think badly of paradox, for paradox is the passion of thought, and the thinker without paradox is like the lover without passion: a mediocre specimen."[21] The paths of love and thought

---

[18] "La pasión maternal es plena pero no tiene el drama de los riesgos de la bestialización por sexualidad fisiológica" (*R* (1987), 147).
[19] "[e]l espléndido 'Hoy' de la Pasión se menoscaba con finalismos. Amar su hoy es el mayor homenaje y servicio al Porvenir" (*NTV* (1994), 339).
[20] "[p]ara todos hay eternidad pero sólo la Pasión plenamente cumplida puede eternizar un instante, es decir la memoria triunfa de la eternidad, la reemplaza por el instante de Pasión del todoamor, acontecido en cualquier etapa de la totalidad del tiempo" (*MNE* (1993), 145). Translator's note: Here I use Schwartz's translation of Macedonio Fernández's neologism "plenoamor" (total love).
[21] See Kierkegaard, *Migajas filosóficas*, 51.

become disoriented by the paradox of passion, an eccentric intersection that only the wise, never the mediocre, will ever encounter.

Consuelo-Eterna, Passion's Body

MNE, written over a span of approximately thirty years, hides in its tangled fictional world the secret of the great Passion that inspired Macedonio throughout his adult life until old age: his *plenoamor* for Consuelo Bosch. This strange relationship was kept under a delicate and dignified pact of silence, honored by both lovers, through a game of agreements, inventions, and anachronistic courtliness. The exact details and biographical events were suspended inside a haze of mystery that removed their intense romance from the public eye. There were no legal, social, economic, or cultural obstacles that might have prevented the protagonists in this peculiar tale from making their profound romantic relationship "official." Nevertheless, they chose to shroud it in an enigmatic air of mutual adoration, without providing any explanations.

Their reservations toward any sort of contract, order, or "paperwork" stemmed largely from Macedonio's anarchic disillusionment, and as such, the lover was chivalrously grateful to his beloved for her tribute and understanding. The Non-Existent Knight carried himself with authentic knightly manners and charm, both in his discourse and in everyday life, an old-fashioned character that typified Macedonio's style and which Consuelo encouraged by never addressing him informally in public and also by responding with ceremonies rich in artifices and elegance: "I have been unfair; me, the one who is and has been throughout this ennobling arrangement as I recall the happiest and freest of the two."[22] Time and again, his texts express his eternal gratefulness to this woman who saved his life, his total dedication embodying the model of Passion his thought had conceived:

> [and] generous as always, or perhaps, because I beg you and long for you, *passionate*, humble in affection, not out of pity, but joyful, happy to give yourself to the fulfillment of the immense feeling of identification, of love, you, fervent woman will speak first.[23]

---

[22] "Injusto fui yo que soy y he sido en este trato ennoblecedor que me acuerda, el más feliz y libre de los dos" (*MNE* (1993), 172).

[23] "[y] generosa como siempre, o quizá, como yo le ruego y ansío, *apasionada*, humilde de ternura, no compadecida, sino gozosa, venturosa de darse a la plenación del inmenso sentir de identificación, de amor, tú ardorosa mujer hables primero" (*MNE* (1993), 172).

Even so, the reader will likely be interested in some proof of this Consuelo-Eterna identification, abundantly documented in countless passages from Macedonio's work. It would therefore be best to mention Macedonio's holographic testimonies, a collection of loose pages he kept separate in a folder, which include lyrical texts that read:

> An endless and immutable poem,
> Of the inconstant Eterna.
> For Consuelo
> Bowed at your feet, before we are discovered by the first word of the poem that today I recite for you, lower your loving countenance and the lucid spirit that with it, furrowed brow or serene, reveals your diligence and your repose, toward me, and toward the sober thought I have always commanded of my art.[24]
>
> Reflections of your soul, Consuelo. For eternal Consuelo.[25]
>
> Oh Consuelo, may your mouth never again pronounce: I am fleeting.[26]

In the novel's first publication in 1967, the proper name in these texts was substituted with the nickname "Eterna," an editing tactic that was applied to every passage in which the proper name appeared, which preserved the secret of Consuelo's presence in Macedonio's romantic life. It is difficult to judge whether this decision was appropriate. There is also no indication regarding what Macedonio might have wanted, considering that the paradoxical construction provides as many arguments for one option as for the other. My decision for the 1993 edition was the opposite, and I must express my gratitude to Adolfo de Obieta for respecting my position, despite having established the previous standard. I believe that readers should be aware of how the text was assembled, with as much accuracy as possible, in cases when credible documents are available. This is my professional stance. However, from a feminine perspective I also do not consider the effacement of Consuelo's value and incredible influence on Macedonio's writing to be fair. In his notebooks, there are a thousand and one fragments dealing with Consuelo as well as annotations referencing her that are labeled with the abbreviation "C." Below is an example taken from the notebook marked "AA" (*c.*1928), p. 33:

---

[24] "Poema sin término, e inmutable, / De la cambiante Eterna. / A Consuelo / Antes que, puesto el pie tuyo, acierte de vos y de mí la primera palabra del decir que hoy para ti comienzo, inclina tu faz amable y el lúcido espíritu que con ella, con ceño o con serena frente, muestra sus labores y sus reposos, hacia mí, y hacia el pensar grave que al arte me impuse siempre" (*MNE* (1993), 290).
[25] "Cambiantes de tu alma, Consuelo. A Consuelo eterna" (*MNE* (1993), 292).
[26] "Oh Consuelo, que en tu boca no se diga más: soy pasajera" (*MNE* (1993), 298).

–Invocation of Art before C.

I do not conceive Art except in the execution of Passion; nor do I want to see it practiced without the powers of Thought, proving the mystery of its Diction in the lucid speech of the mystery of the Whole. May my Art always be this when waiting to lay Words upon C's journey of Passion.[27]

His love for this woman is not the only thing made explicit here; her figure also plays an essential role in his art and metaphysical thought. It is undeniable that Consuelo's hegemonic presence in *MNE* is established in the initial stages of the text's creation, especially if we consider that the document I referred to in my genetic studies as *Manuscrito'29* (1929) was handwritten by Consuelo herself and constitutes an early composition of utmost importance in understanding the project's structure and general circumstances. This is even present in the text: "You write the manuscript of this your novel in which I give you my spirit as you have given me yours."[28] Both lovers, "necessary participants," seal their complicity inside the world of the novel, just as they had conceived it and lived it "to its ultimate consequences" and "they hid the evidence" of their contract inside the fantastic rhetoric of that Secret made known in literature, where it strictly states:

> She is Eterna; in her alone the Secret, our friend, found refuge, arriving so that we may write this page, told only to us, and on which no part of our secret will fade for words cannot tell it all, and if all were said, the secret would not be risked, no one would discover what it is, or what it is like, or if it is a secret in a dream or in reality.[29]

The paradox of the told-secret in this passage—a beautiful key ("a practical joke," Sanders Peirce would say)—reveals and conceals the lovers' joy and romance. It's true that their family and close friends were all aware of the "state of the matter," but they were willingly complicit in the unspoken agreement. My interest here, however, does not lie in presenting an anecdotage of this amorous saga, but

---

[27] "–Invocación de Arte ante C. / No concibo el Arte sino en ministerio de la Pasión; ni quiero verlo tampoco ejercerse sin los poderes del Pensamiento, probando su misterio de Dicción en el decir lúcido del misterio del Todo. Así sea siempre el Arte mío cuando atienda a servir de Palabras el camino de Pasión de C" (*MNE* (1993), 328–9).

[28] "Escribes el manuscrito de ésta tu novela en que te doy mi espíritu como el tuyo me diste" (*MNE* (1993), 127).

[29] "Es la Eterna, aquélla sola en quien el Secreto, amigo nuestro, halló el seguro, que viene para que escribamos esta página, dicha sólo a nosotros, en la que nada de nuestro secreto se desvanecerá pues todas las palabras pueden contarlo, que cuando estuviera todo dicho el secreto no se habrá arriesgado, nadie lo descubrirá, ni cómo es ni si es secreto en un sueño o en lo real" (*MNE* (1993), 180).

rather in bringing forth several testimonies on the Passion that was expressed in writing and on Consuelo's metaphorical and metaphysical transmutation into the character of Eterna.

Since the text's posthumous publication, specialized critics and general readers of Macedonio's work have seen Eterna as the hypostatic figure of Elena Bellamuerte, all of them transfixed by his legendary widowhood, the Idyll-Tragedy that left Macedonio devastated and that no doubt marked his writings with the same force as did his Passion. Nevertheless, such an affirmation does not contradict or diminish the sudden appearance of the new love that rescued him from his death-in-life, which had plunged him into a state of aimless wandering from one boarding house to another, a depressing gray monotony. In the same way that the endless *Prologues* in *MNE* insistently announce the arrival of a new narrative theory, the novel recounts again and again the epiphany of a new Passion, the awe of a Selfless Soul who illuminates and write-thinks this new real dream, this fantastic reality that transforms the universe (life–poetry–metaphysics):

> With this I make clear to the Reader that the first meeting between the President and Eterna was a dazzling light that appeared uncontrollably as if from an inexperienced thinker like him and Eterna, as majestic and profound in her feelings as she was suspicious and disciplined in the self-delusions and easy games of the masculine idea of loving.[30]
>
> When they met, she changed the President's past, such that he could no longer remember any instant in which he had not known her and loved her.[31]

After this spark that ignites the genesis of Passion, Consuelo is present everywhere and always, and she becomes the muse, the force, Eterna the allegory, which propels his think-writing. The author-narrator in *MNE* assembles the exemplary virtues of his love with passion and elegance: "the courage and good sense of a great woman, equaled by none I have ever known, discreet, compassionate, active, pure, and my pride has not suffered."[32] To understand the lover's declaration, we must consider the spiritual gifts as well as the social

---

[30] "Con esto dejo dicho al Lector que el primer conocerse del Presidente y Eterna fue un deslumbramiento que se manifestó sin medida como de un inexperto pensador cual él y Eterna tan majestuosa y profunda en sus sentimientos como suspicaz y maestra en resortes de las auto-ilusiones fáciles, del masculino creer amar" (*MNE* (1993), 166).

[31] "Al conocerse, ella cambió el pasado del Presidente, de modo que no recordó un instant en que no se contuviera el conocerla y amarla" (*MNE* (1993), 220).

[32] "la valentía y sensatez de una gran mujer, sin igual en lo que he conocido, discreta, piadosa, activa, pura, y mi orgullo no ha sufrido" (*MNE* (1993), 170).

lineage and financial wealth of this woman who took charge of everything, careful not to offend the manly "pride" proper to the sociocultural class to which both of them belonged. Eterna, in a self-definition (which is nothing more than the gaze of the narrator), states:

> –I am speaking to you, reader; I am Eterna; perhaps a noble woman, perhaps beautiful and strong of mind, emotionally generous and with a bleak future, perhaps vain and elegant-mannered, perhaps from a sumptuous house and prominent family, with a pristine and severe past, perhaps not happy, and capable of a joy whose exquisite, vibrant, exuberant laugh, resonating as if from some subdued inner depth, could perhaps efface the idea of Death.[33]

The repetition of "perhaps" is not intended to cast doubt on the assertions, rather it serves to mitigate any pretension, which Macedonio detested, while underlining the modesty of a considerate individual who speaks about herself. Consuelo's powerful social status is distressing for the apathetic lawyer, poor and unwilling to resume the work pace needed to be at the level of her circumstances. Yet this inconvenience turns out to be an outstanding advantage for the couple, given that they could rely on a steady, dependable, and "naturally" available source of income. The aristocratic animosity Macedonio felt towards money and the basic modes of obtaining it finds in this comfortable "compliance" a refuge for his helplessness. This removal liberates him from professional work, from marital demands, and patrimonial legal hassles (which he was already experiencing with his own family). This takes us to yet another paradoxical twist in our reading: Macedonio the revolutionary, the great demythologizer of social prejudices, is terrified at the idea of a breakdown in patrician decorum and reluctantly accepts the protection of his beloved. An unstable balance that laid siege to the relationship with its conflicts.

The proliferation of flattery in his narrative discourse steadily transforms Consuelo's beautiful, mature, sensual body into an omnipotent goddess (ethereal and yet concrete in her everyday presence), into a metaphysical category that governs the order of things, into lyrical passion's nocturnal muse, into "ardent fictions" capable of vanquishing Death; I present below one of Macedonio's holographic poems, intimate offerings sent to his beloved:

---

[33] "Te hablo, lector; la Eterna soy; una mujer quizá noble, quizá hermosa y fuerte en el pensar, de sentimiento generoso y de grave destino, quizá altiva y majestuosas maneras, quizá de suntuosa casa y de generaciones principales; con un pasado límpido y severo, quizá no dichosa, y capaz para una ventura cuya risa exquisita, estremecida, rebosante, resonando como desde hondura retenida, sin estrépito, quizá borraría la idea de la Muerte" (*MNE* (1993), 234).

Night Is the Beauty It Pleased You to Wear Yesterday

As if you thought your eyes once asked to be one with night's attire: donning stellar lights—but it was not that, rather the will of your soul, industrious in its adornments and self-transfigurations, its ardent fictions with which your spirit finds fantasy and the strength for Beauty to protect your being from the world, involuntary, limiting cosmos—you feigned pampered petition with your eyes—which, it is true, you shape and name disquiet—it was your vigilant concern that wished to live in the exaltation that renders you impermeable to the Forces of the non-spiritual: Night, Beauty-Sadness: you wanted to exist and you appeared so painfully beautiful to me, incomparable in being, inexplicable in art.[34]

There are many passages that would need to be included among those that realize this metamorphosis of the immediate, the carnal and intimate (with regards to Consuelo) into aesthetic entities, metaphysical categories, and fantastic allegories, but in this selection the reader can appreciate at least the following aspects: (1) the confusing syntax that stretches meaning towards meaninglessness; (2) the baroque conceptism and antiquated tone; (3) the "yesterday" temporal region that gives the text a quotidian order, which simultaneously and contradictorily denotes a personal calendar and an absolute detemporalization; (4) the Night as a metaphor in which the beloved's greatest attributes are concentrated; (5) Consuelo's fictions, always in reference to her grace, her seduction, and her magnificent imagination. The figure of Eterna-Consuelo prevails because of her plenitude, her maturity and majesty, in contrast to the Girl, Elena Bellamuerte, whose poetic portrait is constructed with other traits, though the baroque discourse is the same.

Orbiting throughout this configuration of Eterna are the feminine virtues that Macedonio observes with awestruck curiosity and to which he renders his highest praise. I believe that if we carefully read the "notice" he places at the opening of his text, in the "Dedicatoria a mi personaje la Eterna" (Dedication to My Character Eterna) (written in 1941) we can appreciate the dimension and complexity of what I am attempting to illustrate:

---

[34] "Noche es la belleza que te plugo vestir ayer. / Como si pensaste haberte tus ojos perdido ser una vez parte en el atavío de la noche: luces estelares en ella—mas no fue así sino voluntades de tu alma, hacendosa de decoraciones y transfiguraciones de sí, de ardientes ficciones con que tu espíritu se da fantasía y la esfuerza para que Belleza guarde tu ser contra el mundo, cosmos involuntario y cerrador—fingiste mimada demanda de los ojos—que, es cierto, los figuras y nombras inquietos—lo que en las exaltaciones en que vives para guardarte infranqueable a las Fuerzas de lo no espiritual fue deseo de tu inquietud vigilante: la Noche, la Beldad-Tristeza: quisiste ser y apareciste bella hasta doler en mí, de igualarte en el ser imposible, de explicarte en el arte, también" (*MNE* (1993), 292).

The greatest force of Altruistics, compassion free of any depraved, confusing or demented element in this act of self-sacrifice and assistance [...] her striking and unconditional Act of Compassion. [...] an altruistic leap of succor and engladdening or consolation, with full and instantaneous force which propels each of Eterna's steps. / For / A Superlative Individual / Capable of freezing time. Of annulling death. Of changing the past. / And, though Herself kind, of killing. / With her No / With her forgetfulness / With her comicalness / With her derision / But always pained by her unavoidable, unrelinquishable past.[35]

The great enigma of feminine otherness centers on surrender, on self-sacrifice, on Altruistics, in contrast to masculine egoism. Macedonio defined himself by saying: "I am a civilized man, I am a good egotist."[36] At the same time, speaking poetically about his mother in a text from 1929 (curiously the same year in which Consuelo was copying the manuscript of *MNE*), he says: "because in her there was never / a thought for herself. / Knowing herself eternal / and unconcerned with the terrestrial Today. / Without clinging to the passage of time neither there nor here."[37] This feminine condition freed of the self, letting go of its ties with time and space, holds the most convincing evidence, according to Macedonio, to argue against the fallacies of those categories invented by philosophy. It seems that a mystery resides within the feminine domain that is inaccessible to men, or that is very difficult for them to unravel. Presumably, women "naturally" live with this potential and although not all will reach such exceptional heights, they all certainly possess the possibility. Passion inspires the bold departure toward the Other and eliminates any chronotopic restrictions. This deep conviction in Macedonio's thought involves atavistic acts, both fearful and fascinated, of the most archaic patriarchy. The universal and naturalizing interpretation of the feminine gender gives his judgments a conservative slant inconsistent with his avant-garde positions. The women he reveres are granted virtues that find their origins in the depths of history from Stoicism, to the Judeo-Christian imaginary

---

[35] "El ímpetu máximo de la altruística, de la piedad sin ningún elemento vicioso confuso o demencial en el acto de abnegación y acudimiento lo he conocido en la Eterna. [...] su Acto de Piedad, fulmíneo y total. [...] salto altruístico de socorrimiento o de alegración o consolación con ímpetu total e instantáneo con que se mueven los pasos de la Eterna. / A / Persona Máxima / Capaz de fijar el tiempo. De compensar la muerte. De cambiar el pasado. / Y, si genial en el Sí, de matar. / Con su No / Con su olvido / Con su comicación / Con su avergonzar / Mas siempre dolorosa de su pasado no dimitible, no desasible" (*MNE* (1993), 5–6).
[36] "Soy un hombre civilizado, soy un egoísta bueno" (*Teorías* (1990), 190).
[37] "porque en ella no hubo nunca / un pensamiento para sí. / Sabiéndose eterna / y sin tibieza para el Hoy terreno. / Sin asirse a pasajes del tiempo ni al allá o acá" (*Relato* (1987), 113).

and its hybridizations with the Arab world in his Hispanic lineage, to the *criollo* matriarchs in the aristocratic families of Río de la Plata. Romantic idealization takes hold of this constant secular mixing and constructs feminine silhouettes who are narrated, named, metaphorized, and textualized in discourses that reiterate with determined omnipotence the defeat of discontinuity, of finitude, and the abolition of death.

The peculiar concern for the feminine mystery preserves childhood's spontaneous vivacity while also carrying out extremely acute investigations and interrogations:

> I have dedicated many years to the study of the woman and every day I lose more hope that I will ever feel as she feels, to feel even for an instant one of those emotions of grace, with respect to herself or to the lives of others, or of absolute desperation, with which man is unfamiliar. What must it be like to be a woman?[38]

His metaphysical thought is rooted in sensitivity and takes its primariness, its Ever-Possibility from emotive states, placing the capacity to feel, to experience sensations with absolute intensity within the feminine dimension. At the same time, the fusion with the Other finds its supreme expression in maternal altruism: an amorous couple with asymmetrical relations wherein the child receives care, attention, and the loving awareness of its needs. Macedonio believed (and he practiced this with his own children) that there must always be someone who submits to the capricious control of the child, so that this child may feel that they are manipulating an adult with their ideas. And contrarily, Macedonio adopted the attitude of a temperamental *enfant terrible*, a role he also played in his relationship with Consuelo, who treated him as such. Macedonio complained that this "maternal decline" destabilized the symmetry of the couple, yet at the same time he also enjoyed throwing his tantrums and complying when scolded. He let himself be pampered and reprimanded by *todoamor* [totalove]. These episodes are recorded in various fictional passages, with astonishing autobiographical detail; let us look at some examples:

> And so I recently recall talking about the President's "little wardrobe" and his haste to hide himself away inside it whenever something displeased him, but it was only in his conversations and relations with Eterna, when he was humbled

---

[38] "Estudio mucho a la mujer desde años atrás y cada día desespero más de sentir alguna vez como ella siente, de sentir siquiera por un instante una de esas emociones de gracia con respecto a sí misma o al vivir de otros o de desesperación absoluta, que el hombre no conoce. ¿Cómo será ser mujer?" (*Relato* (1987), 19)

and sad, but not angry, even feeling more in love, that he would go off into his corner. He is unquestionably a perpetual child following around behind Eterna, tugging at her skirt or running away and shutting himself inside the wardrobe.[39]

Then Eterna offered the President a pleat of her dress pressed between her fingers and said: "take hold of this and follow me to your penance."

This is what the President desired—to be treated like a child scolded by his mother—whenever he could no longer handle his ill temper and depression during the frequent conversations where Eterna appeared so secure yet so loving, more correct than he in her coddling and more certain than he of what could derail, destroy or diminish their love. Sulking, dominated, intoxicated at seeing her always more beautiful, affectionate, energetic, perceptive than he, he resigned himself to subtle intelligent thought, which made him happy.[40]

For this reason, the President, knowing her in this way—and not possessing a single emotion of his own—became instantly and forever a child.[41]

The scene of a boy sulking, scolded by an adult, who confidently shows him the way, who reprimands and punishes him while also sheltering and seducing him, allows for at least the following readings: (1) it recreates a factually autobiographical game; (2) it constructs a "theme" within Macedonio's inventions; and (3) it introduces the child-world as a necessary condition for the artist, the thinker, the metaphysician, and the witty, impractical, and fickle writer, poorly equipped for life.

What connection is there between this and Passion? This is Passion's body: in the minimalism of an almost ridiculous scene, where the thinker's potential for passion is dependent on affection, on the beloved's care, on unconditional love, which is accepted and offered when "intoxicated at seeing her always more beautiful, affectionate, energetic, perceptive." The aporetic morass of this masculine–feminine game comes filled with tinges of traditionalism: on the one hand, Consuelo's

---

[39] "Así yo me acuerdo recién de hablar del 'roperito' del Presidente y de sus corridas a guardarse en él cada vez que algo no le gusta, pero sólo en sus coloquios y relaciones con la Eterna, cuando humilde y triste pero sin enojo, aun con más amor, se encamina a su rincón. Es absolutamente un niño siempre para seguir a la Eterna tomado de su pollera, o para alejarse y encerrarse en el roperito" (*MNE* (1993), 109).

[40] "Entonces la Eterna tendió al Presidente un pliegue de su vestido tomado entre sus dedos y le dijo: 'tómese de aquí y sígame a su penitencia'. / Esto deseaba el Presidente—ser tratado como un niño que la madre corrige—cada vez que ya no podía con su malhumor y depresión durante las conversaciones frecuentes en que Eterna aparecía tan segura aunque tan amante, más que él certera en el mimo y cierta más que él siempre de lo que podía descaminar, degradar o embrillecer su amor. Enfurruñado, dominado, embriagado de verla siempre más bella, cariñosa, enérgica, clarividente que él, resignábase con el sutil inteligentísimo pensamiento que lo hacía feliz" (*MNE* (1993), 233).

[41] "Por ello el Presidente, el conocerla tal—y no teniendo una sola emoción de sí mismo—se tornó al instante y para siempre niño" (*MNE* (1993), 235).

authority takes charge of the decision-making, the management of everyday affairs, and of Macedonio's rebellious submissiveness (Administrator, Governess); on the other hand, the undeniable intellectual power exercised by the thinker-artist and the woman's devoted admiration, always referring to him as "Maestro,"[42] indicate a subordinate position that does not attempt to challenge the lover-writer's "obvious" intellectual superiority. The quixotic chivalry of the troubadour-poet and the Lady finds its corresponding connection in popular culture with the orders of the "Matron" and the unarguable authority of the "Husband."

The Passion that metaphysics extends to infinity using such monumental categories as Eternity is incarnate here on earth in the body of Consuelo, in their intimate home life, in the magical world of conversations, and in the fictions that the lovers invent. In this constellation of passionate impetus there must also be humor, which explains why the previously cited "Dedication" includes words like *alegración* (engladdening) and *comicación* (comicalness), lexical creations that twist morphology to express the variance and charm of extravagance. The first term alludes to an environment of relaxation and goodness (at home Macedonio referred to Consuelo as *Buenita* (my little saint)), requirements for the tenderness that Macedonio sought in human relations: a happiness breathed in the air, a fertile mist influencing body language, discourse, and saturating the climate with elegant and hedonic affection. Let me reiterate: *tenderness* and *elegance*, two paramount values in the comportment (or, more technically, the semiotic representations), aristocratic in origin, that characterize Macedonio's style. The late nights spent at home included conversations, playing piano, singing (Consuelo was a gifted singer), readings (they often read together, particularly novels and philosophy), a few games, listening to the radio, and drinking maté. This small ordinary world, secret and known to all, was one of Macedonio's greatest loves: his attachment to his house, his kitchen, the gatherings on the patio, and friends. Despite the stories of his rootless nomadism, his Passion lives nestled inside the comfortable, dependable, soothing space of home—another paradox at the core of his existence and his relationship with Consuelo. He lived with her, while simultaneously inhabiting other spaces of solitary life. Macedonio lived in the servants' quarters of that "sumptuous house" or stayed at La Verde, another of Consuelo's properties outside of Buenos Aires in Pilar, where he would spend periods of retreat and meditation. He was both present and absent, like the coexistence they shared.

---

[42] This nickname is documented in the inscriptions in the books that Consuelo gave to Macedonio. One of them, written in 1943, reads, "Al querido Maestro, guía y amparo de todas las almas puras. […]" (To my dear Maestro, guide and refuge of every pure soul. […]).

The second term, *comicación* (comicalness), refers to the use of the joke, "the art of nonsense," of verbal ingenuity, disguises, witty wisecracks, and clever dialogues—aesthetic and ethical practices (ideological bearers of class, of Río de la Plata idiosyncrasies, of "tribe") that Consuelo was very adept at exercising. This incessant oral source is what encourages his writing and finds its expression in a humoristic tone that is distinctly *criollo*. However, a careful distinction must be made: the text alludes to an everyday life that can be uncovered in various ways, but the novel's dialogues between characters in general, and between Eterna and the President in particular, do not "reproduce" that content, which could be read as another way of resisting and invalidating mimesis as a means for constructing the fictional world. *Comicación* (comicalness) mentions but does not imitate, instead increasing its presence–absence in situations, in the absurdity of narrative programs, in the arrangement of interactions, and, most of all, in the overall "climate" of the novelistic universe. Also, it does not incorporate methods of conceptual humoristics into the direct discourse. Indeed, the Author and the narrator make use of the devices set forth in his theory of Humor; the characters, however, do not.

Furthermore, the feminine world does not employ intellectual humor, devastating and irreverent, in their interventions, but rather displays a shrewd smile, understanding and prudent, in response to masculine criticism and sarcasm. Such discrimination allows for another reading of gender: humor is present throughout all of Macedonio's discourse, but intellectual ingenuity in the paradoxical play of concepts is always formulated within masculine speech. Thus, the *Pasión de la Amistad* (Passion of Friendship) (among men) is the driving force of conceptual humoristic discourse, preferentially embedded in the dynamic of masculine discussions. A rough assessment might conclude that women love and men think, *ergo*, men make witty jokes in the presence of women who smile and yield, yet not without scolding them for their childish stupidity. The feminine universe is not naïve, but rather "beyond good and evil," the bearer of a knowledge that far exceeds the doubt, debate, and investigative disquiet of the masculine universe. In short, the aporia consists in recognizing that women live inside the certainty of passion, extreme sensitivity, and the intensity of emotions, which grants them unassailable power.

Consuelo's body, along with the erotic and intoxicating aura that awoke a Passion so intense in the man known as Macedonio, died of sadness (a stroke) in July 1952, only a few months after the death of her beloved. The biographical events tell a "truly" romantic story. A "story fit for a novel" transformed into an eccentric textual corpus that hides the story and celebrates Passion inside a fantastic labyrinth that reveals it and conceals it, that erects a metaphysical monument to the Selfless Soul and to Ever-Possibility, a virtual and thought-written Museum to house the inexistent existence of a woman named Eterna who rescued him from unhappiness. Macedonio believed that human Passion longed only for a hedonic legacy, a taste of happiness ... And that is what he gave in his greatest toast to Consuelo, Eterna.

4

Macedonio Fernández's Neighborhood Metaphysics: *Belarte*, the Fool of Buenos Aires, and the Evidential Siesta

Gonzalo S. Aguirre

Practicamos sinceramente la Metafísica Cucurbitácea
(We sincerely practice a Cucurbitaceous Metaphysic)[1]
Macedonio Fernández

Introduction

Macedonio Fernández's oeuvre cannot be circumscribed to a strictly literary realm. The lines of thought that he initiated and explored in metaphysics, political theory, economics, ethics, law, and literary theory, and then meticulously articulated throughout his writings, prove that he belongs to a genealogy of great thinkers. The following analysis concentrates specifically on his political and ethical-juridical thinking, while expounding on his theories of art and *valor* (courage/value). It also addresses lesser-known aspects of his life and work. For Macedonio, living, thinking, and writing were intrinsically interconnected. Although he remained at the margins of prominent academic circles and public intellectual debates, he had a particular way of inhabiting Buenos Aires and elaborated a metaphysic for his city.[2] Like the Cynics or the Stoics who

---

[1] "El zapallo que se hizo cosmos" (The Pumpkin that Became Cosmos), in *Relato*, 54. All translations are mine unless otherwise noted.
[2] In Macedonio's creative essay "Sueño o realidad" (Dream or Reality), we can hear a character named Domínguez talking to Thomas Hobbes: "En el barrio de él, Macedonio Fernández, a quien me refiero, goza confianza de haber resuelto todo el problema metafísico, y es tanta la seguridad del vecindario que ya nadie allí estudia ni sabe nada de metafísica; se ha delegado en él saberlo todo en este tópico, y efectivamente es hombre de no ignorar nada que se le confíe y que interese al barrio, como en este

considered it impossible to live other than according to their metaphysical principles, Macedonio applied his own metaphysics to that city located along the Río de la Plata and to the *rioplatenses* who lived there.

Macedonio could not conceive of a life without a metaphysical vision of the world, in which one is left to fend for oneself among the automatic perceptions—"apperceptions" as he defined them—that empirical and scientific knowledge impose on our way of understanding.[3] He was not a modern man in the Cartesian sense, and in his texts Buenos Aires emerges akin to a Greek polis depicted by an ancient philosopher. He even created the conceptual character "el Bobo de Buenos Aires" (the Fool of Buenos Aires) to convey the ethos of his city, the embodiment of the *porteño piola* (a clever and witty local guy). On the other hand, this character also resembles Voltaire's naïf Candide or Socrates, but without the same tenacious questioning of his fellow citizens. The Fool circulates within the city and intervenes in its daily life as if he were just passing by or as if his trajectory through this urban space encompassed the fast pace of city life.[4]

In the middle of the hustle and bustle that modernization brought to the city during the first decades of the twentieth century, Macedonio sought to recover a tradition that the *porteños* were steadily losing: the siesta, which he thought could insert a wedge in the city's frenetic daily life. He was convinced that the afternoon siesta could initiate a threshold for an untimely mediation and induce a metaphysical experience removed from spatial constrictions. In this sense, he writes: "For me the Siesta is the Call to the Path of Mystic Evidentiality, and

caso la metafísica. Se ha hecho cargo de saberlo todo tan bien, que el barrio, fiado en él, ha llegado a una perfección tan extraordinaria de no saber nada de metafísica, que es cosa de no creer que haya alguna vez sabido alguien algo, una pizca de ello" (In his neighborhood, people are confident that Macedonio has resolved all metaphysical problems, and they are so convinced of it that nobody else there studies or even knows anything about metaphysics anymore; so it has been delegated to him to know everything about this topic, and indeed he is one not to ignore anything that has been entrusted to him and that it is of interest to his neighborhood, like metaphysics in this case. He has assumed the responsibility of knowing everything so well that the neighborhood, placing all their trust in him, has achieved such extraordinary perfection of not knowing anything about metaphysics, that now nobody can believe that at one time somebody knew something, even a modicum of it) (*NTV* (2001), 253). This essay has been a critical source and inspiration for writing this chapter.

[3] In "La metafísica," Macedonio writes: "La Ciencia es ante todo industriosa; industria humana para escapar al Dolor, alcanzar el Placer. [...] Su peculiaridad estriba precisamente en huir sistemáticamente del conocimiento del fenómeno. [...] La Ciencia, acrecentando cada día las relaciones y ubicaciones, complica progresivamente las ramificaciones de la Apercepción y aspira nada menos que a expresar toda la Realidad en los términos de una sola y total apercepción causal" (Science is first and foremost industrious; human industry to escape from Pain, to reach Pleasure. [...] Its peculiarity is based precisely on systematically escaping all knowledge of phenomenon [...] Science, increasing each day the [codifications of] relationships and locations, progressively complicates the ramifications of the Apperceptions and aspires to nothing less than expressing all of Reality in terms of a single and total causal apperception) (*NTV* (2001), 63–4).

[4] See Fernández, "Del Bobo de Buenos Aires," in *PRC* (1989).

it is located at the intersection of Darkness and Blinding Light."[5] Macedonio explained, however, that the experience of the Evidential Siesta could only be communicated through metaphors. For instance, we may say that the midday nap expands and intensifies the shortest shadow of the day or, in Nietzschean terms, that it brings closure to the longest mistake in the history of humankind.[6]

For Macedonio the Evidential Siesta beckoned the individual down a passageway from a world created by the representations that he/she projects upon it toward a world created by what he called an *almismo ayoico* (selfless soul).[7] This thought is an obvious evocation of Schopenhauer's *The World as Will and Representation*, but Macedonio adapted his philosophy to develop a local metaphysics and metaphysical practices. In his early essays, as he realized that written language tends to operate at a superficial level when it is still rooted in a fabric of apperceptions, we can already trace his initial ruminations about the obstacles that written language faced when attempting to produce an experience that would give rise to an individual's pure perception of the world. Even Schopenhauer's writing, as Macedonio pointed out, could not always escape the rhetorical devices that empirical and scientific knowledge have infiltrated into our language.[8]

Macedonio never ceased to experiment with how best to provoke this metaphysical experience in both oral communication and written language, but rather than explaining what it meant, he sought to stimulate his interlocutors and readers into living it and feeling it. He only explained that this experience must occur before any distinction between the individual subject and the object could be drawn, and that in order to achieve this state, it was crucial that a *visión pura* (pure vision) be restored, a pure phenomenological perception of the world capable of unraveling the fabric of apperceptions.[9] Furthermore,

---

[5] "Para mí la Siesta es el Llamado al Camino de la Evidencialidad Mística, y está en el ángulo de Oscuridad y Deslumbramiento, [...]" ("Poema de trabajos," in *Relatos* (1987), 136).

[6] See Nietzsche, "How the 'Real World' At Last Became A Myth," in *Twilight of the Idols*.

[7] See Fernández, *NTV* (2001), 243.

[8] Macedonio claimed: "Encuentro que Schopenhauer no alcanzó la total emancipación de todo automatismo o sugestión tomados de las lecturas y este género de defecto en un sistema es más lamentable que el verdadero error o afirmación conciente y errónea, sin embargo. Tomar un error de otros es más deplorable que equivocarse personal y hondamente, pues lo primero es sumamente fácil de evitar en tanto que lo segundo es inevitable a todos en mayor o menor proporción" (I find that Schopenhauer did not reach total emancipation from all automatism [apperceptions] or from the influence coming from his readings. However, this sort of mistake is more regrettable than the true error or conscious and erroneous affirmation of [apperceptions]. Appropriating others' mistakes is more deplorable than making the same mistake by one's own consideration. Since the former is possible to avoid, while the latter is impossible for all of us to different degrees) ("La metafísica" in *NTV* (2001), 66).

[9] See Fernández, "Bases en metafísica," in *NTV* (2001), 43–62.

Macedonio believed that we could only achieve and sustain the intensity of such an experience if we were able to disentangle pure perception from the web of apperceptions, and if we had the *valor* (courage) to grant this pure perception the *valor* (value) to transform our lives.

As we shall see, Macedonio's notion of *valor* bears a double meaning. On the one hand, as mentioned above, it alludes to the individual's bravery in defeating their own fears. On the other hand, this concept implies the idea of an economic value or, more precisely, it refers to the individuals' capacity to assess their affections, as they extricate them from the web of apperceptions, and to transvalue the already assigned value of feelings and things. Macedonio considered that art could trigger this process and the following pages will examine the different techniques and genres in his work with which he experimented to foster a pure vision of the world. In particular, attention will be given to local metaphysical practices, which he believed could spark the same experience on any common day. Drawing this road map into Macedonio's thought will also shed new light on his understanding of individualism, and ultimately on how he translated an experience that seems to be confined to the individual into the possibility for a collective becoming.

Theories of *Valor*, Art, and the State: Toward an *Ayoico* Individualism

Macedonio defined *valor* as the effort invested in the attempt to defeat fear.[10] This struggle entails a physical effort (muscular contraction) and the ability to envision oneself overcoming fear (intellectual attention). He believed that when our soul–body association assiduously confronts this challenge, it can generate the effortless habit of gauging our emotional states in order to release them from their stagnant condition. Otherwise, when our emotions correspond to the automatic perceptions structuring and regulating our life, i.e., if we remain enthralled by this web of apperceptions, they are the objects of a *Culinaria del Sentimiento* (Culinary of Feelings).[11] This Culinary, Macedonio argued,

---

[10] In "Para una teoría del valor," Macedonio defines value as "el fruto de un esfuerzo habitual de destrucción de la *emoción* Miedo no siendo el Valor mismo una emoción" (the fruit of a habitual effort to obliterate the *emotion* of Fear without Value being an emotion itself) (*T* (1997), 77).

[11] Macedonio explains: "He llamado Culinaria a todo arte del placer-sensación, y en Belarte por eso llamo Culinaria a todas las obras de pretendido arte, que recurren a la sensación" (I have called all art of pleasure-sensation "Culinary," and for that reason, in *Belarte* I call all works of alleged art, that resort to sensation, "Culinary") ("Para una teoría del arte," in *T* (1997), 238).

is a system that rigidifies our cognitive apparatus as it assesses and classifies the images and feelings that we perceive and create by way of our intellectual attention or muscular contractions. More precisely, it operates at the level of emotional states generated by automatic perceptions. It nourishes our desires either through the repetition of images that capture our attention or by triggering sensations that we have retained in our memory.

The Culinary of Feelings administrates our sensations, desires, and customs. It also generates them, cooks them, and articulates them in order to weave the fabric of apperceptions in which we are embroiled. For this reason, Macedonio argued that all art should be *Belarte*: a form of art capable of suspending the Culinary and recuperating the artistic experience as a hermeneutic practice on oneself. But *Belarte* also implies the art of having the courage to assess the constant psychic–corporal affections that constitute our will.[12] According to Macedonio, we express affections as we gauge the manifestations of our soul–body at three different levels: (a) as a spontaneous reflex that expresses our acquired customs and/or our previous attempts to cope with affections still caught in the matrix of apperceptions; (b) as an initial attempt to extricate our emotions from this matrix, which is the first effect of *Belarte*; and (c) as an effortless habit of valuing our affections.

The Culinary shapes and controls the emotions that we cannot apprehend in their pure state because they are determined by our own fear. Thomas Hobbes explained in his *Leviathan* that the most intense feeling we produce is fear, and that it causes us to live on guard, in a state of alertness, and consequently, awake.[13] Thus, fear predominates over other emotions and lures us into accepting the social agreement that subordinates us to the power of the State. However, for Macedonio, we cannot distinguish the dream world from the real world because there is no ontological difference between the two. We may see other people around us as imminent threats, but the fear that we feel is the same that a child may feel in his/her worst nightmare. Macedonio believed that the task of *Belarte* should specifically consist in unveiling a continuum between wakefulness and dreaming and exposing our attention to an experience devoid of fear that should

---

[12] Macedonio writes: "La Voluntad es el símbolo animado de la unidad psico-fisiológica, del consorcio alma-cuerpo, y, por ello, admirablemente se presta para expresar la esencia metafísica de la Realidad, como con tanta lucidez lo ha visto Schopenhauer" ([human] Will is the animated symbol of a psychical-physiological unity, the soul-body consortium, and, consequently, it admirably lends itself to expressing the metaphysical essence of Reality, as Schopenhauer himself so lucidly saw it) ("Para una teoría del valor," in *T* (1997), 87).

[13] See Thomas Hobbes, *Leviathan*, chapter 2, for his definition of wakefulness, and chapter 13, for his analysis of the notion of the individual's fear.

propitiate a pure form of attention capable of undermining both the power of the State and the social pact.

Belarte induces us to transvalue emotional states still fixed within the matrix of apperceptions. In this sense, Macedonio writes: "The instrument of any *Belarte* should be monotone."[14] Strong emotions are feelings entangled by the Culinary of Feelings. On the contrary, *Belarte* should create an experience that tempers the emotions that are fueled by fear. Furthermore, Macedonio thought that *Belarte* should provoke disaffection with these emotions in order to free our perceptions from the web of apperceptions. It should give us the opportunity to inhabit the world as if we were a *recienvenido* (newcomer) to our own life and prepare us to embrace the unexpected as a common routine.[15]

Macedonio's definition of a mystical state sheds more light on the experience that *Belarte* initiates and that a newcomer performs: "[a] mystical state is living as an uncreated self-existent being; and I think that it is also living without the distinction between image-sensation, dream-reality, and without the distinction between newly-remembered, newly-already-known. Therefore, a mystical state is living without any motive for action."[16] *Belarte* is similar to the experience of the newcomer insofar as it disrupts the matrix of apperceptions by destabilizing the link between apperceptions and the formation of our feelings and desires. However, as mentioned above, it is dependent upon our courage to confront our fear and reclaim our intellectual attention and muscular contractions. This effort should ultimately prepare us for the "habitual culture of inhibiting an emotion: Fear."[17]

Macedonio also claimed that individual anti-fear efforts should aim to release perceived images, those that feed emotions, from the Culinary, so that one might relate to them as affective states rather than as automatic perceptions. Once the illusory fabric of apperceptions that determine one's life and desires is suspended—here I am following Hobbes's theory of the formation of the modern State—then there would no longer be a need for the State. If fear could be defeated, the enveloping social mesh of automatic perceptions that subordinates the individual to the power of the State could be dissolved. For Macedonio, free

---

[14] "El instrumento de cualquier Belarte debe ser un monótono" ("Para una teoría del arte," *T* (1997), 251.)

[15] See Fernández, "Para una teoría del valor," *T* (1997), 77.

[16] "Estado místico es vivir como autoexistente increado; y creo que es también vivir sin la discriminación imagen-sensación, ensueño-realidad, y sin la discriminación nuevo-recordado, nuevo-ya-conocido. Por todo lo cual estado místico es vivir sin motivo ninguno de acción" ("Descripcio-Metáfisica," in *NTV* (2001), 362).

[17] "cultura habitual de la inhibición de una emoción: el Miedo" ("Para una teoría del valor," *T* (1997), 80).

self-interested individuals invented the State, and he was convinced that if one's efforts at courage intensified and prevailed, people would spontaneously begin to cooperate with one another. As he explained in an early essay: "communism, if fertile, not impoverishing, will take place spontaneously, not by Law."[18]

There is a peculiar coincidence here between Hobbes and Macedonio. Both believed that if there were people without fear, there would no longer be a need for a State. Nonetheless, for Macedonio these fearless individuals would also debunk Hobbes's assumption of a pre-social State of Nature, which hunts civil society as a potential threat that prevents it from questioning the State's legitimacy. Macedonio maintained that the State and the law could only be founded on a juridical-political apparatus that exerts its coercion upon individuals. But he also pointed out that this force manifested the symptomatic lack of the people's courage to confront their fear. Spinoza's philosophy illuminates this thought: As long as there are not "adequate" ideas, if individuals cannot discern how their affections are configured by their own fear, the power of the State will emerge as if it were necessary to regulate their interactions, because they project "inadequate" representations of the world.[19]

The State crystalizes a specific mode of shaping and administrating individuals' affections, which stem from their "inadequate ideas" and which, at the same time, express a "conatus" or a desire detached from itself and distorted by the individuals' fear or hope.[20] However, there would also be the possibility of a conatus that Macedonio defined as valuating, as long as it was capable of expressing itself without being subsumed by the individuals' fear or hope, which determine a fixed conatus according to inadequate ideas and exterior images. Spinoza explains that basically we suffer because we imagine.[21] But when fear constricts the civil society, which is an axiom embedded in Hobbes's doctrine, it should be considered as a specific mode of affective composition that tends to preserve within its own being a passive conatus imbued with fear and detached from its valuating potentiality. Without the individuals' courage and anti-fear efforts that Macedonio postulated, it would be impossible to configure alternative affective encounters that are not tainted by fear or hope, which diminish the individuals' capacity to value their affections. Nonetheless, alternative social

---

[18] "el comunismo si es fecundo, no empobrecedor, vendrá por la espontaneidad, no por la Ley" ("Para una teoría del estado," in *T* (1997), 151).
[19] See Spinoza, *Ethics*, Part 3, Def. 1.
[20] See Aguirre, "Filosofía política y política gnoseológica," 8.
[21] See Spinoza, *Ethics*, Part 3, specifically, note 2.

formations remain a possibility even under societies and political regimes that have been founded on inadequate or confusing ideas.[22]

If individuals dared to live in the world as newcomers, they would constantly assess the order of things without accepting the imposition of pre-given values, of a social and political regime, and ultimately of the State as the legitimate representative of the people's will. For Macedonio there was only one element that remained constant: the potential courage of individuals. Nevertheless, in order to actualize this force, the fearless individuals should first understand that a juridical-political apparatus does not actually exert its power upon their bodies and souls, but rather it uses force to shape them as subjects. Thus, the notion of *almismo ayoico* is a precondition for a pure perception, which exposes the impossibility of fixing values and imposing a social and political order. Such impossibility explains Macedonio's theory of *valor* (value/courage), alternatively defined as the individual's act of creating a surplus value that constantly exceeds the already-assigned value of things and that inevitably questions any order already imposed.[23]

Macedonio's political and juridical-ethical thinking seems to champion a defense of individualism, while his metaphysics posits a selfless *almismo ayoico* as the ontological foundation for the development of pure sensitivity. Therefore, to clarify his notion of individualism, it is fundamental that we redefine the notion of individuality according to this principle. In this sense, we should first consider that Macedonio sought to trigger processes of *subjectivation* that, while individuals as newcomers develop their pure perception, would lead them into a constant state of assessment, dislocating not only any form of coercion and law, but also the very notion of the individual person, the cornerstone of the modern juridical apparatus.

---

[22] In *A Political Treatise*, Spinoza writes: "Man, I say, in each state is led by fear or hope to do or leave undone this or that; but the main difference between the two states [natural or civil] is this, that in the civil state all fear the same things, and all have the same ground of security, and manner of life; and this certainly does not do away with the individual's faculty of judgment. For he that is minded to obey all the commonwealth's orders, whether through fear of its power or through love of quiet, certainly consults after his own heart his own safety and interest" (302).

[23] Macedonio's theory of value reverberates with Nietzsche's notion of transvaluation. For the German philosopher any form of value was already a transvaluation, any act of one valuating an experience already implied a transvaluation. According to Nietzsche's aphorisms 46 and 203 in *Beyond Good and Evil*, this concept basically implies removing fixed values attributed to affects and things. As their anchor value progressively loses its potential value, this potency depends on a sort of constant state of transvaluation. However, Macedonio's postulates clarify that this attitude, the habit of transvaluing, should be "sin esfuerzo actual" (effortless) (*T*, 89), and this it should also rely on another key state of mind: the "inhibición activa" (active inhibition) (91) of moral reflexes. Or, following Nietzsche, we may say that this state entails losing the habit (*sich abgewöhnen*) of preserving morally stagnant affections, which neglect the human beings' power to fully develop their transvaluating acts. See aphorism 39 in *Human, All Too Human: A Book for Free Spirits*.

In Macedonio's thought, the notion of personhood in fact expresses a symptom: the inability to assess each experience as a singular phenomenon and to defeat fear. These scared individuals are therefore unable to achieve an *ayoico* phase and a pure perceptive state. One of Macedonio's Zenonian paradoxes, which he often celebrated, seemingly appears: as individuals attempt to defeat their own fear by increasingly valuing themselves as singular entities, they will show a decreased capacity to transvalue the fixed values attached to their pre-given notion of personhood. Nonetheless, this paradox explains why his theory of the State has been sometimes labeled as simplistic, or that it swiftly resolves critical issues. Because for Macedonio any embodiment of personhood expresses the individuals' fears, and can only be defined and molded through the State apparatus' acts of violence and force, his anarchism would be incapable of postulating individual freedom. However, his political thinking should be considered not only as anti-Statist, but also as against individualism. It is an *ayoico* anarchism, which always arrives at an unfinished definition of the notion of personhood, never drawing definitive contours or assigning a specific essence to the idea of the individual person.[24]

Artistry of the Word: Novelistics and Humoristics

> *There is no art beyond technique: the invention of the [artistic] "affair" is an innocent game compared to the richness of plots and topics in daily life. Life is absolute-possibility; there is no character, act, or material event any less plausible than another.*[25]

For Macedonio, art would tear apart the networks that instrumental rationality articulates in our life. But he clarifies: "Art is only found in the technique of eliciting states that do not exist in life, neither in the reader nor in the author, without this technique."[26] A reader, for instance, should no longer read a text confident that he/she is performing a utilitarian practice, which dictates that a lineal way of reading, like a chronological accumulation of knowledge, is useful.

---

[24] For further development on this topic, see Luis Othoniel Rosa, *Comienzos para una estética anarquista* (2016).

[25] "Fuera de la técnica no hay arte; la invención del 'asunto' es un juego inocente frente a la riqueza de tramas y temas cotidianos. La vida es la todo-posibilidad; no hay *carácter, acto* ni *suceso material* que no sea tan posible como cualquier otro" ("Para una teoría del arte," *T* (1997), 236).

[26] "El Arte está sólo en la técnica de suscitación de estados que no están en la vida, ni en el lector ni en el autor, sin esa técnica" (*T* (1997), 241).

Instead, Macedonio claimed that writing must dislocate the reader's rationality. It should transform the *Lector Seguido* (Orderly Reader) into a *Lector Salteado* (Reader Who Skips Around) either through Novelistics or Humoristics.[27] In a similar manner, the useful and intelligent citizen still trapped by the Culinary and enmeshed within the fabric of apperceptions should be transformed by the Fool of Buenos Aires's Humoristics into a skipping individual and into a skipping smart person. This conceptual character offers us an operative example of how the latter technique can be used when one rainy day he warns a passing pedestrian: "Watch out, sir! Your umbrella is getting wet!"[28]

Belarte generates a perceptive commotion, a mental fragility that Macedonio defines as *inverse paramnesia*: the conviction of unknowing what is known.[29] Without this sensation, which marks another stage or point of entry into a pure experience, it would be impossible to acquire knowledge that concurs with what is unknown, without reducing it to previous orders of knowledge. Macedonio finally concluded that of all the forms of *Belarte*, "the written word […] has the privilege of being free of all sensorial impurity."[30] Thus, it seems that logos is the most appropriate scaffolding for bringing about the so-called inverse paramnesia in people's attention, but it should be understood that this could only occur as long as the Culinary of Feelings has been deactivated. In this sense, he writes: "The spoken word, without sonorities, inflections, beautiful voice, gestures, has the same value as the written word does for Prose, but the human voice always has a sensitivity; the dull scribble is victorious, a twisting wire called writing, which no other art possesses, absolutely free of impurities."[31] While *Belarte* can occur through oral communication, Macedonio thought that only by delving into the process of writing could one achieve *Belarte*'s highest form of expression, which he called "Artística de la Palabra" (Artistry of the Word).

---

[27] In one of the prologues in *MNE*, Macedonio writes: "Te dedico mi novela, Lector Salteado; me agradecerás una sensación nueva: el leer seguido. Al contrario, el lector seguido tendrá la sensación de una nueva manera de saltear: la de seguir al autor que salta" (1975, 129); "I dedicate my novel to you, Skip-Around Reader; you, in turn, should be grateful to me for a new sensation: reading in order. On the other hand, the orderly reader will experience a new way of skipping: the orderly reading of a skipping-around author" (Schwartz, 119).

[28] "Señor, vea que se le moja el paraguas" ("Del Bobo," in *PRC* (1989), 109).

[29] See Fernández, "Descripcio-Metafísica," in *NTV* (2001), 361.

[30] "la palabra escrita […] tiene el privilegio de hallarse exenta de toda impureza de sensorialidad" (*T* (1997), 245).

[31] "La palabra hablada, sin sonoridades, inflexiones, bella voz, gestos, vale lo mismo que la palabra escrita para la Prosa, pero siempre la voz humana tiene alguna sensorialidad; victorioso queda el insípido garabato, gusanillo del papel, que se llama escritura, que ningún arte posee, absolutamente libre de impurezas" (*T* (1997), 245).

According to Macedonio, writing should not consist in telling stories that rely on facts. He advocated for a "prose of thought" or a "prose of attention," which specifically seeks to affect and subvert the reader's attention.[32] Furthermore, he believed that the story did not matter because for him writing a plot would be akin to laying the dance floor. The process of writing should compose a minimal assemblage, providing readers with a steppingstone that they should then abandon and return to later. Thus, Macedonio's Novelistics aim to achieve a monotonous rhythm that releases the processes of writing and reading from any constrictions imposed either by the fabric of apperceptions or by the violent coercion of the State apparatus. He thought that Novelistics should capture an amount of time or, more specifically, an amount of the reader's memory in a pure state.[33]

Beyond the monotone that any *Belarte* should convey, Macedonio also offered the following guidelines for developing the technique of Novelistics: (a) avoid descriptive information; (b) do not provide readers with any sense of direction or finality; and (c) do not depict or provoke emotions in readers that might reassure them that they are only readers. He sought to push language beyond its own limits, i.e., beyond representation, and explore discursive practices that undermine language's own meaning. In doing so, through Novelistics, he thought language could reveal itself as a pure form of expression that presents the unreal as authentic, and consequently, provokes an inverse paramnesia in the reader's sensitivity, which will suspend their certainty of being an (inattentive) Orderly Reader.

Museo de la novela de la Eterna (*The Museum of Eterna's Novel*) (1967) should be read along these lines. The novel articulates a complex literary device that follows the development of a novelistic conspiracy spilling over the limits of the text to provoke a sort of great inverse paramnesia in Buenos Aires. The goal of the plot is to induce the city's people to awake from the spell that has subsumed them under the power of a State and shake themselves free of the lethargy that characterized their daydreaming daily life. If they were to gain access to the pure

---

[32] I am following here Miguel Morey's reflections on alternative processes of writing as he elaborates in his article "Traducir los *Pequeños tratados*," which is a selection from the lecture he delivered in the context of the colloquium "Pascal Quignard. L'écriture et sa spéculation" on December 7–9, 2017, in Paris.

[33] Macedonio thought that "la Memoria es la Atención" (memory is Attention) ("Metafísica," in *NTV* (2001), 200). However, as mentioned before, the inverse paramnesia sensitivity that he sought to provoke through the artistic experience disarticulates the regime that structures the order of what is already known. So, it opens the opportunity for mystical self-contemplation of a pure memory, an absolute instant that may be more or less expanded. The Evidential Siesta, as we shall see, is the ultimate example of this.

experience brought about through the underground interventions carried out by conspirators throughout the city, they would be able to reach the epiphany that the Evidential Siesta reveals.

Humoristics, the second technique that Macedonio elaborated and which may also be considered a theory in his system of thought, can coexist with Novelistics. But Humoristics can provoke the inverse paramnesia effect through oral communication and casually during everyday life. Macedonio writes:

> [...] two moments, unique and genuinely artistic, can be created in the reader's psyche: the moment of intellectual nothingness via Conceptual Humoristics [...] and the moment of the conscious being's nothingness, utilizing the characters (Novelistics) for the only artistic purpose they should ever fulfill, not to make a character or a story believable, but to make the reader believe, for an instant that he is a character himself, snatched away from life.[34]

If Humoristics is not conceptual, then it remains within the realistic field proper to the Culinary of Feelings and the laugh that it provokes only serves to pamper the order of things and the stagnant emotions still trapped within the fabric of apperceptions. Conceptual Humoristics implies a form of art, as does Novelistics, and its main purpose is to create "the comic tickle [...] where one discovers oneself in a state of mental fragility" using three different methods: conveying an inauthentic sense that tears apart one's conscious certainties, exhausting the apperceptive mode (not only exposing its dubious procedures), and stimulating optimistic affections (a radical contrast with the pessimistic root that structures Schopenhauer's thought).[35]

As suggested before, the Fool is the herald of Humoristics. Roaming the streets of Buenos Aires, this character spreads his fugacious and hilarious interventions as if he were a spy already working for the conspiracy yet to be hatched in *MNE* or as a long-range reconnaissance agent who has infiltrated the city to prepare the terrain for the covert operations of Eterna's messengers. Nevertheless, in one of the Fool's letters we can see that he does not only embody Humoristics:

> Mister John Doe: I congratulate you on the fact that the fire reported today by "The Siesta" was only an alarm, and also that it took place in a private home that,

---

[34] "[...] pueden crearse dos momentos, únicos genuinamente artísticos, en la psique del lector: el momento de la nada intelectual por la Humorística Conceptual, [...] y el momento de la nada del ser conciencial, usando de los personajes (Novelística) para el único uso artístico a que debieron siempre destinarse, no para hacer creer en un carácter, un relato, sino para hacer al lector, por un instante, creerse él mismo personaje, arrebatado de la vida" ("Para una teoría de la humorística," in *T* (1997), 260).

[35] "La cosquilla chistosa está en que la gente se pesca a sí misma en fragilidad mental" (*T* (1997), 304).

fortunately, is not yours. One is happy to think that you are not the only one in our great city who does not reside in the house that could have started to burn down, and so one is also led to think that if the heart of the projected fire had been located inside your home, my pleasure would not change, considering that the number of undamaged residences and people would still be the same, and very considerable.

I hope you will acknowledge receipt of this letter: I have been writing these congratulations all morning for every house in Buenos Aires, and if by chance, due to some enviably notorious bad luck, you are the occupant of the house that was about to catch fire yesterday, return these congratulations so that I can replace them with a unique letter of condolences that I have already written, trying to hide my envy [for your notoriety].[36]

This letter presents the central pillars that have been discussed up to this point: Novelistics, inverse paramnesia, the idea of writing as a continuous process, the nuances of oral language, an intuited conspiracy behind events that could have taken place, the Siesta, a neighborhood metaphysics, the realistic, the Culinary, and of course Buenos Aires.

The Fool writes a letter that turns out to be perfectly useless and whose only eventual purpose demands an expense that surpasses all realistic parameters. The letter is impossible but, at the same time, for the Fool of Buenos Aires it is necessary. Based on the non-news announced by "The Siesta," inconceivable as a name for a newspaper (they tend to appeal more to an idea of vigilance and attentiveness, i.e., the fabric of apperceptions), the letter congratulates someone for something that has not happened. The only difference would be that the event that did not happen was about to happen to the addressee and not to anyone else, although from a metaphysical point of view something is always about to happen to all of us. Hence, "The Siesta" could be lying, but in turn it allows us to discover the truth: the media creates news where there is not the possibility for any. The realistic silliness of the Fool's letter, his not knowing much, exposes this crack in the "real" world and suggests that napping could potentially be evidential.

[36] "Señor N. N.: Lo felicito a usted por haber sido sólo una mera alarma el incendio que relata 'La Siesta' de hoy, ocurrido en un domicilio particular, que, además, felizmente no es el de usted. Uno se siente feliz al considerar que en nuestra gran ciudad no es usted el único que no tiene el domicilio en la casa que pudo empezar a incendiarse, y es llevado a pensar que si el foco del incendio proyectado hubiera radicado en el domicilio de usted, no por eso se alteraría mi placer de considerar que el número de domicilios y personas exentas del daño sería el mismo, y muy considerable. / Espero se sirva usted, acusarme recibo: durante toda la mañana he escrito esta felicitación a cada casa de Buenos Aires, y si acaso es usted, por una mala suerte de enviable notoriedad, el ocupante de la casa a punto de incendiarse ayer, devuélvame esta felicitación para canjeársela por una única de condolencia que he redactado, disimulando mi envidia" (*PRC* (1989), 112).

Between the *Bobo* and the *Piola*: Genealogy of the Fool of Buenos Aires

The conceptual character of the Fool embodies a *porteño* way of being. Thus, he is a key native informant for understanding local notions of value and the *almismo ayoico* as a universal experience. However, the Fool's trajectory not only reveals his ontic status in this milieu. He also expresses similarities with the experience of the newcomer. The Fool and the newcomer were figures that strongly resonated within the socio-cultural context of Buenos Aires during the first half of the twentieth century. While the former might reflect the wittiness of the *porteño piola* (a clever and witty local guy), the latter was seen on the faces of thousands of immigrants arriving from the provinces and/or from Europe to Buenos Aires at the time. An Orderly Reader would easily identify them and ground these literary figures as representations of historical characters. However, the dialectical relationship that this type of reader could establish between fictional and real characters would probe their lack of attention to a process of reading that should lead them to undermine the logic behind a realistic representation.

The Fool is similar to a newcomer from and to Buenos Aires, a local manifestation of a universal ontological base. On the one hand, he seems to act as a *porteño piola*. On the other, however, the Fool may echo certain characterizations sardonically projected upon newcomers to the big city, those arriving from the provinces (where the siesta is often still religiously practiced) and who were considered silly, lazy, or slow people in need of a nap. Meanwhile, Buenos Aires was rapidly becoming a modern city in which its citizens no longer napped or, in other words, a city that never slept. It was becoming a wakeful city, always on alert, attentive, fast-paced, and extremely *piola*.

There is a resulting deep tension that arises between the Fool and the *piola*. The latter is a quick-witted person who moves within the city, but always pushing the limits of its rules in order to gain well-calculated benefits by investing less effort than was anticipated. The Fool, then, is not someone who cannot conform to the realistic and utilitarian rationality of life, but rather one who, in Buenos Aires, cannot conform to the game that is taking place at the limits of that same rationality. Thus, it has been assumed that the *Bobo* is commonly the victim of the *porteño piola*. Nevertheless, considering the *piola*'s quick thinking, which is above the city's average, and the slow way of thinking that characterizes the Fool, we can formulate yet another Zenonian (or Macedonian) paradox: the *piola*'s quickness cannot catch up to the Fool's slowness because each of them develops different flows or velocities.[37]

This paradox explains why Macedonio elevated both the Fool and the newcomer to the ontic status of conceptual metaphysical characters. Following the reflections of Gilles Deleuze and Felix Guattari on the notion of limit, we may think that while the *piola* moves inside the city's limits, which they are always trying to extend, they cannot fracture the apperceptive fabric that codifies this milieu. The Fool, like the trajectory of the newcomer, always moves toward a threshold beyond which a new assemblage is created.[38] The process of this character's *subjectivation* can be traced as a constant movement through liminal spaces or, perhaps, through a liminal language, but rather than taking advantage of the breaks in realism that he traverses, as the *piola* would, the Fool develops fracture lines that destabilize the grid imposed upon the city's people by apperceptions. As Nietzsche would have said, the Fool is an *Über-piola* who untangles the realistic social fabric.

Certainly, it can be said that Macedonio sought to transform the smart and quick-thinking person (the Orderly Reader or citizen) into the Fool. But he did not merely want to show this type of reader or citizen as a fool—in a way that no *piola* could. He wanted to recruit them for his cause. Therefore, while the Fool pretends to be dumb, he is in fact the keystone of an organized army of Fools set to infiltrate the city, undermine the mechanisms that have subsumed its people under the central power of a State, and take back Buenos Aires. In other words, his mission is to transform every *porteño* into a newcomer, an individual who would not only recover their ability to enjoy the siesta, but also the ability to be heedful of this experience, heedful of the hour of the Evidential Siesta.

H. A. Murena noted that the humidity in Buenos Aires has become a metaphysical entity that inhabits the city: the *Humedad*.[39] Similarly, the *porteño bobo* or *piola* could be transformed into the Fool of Buenos Aires, and the ongoing provincial tradition of the siesta could be recovered as the Evidential Siesta: a local mystical contemplation that underpins critical thresholds in the

---

[37] The asymmetry between these two flows or orders of velocity resembles the relationship between two other conceptual characters: Inspector Clouseau and the Pink Panther, created by Blake Edwards. These characters provide us with an interesting picture of this Macedonian paradox formulated within the parameters of his Conceptual Humoristics.

[38] See Deleuze and Guattari, *A Thousand Plateaus*, 438.

[39] In *Los penúltimos días* (The Penultimate Days) (1949), Murena writes: "The *porteños* talk a lot about the humidity, they talk about it like a homemade Ahriman who can be blamed for all the maladies. They talk about it like a metaphysical principle for common and everyday use. And they are right" (41).

city. *Belarte* would also spark this inverse paramnesia, but only once one has been able to defeat their own fear and restore their intellectual attention. Then, and only then, can *Belarte* drive individuals to achieve this mode of pure perception through written and/or oral interventions. The Evidential Siesta, on the other hand, could provoke a sustained inverse paramnesia that highlights a form of attention lying between the limit of intellectual and non-intellectual attention.

In this experience, characterized by absolute inattention, Macedonio noticed the possibility for a superlative form of attention, which seems to directly operate within the individuals' cognitive apparatus. Nonetheless, we should remember that this experience could only be communicated through metaphors or, more precisely, through the process of searching for these metaphors. Thus, even though there are previous traces in some unpublished texts, it should not be a surprise that the first quasi-allusion to the Siesta did not appear in a text by Macedonio until 1940.[40] Also, it would be important to notice that when he actually sought to draw the contours of this experience through his writing, he did so appealing to poetic language, which expresses the maximum level of abstraction and intensity of the literary world. In his text entitled "Poema de trabajos de estudios de las estéticas de la siesta (En busca de la metáfora de la Siesta)" (Poem on Investigations into the Aesthetics of the Siesta (In Search of the Metaphor for the Siesta)), he points out the limits of the Artistry of the Word in conveying the meaning of the Evidential Siesta.[41]

Even though in this text Macedonio offers a set of indications and guidelines about the Siesta, they should be considered as aesthetic formulations elaborated through a study focused on this experience and utilizing an intellectual attention capable of perceiving it. They are metaphors or elements of a poetic imagination that assume their limitations, only obliquely grasping the experience that they are trying to convey and, consequently, to define. The poetic voice departs in search of these metaphors for the Siesta and concludes with the following sentence placed between parentheses: "(But this must be given in translation,

---

[40] In Volume 7 of Macedonio's *Complete Works* there is also a poem dating back to 1900 titled "The Siesta" (95) and in the footnote to "Poema de trabajos de estudios de las estéticas de la siesta" (Poem on Investigations into the Aesthetics of the Siesta), Adolfo Obieta indicates the presence of several references to the siesta in other papers.

[41] In "Para una teoría del arte," Macedonio writes: "El arte literario tiene tres géneros puros: la Metáfora o Poesía (que incluye lo Fantástico Tierno, no las futilezas de invención del Ensueño y la Imaginación), la Humorística Conceptual y la Prosa del Personaje o Novela. Son las solas belartes puras de la Palabra, o Prosa" (Literary art has three pure genres: the Metaphor or Poetry (which includes the Tender-Fantastic, not the inventive futilities of Fantasy and Imagination), Conceptual Humoristics and the Prose of the Character or Novel. They are the only pure *belartes* of the Word or Prose) (*T* (1997), 247).

that is, as a metaphor, not as a definition. Whoever has the metaphor for the Siesta, hand it over. I'll ask for it from the sleepless rooster of the Night of the Siesta. We must make the mystic, Passion, into Art, but not the Real, not the passion for living.)"[42]

On any given day Macedonio experimented with this local metaphysical practice in Buenos Aires to delve into a pure perception of the world devoid of fear. But if the mystic state induced by the Evidential Siesta reveals its specific geographical location, as it demands an oblique form of attention rather than a rational and empirical sensitivity, which inevitably annihilates it, it could also show us the opportunity for a universal experience. According to Macedonio's theory of art, *Belarte* can also lay the groundwork for assuming this perspective and restoring a pure attention of affections removed from objective circumstances. Nevertheless, in order for individuals to be able to develop this hermeneutic practice on themselves, they must have the courage to face their own fear, to reassess their affections and transvalue the weight with which the fabric of apperceptions has invested them. Macedonio could not conceive of this liberation process as the singular experience of an isolated and individual self. The *almismo ayoico* that he postulated as a precondition for a pure perception of the world intrinsically signifies becoming collective.

---

[42] "(Pero esto ha de ser dado en versión, es decir en metáfora, no en definición. Quien tenga la metáfora de la Siesta, la dé. Yo se la pediré al gallo insomne de la Noche de la Siesta. Hay que hacerle arte al místico, a la Pasión, pero no a lo Real, a la pasión de vivir.)" (Fernández, "Poema de trabajos," in *R* (1987), 177).

Part Two

Philosophy, Affects, and Politics

Macedonio Fernández: The First Egocide in the Río de la Plata*

Diego Vecchio

The Two Births

In one of his autobiographies, Macedonio reduces his existence to two originary events: his birth as a self and his birth as an author. Regarding the first, and evoking Schopenhauer, he states: "The Universe or Reality and I were born on June 1, 1874 and it's easy enough to add that both births occurred not far from here in a city called Buenos Aires. There is a world for every birth, and not being born is nothing personal, it simply means there is no world." Regarding the second, he writes: "I have moved on from being a lawyer; I am new to Literature and since none of my clients came along with me, I have yet to find my first reader."[1] In many ways, these two events seem to stand in opposition to one another. The first birth presents a correlation between the world and the self; it is impossible to conceive of a self without a world or a world without a self. In contrast, the second birth presents a disjunction between author and reader; in this case it is impossible to conceive of an author with a reader or a reader with an author. Why did Macedonio establish an intrinsic connection between the world and the birth of his self, yet a dissociation between the reader and his birth as a writer? What could have happened between the two births?

"Nothing remarkable," Macedonio would likely answer, but he would be lying—the autobiography is the genre of deceit par excellence. We know for a fact

---

* Translated from the Spanish by Sean Manning.
[1] "El Universo o Realidad y yo nacimos en 1° de junio de 1874 y es sencillo añadir que ambos nacimientos ocurrieron cerca de aquí y en una ciudad de Buenos Aires. Hay un mundo para todo nacer, y el no nacer no tiene nada de personal, es meramente no haber mundo […] De la Abogacía me he mudado; estoy recién entrado a la Literatura y como ninguno de la clientela mía se vino conmigo, no tengo el primer lector todavía" (*PRC* (1989), 83).

that death intervened. More precisely, the death of the other. Or the death of the self. Or, better yet, the death of the other, which brought about the death of the self. Then and only then was his transformation possible: changing professions, leaving law for literature, giving birth to Macedonio Fernández the author and to a literature strictly aligned with a radical critique of the idea of the subject; a literature whose motto would necessarily be: the self must be eliminated.

Dudarte (The Art of Doubting)

For Macedonio Fernández, there is neither literature without theory nor production without speculation. Acting is inseparable from thinking, and thinking is inseparable from doubting; consequently, to name his theory of literature, he coined the term *Dudarte*. Macedonio presumes that literature consists of three subgenres: *poemática* (poematics), *humorística conceptual* (conceptual humoristics), and *novelística* (novelistics), each with its own particular writing technique.[2] "Poematics" makes use of the metaphor, which seeks to recreate the author's feelings within the reader by establishing a similarity between two unlike objects. "Conceptual humoristics" uses wit to induce a momentary belief in the absurd, i.e., content that is mentally impossible to represent. "Novelistics" generates a particular type of *mise en abyme* that consists in offering the reader a novel in which the characters are reading so as to make the reader also feel like a character.

This theory of literature is not governed by any principle of consistency. Macedonio takes the classical opposition between prose and poetry and adds an entirely heterogeneous third term: humor. It is not surprising then that these distinct subgenres and techniques overlap. Macedonio's conceptual witticisms are metaphors that establish a relationship between a present or existent object and another that is absent or nonexistent, and very often the *mise en abymes* are formulated as witticisms. There is one thing, however, that these three techniques have in common: the disruption of the reader's consciousness, whether it be by making them feel what the author feels by way of metaphor, by confounding their sense of reason with wit, or by filling them with a feeling of unreality through the novel.

---

[2] In "Para una teoría de la novela," and "Para una teoría de la humorística," Macedonio develops this Art of Doubting as well as other aesthetic doctrines. See *Teorías. Obras completas*, vol. 3 (1990).

Such dizzying play between reader, author, and character is found throughout his work, from his *Museo de la novela de la Eterna* (*The Museum of Eterna's Novel*) (1967) to the humoristic prose of *Papeles de recienvenido y continuación de la nada* (The Newcomer Papers and the Continuation of Nothingness) (1944). Macedonio's literature seeks to produce a philosophical effect by questioning the existence of the self. For this reason, his aesthetic project can also be considered a metaphysical project. In one of his notebooks, he states that "Art sets out to do the same as Metaphysics; it is a different way of inducing a mystic state, which is the enucleation of the notion of being, of personal identity and the historical-personal continuity."[3] It is not for nothing that Raúl Scalabrini Ortiz considered Macedonio Fernández to be the first metaphysician in Buenos Aires.[4]

Metaphysics

What exactly is Macedonio's understanding of metaphysics? In several of his early writings we find that metaphysics is for him a return to *vision pura* (pure vision).[5] By pure vision, he refers to that moment in our experience when there is still no experience, like the first perceptions of a newborn. Through pure vision, we are not required to identify a phenomenon as an artifice in order to reconstruct what has been lost forever (its origin). Instead, we can see it as the fable and method that created it, like the *tabula rasa* invented by the empiricists.

The empiricist method contrasts with a transcendental approach, which describes the experience from the outside and relies on the idea that the individual subject is the fundament of their experience, that the experience happens to this subject. The empiricist method, on the other hand, prefers to describe the experience from an immanent perspective—from inside the experience itself—without transcending the objective perception of the experience. It asserts that the experience does not happen to the subject, but rather it is the subject who is produced by the experience.

In this sense, Macedonio's definition of metaphysics does not imply a regression to an archaic and (pre)conceptual perception; it is the construction of an immanent perspective. If, for the adult individual, reality is a system of

---

[3] "El Arte se propone lo mismo que la Metafísica; sería una forma diversa de provocar el estado místico, que es la enucleación de la noción de ser, de la identidad personal y la continuidad histórico-personal" (*Todo y nada* (1992), 141).
[4] See Scalabrini Ortiz, *El hombre que está solo y espera* (1931), 123.
[5] See Fernández, "Bases en metafísica," in *NTV* (1990), 43–62.

perceptions and affects organized according to the subject–object dualism and to temporal, spatial, and causal categories, then for the newborn an experience is a collection (and nothing more) of sounds, colors, smells, tastes, tactile sensations, pain, and pleasure. In other words, pure vision, like the newborn experience, is an immanent field of phenomena.

Phainomenon, in accordance with its etymology, is that which reveals itself. Nevertheless, this is not entirely correct. Either the phenomenon is what it reveals, in and of itself, i.e., the being and the phenomenon coincide, or the phenomenon reveals what it is not, i.e., the being and the phenomenon diverge. The phenomenon is pure appearance that hides and distorts the being of things. Naturally, to be able to speak about an immanent field of phenomena, we must opt for the first sense. Inside this immanent field, there is no beyond—behind, beside, or outside—the phenomenon; there is nothing. Therefore, Macedonio is opposed to any variety of theory that divides the Real into a sensible world and an intelligible world (Plato), a phenomenal world and a noumenal world (Kant), or a conscious world and an unconscious world (Freud). This immanent field of phenomena allows itself to be described neither according to the subject–object dualism (or in its different expressions: exterior/interior, physical/psychic, material/spiritual) nor according to spatial and temporal categories. For Macedonio, such notions (subject and object, space and time) are the aftermath of adulterated pure vision, when original perceptions become derivative perceptions.

Our psyche is governed by the law of association. Perceptions that occur subsequent to pure vision are automatically associated with each other, creating sequences in which it is possible to identify perceptions that are anterior and posterior, proximate and distant, exterior and interior, causes and effects. As a result, the immanent field of phenomena becomes a system: a subject opposite an object, determined by time, space, and the law of causality. In place of our initial pure perceptions, we have what Macedonio calls *apercepciones* (apperceptions).[6] Philosophical tradition typically defines apperception in terms of self-reflection. Apperception is a perception accompanied by consciousness: apperceiving is perceiving that one is perceiving. But Macedonio follows the German psychologist Johann Friedrich Herbart (1776–1841), who defines perception in terms of the association between states of consciousness. On this, Macedonio writes: "when my psyche is moved by just one of the many perceptions that an object is capable of providing—for example, color—images of every other

---

[6] See Macedonio, "Bases en metafísica," in *NTV* (1990), 43–62.

sensation that this concrete body can offer us and has offered us many times before immediately arise within our consciousness."[7]

According to Macedonio, instead of making our world more intelligible, apperception makes it paradoxically more abstruse. Instead of helping us to know the world, it renders it completely incomprehensible. What is intended to guide us in fact leads us astray. When certain exceptional circumstances allow for pure vision to occur once again, rather than familiarity, we experience a sense of uneasiness, a confusion of being, a strange bewilderment. What was once known to us now appears as something unknown. What was once familiar to us emerges as something foreign. Metaphysics then, for Macedonio, is the dissolution of this bewilderment, transforming impure perceptions into pure perceptions. And by dissolving impure perceptions, he means that we must eliminate them, or, more precisely, that we must eliminate the ego. As we shall see, his metaphysics is a plot to overthrow the ego. Indeed, Macedonio was the first to commit *egocide* in the Río de la Plata.

On the Notion of Ego

Like Macedonio, the ego also experienced two births. It was first born following the labor of philosophical argumentation in Descartes' *Discourse on the Method*, published in 1637. But in 1641 it was born once again in his *Meditations on First Philosophy*, but this time, we might say, as fiction. In this text, Descartes searches for an apodictic principle that is unconditionally true and, like bedrock, can serve as a foundation for philosophy. To find this principle, he conceives a method—hyperbolic doubt—and a staging for this method—the fiction of a character who doubts to excess, hereafter referred to as the Doubter.

There is a difference between simple doubt and hyperbolic doubt. In the latter, the Doubter not only doubts patently false knowledge, founded on error or obvious bias, but he also questions knowledge that is probable but not absolutely certain. The Doubter's doubt does not allow for degrees or shades, hence its hyperbolic character. Anything susceptible to doubt is automatically considered to be erroneous and false, and consequently rejected. Sensorial knowledge is

---

[7] "[...] cuando mi psiquis es actuada por una sola de las muchas percepciones que un objeto puede proporcionar, el color, por ejemplo, brotan instantáneamente en la conciencia todas las imágenes de las demás sensaciones que ese cuerpo concreto puede procurarnos y nos ha procurado muchas veces" ("La metafísica," in *NTV* (1990), 80).

therefore the first to collapse under the weight of this doubt, given that the senses can sometimes be misleading, and according to this principle it is always wise not to trust those who have deceived us before. However, by rejecting certain clearly evident knowledge attained via the senses (for example, "I am here, seated by the fire, attired in a dressing gown, having this paper in my hands"[8]), the Doubter resembles, not without some risk, those insane individuals "devoid of sense, whose cerebella are so troubled and clouded by the violent vapours of black bile, that they constantly assure us that they think they are kings when they are really quite poor, or that they are clothed in purple when they are really without covering [...] or are made of glass."[9]

However, we should not diagnose insanity so quickly. This argument is best reserved for later to destroy more-resistant evidence. For us to reject sensorial knowledge, it is sufficient to recall that in dreams we often witness the same things, in the absence of the exterior world, that we perceive when we are awake. The Doubter declares that he has dreamt many times that he was "dressed and seated near the fire, whilst in reality I was lying undressed in bed!"[10] All forms of sensorial knowledge collapse under the weight of this argument, even the belief in the existence of our own body. Nevertheless, the impossibility of definitively differentiating between sleep and wakefulness calls into doubt the particular but not the universal; it causes sensorial knowledge to founder but not intelligible knowledge; it denies the principles of physics, astronomy, and medicine, but not those of arithmetic or geometry. Whether asleep or awake, two plus three will always equal five and a square will never have more than four sides.

In order to question mathematical principles, extreme doubt must be pushed to the point of paroxysm. The Doubter invents a sort of demiurge of errors, who is the contrary of God's absolute Truth and Goodness. This demiurge manifests itself inside an evil genius who is determined to deceive the Doubter, making him believe that the sky, the air, the earth, colors, shapes, and sounds are nothing more than illusions, that he has no hands or eyes or flesh or blood, that two plus three equals six, that a square has three sides, and so on. In short, everything is false. At this point, the Doubter discovers something that manages to resist hyperbolic doubt. Even if the Doubter accepts the extreme hypothesis that a certain powerful and clever trickster is dedicated to constantly deceiving him, he

---

[8] Descartes, *Discourse on the Method*, 59.
[9] Descartes, *Discourse on the Method*, 59.
[10] Descartes, *Discourse on the Method*, 60.

notices that "without a doubt I exist."[11] The evil genius can deceive him whenever he likes, but he will never be able to reduce the Doubter to nothing as long as the Doubter thinks that he is something. The Doubter concludes: "So that after having reflected well and carefully examined all things, we must come to the definite conclusion that this proposition: I am, I exist, is necessarily true each time that I pronounce it, or that I mentally conceive it."[12]

Descartes posits that doubt ceases when confronted with a simple and immediate piece of evidence: the existence of a thought that perceives itself perceiving. One can doubt everything, except for the fact that there is someone who is doubting. Or in other words, while hyperbolic doubt affects the various subjects of a statement ("there is no sky or earth or air," "I have no body," "two plus three are not five," and so on), it makes an exception for the subject of the enunciation ("I exist"). As an indestructible certainty, the pronouncement "I am, I exist" can be considered philosophy's first truth. This apodictic principle is not the result of deduction or inference, that is, of reasoning, but rather of intuition. For Descartes, the knowledge that we possess of ourselves is transparent. Thoughts cannot exist inside us without us instantly having knowledge of those thoughts. The experience of thought only makes sense in the first-person singular, as we recall from the celebrated formula: "cogito ergo sum / I think, therefore I am."

But what is the ego? In Descartes' "Second Meditation," the first person states: "I am not more than a thing which thinks."[13] Indeed, the word "thing" suggests a material entity. By describing the ego as a thinking thing, Descartes is relating two ideas: immateriality and substantiality. The immateriality of the cogito stands in contrast with the materiality of the body. Substantializing the ego is a way of giving it consistency. Therefore, a fundament of Descartes' thought is that the ego remains, persists, and subsists despite changes in qualities and accidents.

And what is a thinking thing? A thing that thinks is a thing "which doubts, understands, conceives, affirms, denies, wills, refuses, which also imagines and feels."[14] The Cartesian cogito cannot be reduced purely to the verb "to think" but exists over a series of verbs—or a collection of faculties—such as "to think," "to want," "to imagine," and "to feel." The ego is the unifying principle. However, in

---

[11] Descartes, *Discourse on the Method*, 64.
[12] Descartes, *Discourse on the Method*, 64.
[13] Descartes, *Discourse on the Method*, 65.
[14] Descartes, *Discourse on the Method*, 66.

Descartes' meditations doubt is the other face of certainty, and the Doubter, the main character of this fictional story, disappears suddenly from the scene at the very moment the reign of Descartes' hero—the ego—begins.

Various prominent voices emerged to speak out against this new ruler. One of them was David Hume, who in the first version of his *A Treatise of Human Nature*, published in 1739, dedicated a section to the problem of personal identity. Like Descartes, Hume opts for a journey inside himself in order to confirm that there is no self, casting doubt on the transparency of the self-reflective experience. As an empiricist, Hume believes that every idea is a copy of an impression. An idea can only exist if there is a corresponding originating impression. But, if the self exists, then what is the impression that gave it its origin?

During his introspective journey, Hume always encounters one particular perception or another, whether it be hot or cold, light or dark, love or hate, pain or pleasure. However, he is never able to find his self except through a perception, and once those perceptions disappear, as in dreams, the self disappears along with them. There is in fact no impression that has given rise to the self. There are only perceptions and affects. The supposed self does not exist. The mind is nothing more than a bundle of different perceptions, one succeeding another at inconceivable speeds, in a constant state of flux and movement. Or rather, the mind is a sort of theater in which distinct perceptions appear successively; they happen, they happen again, they fade, and then they fuse with an infinite variety of positions and situations. It would be a mistake to attribute this collection to a center and this theater to a director, whether postulating the existence of a self or an ego.

Contemplation

Pure vision is not limited to the first perceptions of a newborn; it is also possible as artificial vision, as perception purified of its reminiscences and apperceptive attachments through an act of dissociation or, as Macedonio would say, through contemplation. In this sense, contemplation is a critique of knowledge through an examination of our perceptions, which causes us to refute notions of self, matter, time, and space. Once this critique of knowledge has been realized, one achieves what Macedonio calls "the mystic state," which he defines as the experience of dwelling without being in the world, ceasing to be an individual subject that perceives objects, existing free of the self.

In truth, for Macedonio the mystic state occurs spontaneously and effortlessly every night while we are sleeping. He considers sleep not as a regressive activity but rather as the construction of an immanent perspective through which the various avatars of the subject–object dualism (waking and dream states, exterior and interior worlds, perception and memory) perish. His writing relentlessly repudiates such dualisms, following the argumentation of Schopenhauer, who in the fifth book of *The World as Will and Representation* recalls Hobbes's warning that when we fall asleep without undressing or when a project or business matter has taken over much of our attention, it can be very easy to confuse dreams with wakefulness. Macedonio recalls this text as he creates a fiction in which Hobbes becomes a protagonist who travels to Buenos Aires and takes a room in a hotel. At a particular point in the story, Hobbes, fully dressed, decides to sit in an armchair to rest when suddenly he is seized by doubt. He is not certain if he has fallen asleep or if he is awake. What is more, he remembers having seen a man enter his room and search through his suitcase before fleeing. Hobbes also remembers that he leapt to his feet to chase the intruder to the front door of the hotel, but never found any indication that he had been real. Perplexed, Hobbes shares this anecdote with Domínguez, his *Porteño* guide, who suggests that he should consult a neighborhood metaphysician named Macedonio Fernández. Hobbes accepts his advice and Macedonio Fernández has him read a manuscript that begins like this:

> The field of phenomena that we call World, Being, Reality, Experience is one and the same and thus unnameable: we will still call it "what is sensed," neither external nor internal, neither psychic nor material. Anything that does not happen for me, within my sensitivity, does not happen at all neither in psychic fields (other supposed souls), nor in the supposed material field [...].[15]

No toda es vigilia la de los ojos abiertos (Not All Wakefulness Is with Open Eyes) (1928) is constructed using the technique of *mise en abyme*. Macedonio writes a metaphysical essay that includes a fictitious story about Hobbes in which Hobbes reads the metaphysical essay written by Macedonio. It leads to Hobbes's annihilation, thus, a few pages after Hobbes's encounter with Macedonio Fernández, he writes:

---

[15] "El campo fenomenal que llamamos Mundo, Ser, Realidad, Experiencia, es uno solo y por tanto indenominable: el de 'lo sentido' le llamaremos todavía, ni externo ni interno, ni psíquico ni material. Nada que no ocurra para mí, en mi sensibilidad, no ocurre de ningún modo ni en campos psíquicos (otras almas supuestas), ni en el campo supuesto material" ("El mundo es un almismo," *NTV* (1990), 255).

It pains me to know that Hobbes and the kindhearted Domínguez, who brought him to me, will die at the onset of my definitive answer to this problem, since one of my first affirmations, absolutely essential if I am to answer Hobbes' trust with the comprehensive solution that he deserves, demands the extinction of his personal entity. The main thesis of my answer is the uniqueness of Sensitivity, the inconceivability of a plurality within Sensitivity. I regret that Hobbes' request and the promptness of my cooperation have turned out to be so fatal for him.[16]

Macedonio's metaphysics not only pronounces philosophical statements (it is not possible to know other psyches), but it also acts, creates, or in this case destroys (Hobbes is exterminated upon reading this thesis). The indiscernibility between dream and waking states is not only formulated, it is also performed by vertiginously blending different narrative planes: fiction (Hobbes's visit to Buenos Aires) and reality (Macedonio Fernández's manuscript that Hobbes reads). Just as dream and waking states represent a continuum, Macedonio creates a continuum between fiction and reality. Reality is a fiction, and wakefulness is a dream. Hence reading's proximity to dreaming.

This theory of being is captured inside several of Macedonio's formulas: "The world, being, reality, everything is a dream without a dreamer, one single dream, only a dream and one's own dream only, and thus, no one's dream; the more real it seems, the more it is entirely a dream."[17] Or: "The states that we associate with perception exist as states, but without an object; being and the world do not belong to perception. There is no Object; we are what is perceived; and what we 'are' when we perceive is nothing but the state of perception without a subject."[18] Or: "For this reason I call the Being an *almismo ayoico*' (selfless soul)."[19] However, despite the variety of subjects (being, world, reality) and predicates (soul, dream, perception), these formulas share several points of contact.

First, the world is defined using terminology grounded in psychology ("soul," "dream," "perception"). In doing so, Macedonio attacks those dualistic philosophies

---

[16] "Me duele tener que anticipar que Hobbes y el gentil Domínguez, que me lo trajo, mueren al principio de mi respuesta definitiva al problema, pues una de mis primeras afirmaciones, absolutamente irrenunciables si he de responder a la confianza de Hobbes con una solución plena y digna de él, exige la extinción de su entidad personal. Es tesis principal de mi respuesta: la unicidad de la Sensibilidad, la inconcebilidad de una pluralidad en la Sensibilidad. Deploro que el encargo de Hobbes y la presteza de mi comedimiento le hayan resultado tan fatales" ("Ley de asociación," *NTV* (1990), 271).

[17] "El mundo, el ser, la realidad, todo es un sueño sin soñador, un solo sueño, sólo un sueño y el sueño de uno solo, por tanto, el sueño de nadie, tanto más real cuanto más es enteramente un sueño" ("La metafísica, crítica del conocimiento," *NTV* (1990), 194).

[18] "Los estados que llamamos de percepción existen como estados, pero sin objeto; el ser, el mundo, no es de percepción. No hay Objeto; somos lo percibido; y lo que 'somos' cuando percibimos nada es sino el estado de percepción sin sujeto" ("La metafísica, crítica del conocimiento," *NTV* (1990), 195).

[19] "llamo por eso al Ser un almismo ayoico" ("El asombre de ser. Idealismo absoluto," *NTV* (1990), 243).

that contrast psychic reality and physical reality, body and soul, matter and spirit, exterior and interior, wakefulness and dreaming, objects and ideas. In their place, he offers a monism: the world is one. This does not mean to say that the world represents a unity. Declaring that the world is one means that everything is made up of one unique substance and that this substance is psychic in nature, that is, it is immaterial. Herein lies the complicit wink of *NTV* (Not All Wakefulness Is with Open Eyes). In this title, Macedonio disrupts the dualism between eyes that are open and eyes that are closed, between wakefulness and dream states, producing a syntactical twist with argumentative value between wakefulness and open eyes and denying all reality of the exterior world. For this reason, Macedonio, on various occasions, declares himself to be an idealist. However, idealism is a subject-centered philosophy, and for Macedonio this material originating in the psyche is not embodied by any subject form. He is in reality a radical empiricist.

Second, with terms like "selfless soul," "dream without a dreamer," "perception without subject or object," Macedonio is proposing a neutral subjectivity, free of distinctive qualities, sufficient in and of itself with no need to refer to an ego. This leads to certain linguistic complications. Instead of saying *yo soy* (I am), *yo pienso* (I think), or *yo sueño* (I dream), one would have to say *se es* (it is), *se piensa* (it thinks), or *se sueña* (it dreams), employing the verbs impersonally, just as one says "it rains" or "it snows."

And lastly, this subjectivity is indestructible because it escapes any temporal determination and, therefore, the categories of beginning or end. It refers to something that is "self-existent and uncreated."[20] By eliminating the self, Macedonio believes that he is also destroying the idea of death. In *NTV*, he writes: "The destruction of the self is progress: it is followed by the mystic state. If there were a self within a being, that would be the only part that was mortal."[21]

Passion

If oneiric states disrupt the dualism of wakefulness and dreaming, then passion cancels the dualism of ego and alter-ego. Macedonio does not consider passion to be the negative of action. Here, passion is not the state in which something is affected by an action, as it was for classical philosophers, like, for example, when

---

[20] "autoexistente increado" (Macedonio, "Descripcio-Metafísica," *NTV* (1990), 362).
[21] "La anulación del Yo es un acrecimiento: a ella sigue el estado místico. Si en el ser hubiera un 'yo' eso sería lo único mortal" (*NTV* (1990), 339–340).

something is "cut" through the act of "cutting." Passion is also not an affection of the soul, as it is for modern philosophers, i.e., the soul experiences love, hate, desire, happiness, sadness, etc. and is altered. For Macedonio, passion is a sort of *egocide* by *traslación* (transferal): "the death of the ego substituted by the other-ego" or, in other words, it is the "complete and constant substitution of living for oneself with 'living for another.'"[22]

In this sense, passion must be differentiated from what Macedonio refers to in *NTV* as sexual frenzy or fantasies (filial love or love for an ideal). In sexual frenzy, there is too much sensorialism and in fantasies, too much asymmetry. In neither of these cases is there an elimination of the ego. Passion, which is a transferal of the psyche, assumes a reciprocity that only occurs in love between equals. Hence the similarity that exists between passion and friendship. By Macedonio's own definition, his theory of passion is a metaphysics of the *Todo-amador* (Total-lover).

There are three phases in *Todo-amor* (Total-love). First, an experience of radical fondness is initiated between the lovers. During passion the other's feeling become one's own. The lover experiences his or her psychic states emotionally, not sensorially, and the other receives no direct information from these states, only indirectly through the expressions of the lover's body. One feels happy when observing the other's happiness, and one feels sad when observing the other's sadness. In this way, the lover begins to live the life of the one who is loved, at first, secondarily, and later, by nullifying his or her own life. Accordingly, Macedonio is able to describe *Todo-amor* as an *Altruística* (Altruistics), not in the sense of a philanthropical intersubjective experience but as a trans-subjective experience. It is a transferal experience that brings about the subjective displacement of the lovers.

The second phase in *Todo-amor* is fission. Passion causes the bond between the body and the psyche to be disrupted, culminating in a true psychic release: the lover's psyche separates from its own body through its intimacy with the other's body. And vice versa, the other's psyche separates from its own body through its intimacy with the lover's body. As such, passion subverts the notion of "my body," that is, a body of one's own that was not chosen and to which the psyche would otherwise be fatally linked. The consciousness is able to abandon its own body and enter that of another, without perishing.

---

[22] "la muerte del Ego sustituido por el ego-otro;" "sustitución completa y constante del vivir para sí mismo por el 'vivir otro'" ("La idilio-tragedia," *PA* (1981), 147).

There is an analogy here between passion and death, not because *Todo-amor* is a miniature death experience; on the contrary, death is an amplified and intensified experience of *Todo-amor*. Death is a repetition of passion's mechanism, not the other way around. For Macedonio, death is also less an experience of destruction than it is of fission. If the consciousness can separate from its body without dying, then we can assume that the consciousness continues to exist after death despite the disappearance of the body. Simply because the body disappears, the consciousness, which has accompanied the body throughout life, does not necessarily have to disappear along with it.

In this theory of passion, the term "consciousness" denotes something completely unrelated to the psychological concept of consciousness or the classical philosophical notion of the soul. In psychology, consciousness is an organization conditioned by temporality, that is, by appearance and disappearance, by birth and death: psychology's consciousness is mortal. In modern philosophy, the soul is contrasted with the body, as is the spiritual with the material. Philosophy is decidedly dualistic. On the other hand, Macedonio's consciousness is something that cannot be conceived either in temporal or dualistic terms. This consciousness is one of many names given to that universal soul, impersonal and neutral, indifferent and independent of temporal determinations such as beginnings, interruptions, and ends. Consequently, it is no longer characterized by unity and identity, as occurs with the individual ego, but rather by indestructibility.

The third and final phase of *Todo-amor* is chiasmus. Passion establishes associations between the unassociated via fission's intermingling of bodies, psyches, and subjects. One's psyche corresponds to the other's body, and the other's psyche corresponds to one's own body. Or also, one's body corresponds to the other's psyche, and the other's body corresponds to one's own psyche. Chiasmus implies a confusion of the subjects' identities, which seems to be encapsulated in this formula that Macedonio scrawled across a page he titled "Metafísica del amador" (Metaphysics of the Lover): "vivir a Ella es su yo" (living for Her is his self).[23] Or in this other formula in *NTV*: "Only in me is there a Self; not mine, but Hers, says the Lover; not mine, but His, says the Beloved."[24] The self and the other quickly become confused inside an equation that destroys the identity of both the ego and the alter-ego. This *egocide* that passion realizes is also a form of "altruicide."

---

[23] Fernández, "Metafísica del amador," in *NTV* (1990), 223.

[24] "Sólo [en la Pasión] hay un Yo; no el mío sino el de Ella, dice el Amante; no el mío sino el de Él, dice la Amada" (*NTV* (1990), 232).

Novel

In addition to contemplation and passion, there is a third method for overthrowing the ego: the novel. Macedonio Fernández wrote two of them: *Adriana Buenos Aires, última novela mala* (Adriana Buenos Aires, the Last Bad Novel) and *El Museo de la novela de la Eterna (primera novela buena)* (*The Museum of Eterna's Novel, the First Good Novel*). Both of these novels constitute a single aesthetic-metaphysical project, which Macedonio explained in an autobiographical note, published in the journal *Sur*, in the following terms:

> My opinion, which is perhaps not shared by others, is that the novel that has been used (and which I will utilize [*sic*] previously in the "last bad novel": *Adriana Buenos Aires*), one of delusions, that is, one that makes the reader participate in the happiness and suffering of the characters, is hopelessly naïve; a novel will only be artistic once it proposes—and, to a lesser degree, achieves—the ultimate objective of a complete disruption of the consciousness, a disruption that will be the greatest opening into the absolute metaphysical enigma.[25]

His two novels were presented to the public as quarrelling twins, a quarrel founded on a twofold dispute: a qualitative dispute (one is good and the other is bad) and a temporal dispute (one is the last and the other is the first). According to the temporal dispute, there is something that begins and something that ends. What ends—that is, what was done in the past, what has already been used—is bad. Alternatively, what begins—that is, what is done in the present and what will continue to be done in the future—is good.

Macedonio thus reformulates the eternal debate between the ancient and the modern. By modern, we must understand the equivalence between good, first, and present. Subsequently, all that is ancient, or past, must necessarily be bad and last. Now, if the present is what slips away, what is slipping away, and what never stops slipping away, then how can a correlation be established between what is good, first, and present? Modernity continues to be uncertain, inconstant, and elusive. In this sense, the notion of ego could be considered anti-modern. The

---

[25] "Mi opinión, que quizá no será compartida, es que la novela que se ha usado (y que yo practicaré [*sic*] previamente en la 'última novela mala': Adriana Buenos Aires), la de alucinación, o sea de hacer participar al lector en las alegrías y penas de los personajes, es irremediablemente pueril; que sólo será artística una novela que se proponga –y obtenga menos intensamente– el supremo resultado de una conmoción total de la conciencia, conmoción que será la más plena apertura hacia el total enigma metafísico" (*PRC* (1989), 91-2).

ego imposes identity and permanence while modernity celebrates difference and becoming. For that very reason, it is Macedonio's treatment of the ego—either enthroning it or overthrowing it—which allows him to walk the line between modern and ancient, last and first, bad and good.

In the bad twin, the enthronement of the ego is described as a delusion. The reader identifies with the characters, deriving pleasure from their pleasure and feeling sorrow at their suffering. Confusion arises from this sort of identification because the reader reads the novel as if it were a real depiction of life, mistaking the world of the characters for the world of people. As a result, the bad novel is accepted as literary realism. For Macedonio, a realist novel is a novel that practices verisimilitude, producing an illusion of reality, concealing its fictitious nature.

In the good twin, the overthrow of the ego can occur through a process of distanciation or disruption. The good twin creates a distance between fiction and reality, reading and life, wakefulness and dream states, open eyes and closed eyes, that will prevent any delusions, denounce any illusions, and destroy the story's verisimilitude through a systematic practice of contradictions and incongruencies. However, when Macedonio introduces his quarreling twins, he is not exactly contrasting delusion with distanciation, but rather delusion with disruption. The good twin seeks to precipitate a disruption in the reader's consciousness that will lead him or her to believe, even if only for an instant, that he or she is a character instead of a person. Rather than offer an illusion of reality, this twin attempts to produce an illusion of irreality.

To bring about this illusion of irreality, Macedonio invents a speculative process that he calls the "Double Novel," which consists of making the reader read a "novel of readers," i.e., a novel in which the characters are also readers:

> My plan, which I will possibly never realize, was to create a novel about the experiences of two or three people who regularly meet to read another novel, and in doing so these people reading the novel become intensely enlivened for the reader when compared to the characters in the novel they are reading. The protagonists in the "novel of readers" seem to be living beings due to the constant weakened presence of the protagonists in the "novel being read." And understand that what I hope comes of this constant parallel opposition, inside the mind of the reader who is you, is that by providing the simultaneous effect of devitalizing the figures or ghosts of the novel being read through the emphasis given to the protagonists in the novel of readers, is that you, the reader, alive,

doubt for a moment that you are a living being who is reading, and shudder at the thought that for an instant you were suddenly a character being read.[26]

The problem here is that there is no genuine opposition between delusion and disruption, which is to say, the twins really have no reason to quarrel. It is true that Macedonio did everything in his power to direct his readers toward an antagonistic reading: pitting good against bad, last against first, antirealism against realism. However, it is also true that delusion contrasts with distanciation, but not with disruption.

What is the difference between a novel that is bad and realist—one that causes the reader to confuse fiction with reality by believing that characters are people—and a novel that is good and antirealist—one that causes the reader to confuse reality with fiction by believing that people are characters? What separates a delusional reader, like Don Quijote, for example, from Macedonio's reader who feels that they are a character when reading a chapter of MNE in which the characters are also reading a novel? Nothing, besides perhaps that there is a change in sign: the negative becomes positive or vice versa. But as far as logic is concerned, there is no difference.

In this sense, the good novel's antirealism is not the negation of the bad novel's realism, but rather an inverted realism, which inverts nothing. Or, in other words, the principle that allows us to differentiate the bad novel from the good novel does not in fact differentiate them. The bad novel and the good novel are part of a continuum. When the characters in the good novel begin to read another novel in order to provoke that disruption within the reader's consciousness, they choose a passage from the bad novel: a passage in which Eduardo de Alto, who is the narrator, watches Adriana as she sleeps. Once the two characters are read, they have exited the bad novel and entered the good novel, producing a moment of vertigo. The twin novels are in fact conjoined novels with certain parts in common. This raises confusion between good and bad, last and first. The *mise en abyme* is a *mise en scène* that features a reader, a fictitious character, who when

---

[26] "Mi plan, que quizá nunca realizaré, era hacer la novela de lo que les pasaba a dos o tres personas, que se reúnen habitualmente a leer otra novela, de tal manera que estas personas que leen la novela se vivifiquen intensamente en la impresión del lector en contraposición con las personas protagonistas de la novela leída. Así que los protagonistas de la 'novela de leyentes' parecen seres vivientes, por la constante figura debilitada de las actitudes de los protagonistas de la 'novela leída'. Y nótese que lo que espero de esta constante contraposición paralela, en la mente del lector viviente que tengo en usted, al surtir el efecto simultáneo de la atenuación de las figuras o fantasmas de la novela leída por el relieve que asumen los protagonistas de la novela de leyentes, es que el lector, usted, viviente, dude por un instante de ser un existente que lee, y se estremezca de creerse por un instante sin más ser que el de un personaje leído" (PRC (1989), 91).

reading that the characters are reading thinks, "In this moment, I sense that I do not exist." However, this is not the only *mise en abyme* that radicalizes the double-novel method.

Macedonio versus Descartes: The Return of the Doubter

Throughout Macedonio's novels and humoristic prose, there are numerous examples of another particular type of *mise en abyme* that involves the author as a character who lists the books he imagined but fortunately did not write, or who openly apostrophizes the reader to announce that he is not in fact writing: "One moment, dear reader: right now, I am not writing anything."[27] In these texts, there is also a very particular type of reader. It is a reader who is rejected by the novel or a reader who rejects the novel; a reader who reads so slowly that the author must leave to occupy himself with something else or a reader who reads so quickly that he or she gets ahead of the author and begins to reads what the author has not yet had time to write: "Do not read so hurriedly, my dear reader; my writing cannot keep up with your reading."[28] Here, it is not a matter of presenting a reader who ceases to exist when reading that other characters are also reading, but rather an author who does not write and a reader who does not read. They are subjects who emerge from the contradiction between what they say and what they do.

The novel's paratext displays this same negation but presented in the form of procrastination. Its kilometric title—*Museo de la novela de la "Eterna" y la Niña de Dolor, la "Dulce-Persona" De-Un-Amor que no fue sabido, primera novela buena* (*Museum of "Eterna's" Novel and Melancholy's Child, the "Sweetheart" of an Undeclared Lover, the First Good Novel*)[29]—has no other function but to extend the preliminaries and preparations required to enter the book. This results in slippage: the title moves to free itself from the text that it denotes. The periphery moves to position itself as the center of attention. From the outset, there is a breaching of the borders that continues with the proliferation of prologues. Rather than orienting and explaining, these prologues serve only to further distance the reader from the novel, frustrating all horizons of expectation.

---

[27] "Un instante, querido lector: por ahora no escribo nada" (*PRC* (1989), 14).
[28] "No lea tan ligero, mi lector, que no alcanzo con mi escritura adonde está usted leyendo" (*PRC* (1989), 29).
[29] Translator's Note: This is Margaret Schwartz's translation of the novel's title (Open Letter, 2005).

Instead of escorting the reader inside, they create more obstacles. Instead of introductions, the reader suffers more and more delays. By systematically postponing the novel for later, the reader must read, while still not having read anything, and the writer must write, while still not having written anything.

In Macedonio's writings, these strategies were accompanied by a genuine transition into action: his books were also rejected or delayed for publication. Before the novel was a novel-book, it was a novel-promise (for thirty years Macedonio informed various correspondents of his forthcoming novel, which he never published during his lifetime) or a novel-performance (a series of events that he conceived and often carried out, like announcing his run for presidency and printing leaflets with his unusual first name, or circulating fragments of his novel throughout the streets for the public to find). Similarly, what happened to the fictitious readers also happened, to a certain extent, to the factual readers. His first audience was made up of readers who did not read him, who could not read him, because his novel was placed in negative circulation through a potential presence that only confirmed its absence. For Macedonio, literature was the possible encounter between an author who does not write and a reader who does not read, or more precisely, between a writer who writes that he is not writing and a reader who reads that he or she is not reading. Through this negative specularity, a subject (the reader, the writer) is assigned an attribute that disqualifies it as a subject (not reading, not writing).

Within the history of literature, this project can be considered to be one of modernity's characteristic acts, summed up by the following formula: "release the power of the negative." Reader-response criticism or most of reading theory is founded on one assumption, namely, that there is a transaction (Wolfgang Iser), a cooperation (Umberto Eco), an interpretive community (Stanley Fish) or a mutual understanding (Julio Cortázar) between the reader and the text. Macedonio developed a theory of negative reception between the reader, the author, and the text, or, if you prefer, he incited divergence, disjunction, and disagreement between the reader and the author. For that very reason, publishing meant not allowing the book to be read, taking it out of circulation. As such, Macedonio not only committed *egocide*, but he was also responsible for the death of the reader.

Within the history of philosophy, this project can be understood as a dual mechanism of fiction and thought, which, by eliminating the reader, seeks to once again refute the Cartesian cogito. This is exactly what Macedonio states in one of the novel's prologues, titled "Prólogo que cree saber algo, no de la novela, pues ello es incompetente a prólogos, sino de Doctrina de Arte" ("Prologue That Thinks It Knows Something, Not about the Novel (It's Not Allowed That), but about the Doctrine of Art")[30]:

> Whoever experiences even a moment of the state of belief in not existing and later returns to the state of belief in existing, will forever understand that the whole content of the verbalization or notion "not to be" is the belief in not being. It's not possible to believe that one does not exist without existing.[31]

In this passage, Macedonio is elliptically rewriting Descartes' "Second Meditation," bringing back the Doubter in order to denounce one of the French philosopher's assumptions, specifically, "without a doubt I exist," given that the evil genius "deceives me, and let him deceive me as much as he will, he can never cause me to be nothing so long as I think that I am something."[32] If there is an evil genius who can make me believe that two plus two equals five, it would not be absurd to say that the same genius can also make me believe that I exist. If mathematical principles can be called into doubt, then the principle of existence must also be called into doubt. The Doubter should have been more consistent in his method. Instead of accepting an exception, he should have also applied hyperbolic doubt to the subject who made the statement and conclude: "I do not exist."

However, this statement presents a glaring contradiction. If we take it literally, then we succumb to the absurd or to spiritualism. The verb "to exist," just like the expression "to be silent" or "to be dead," cannot be conjugated for every tense and for every person without producing an oxymoron.[33] In order to say, "I do not exist," I must exist. I cannot say "I am silent" without speaking. It is not possible to say "I am dead" without being alive. By the same token, it is not possible to be a reader and read that I am not reading or be an author and write that I am not writing. All of these verbs have something in common: they reject certain forms of self-referentiality. When conjugating the verb "to exist" in the present indicative tense and using the negation and the first-person singular form, an antinomy arises between the statement's author and the statement's subject. Macedonio disorients the Doubter, transforming him into someone

---

[30] Fernández, *MNE*, 36; Schwartz, 32.
[31] "Quien experimenta por un momento el estado de creencia de no existir y luego vuelve al estado de creencia de existir, comprenderá para siempre que todo el contenido de la verbalización o noción de 'no ser' es la creencia de no ser. El 'yo no existo' del cuál debió partir la metafísica de Descartes en sustitución de su lamentable 'yo existo'; no se puede creer que no se existe, sin existir" (Fernández, *MNE*, 37; Schwartz, 33).
[32] See Descartes, 64.
[33] See Dardo Scavino, "El autor y su musa," 13–31.

who ignores the speech present in what he is speaking, or who negates what he says with what he does.

Museo de la novela de la Eterna (*The Museum of Eterna's Novel*) can be read as a repudiation of *Meditations on First Philosophy*, which rather that enthroning the ego, carries the Doubter's doubt to its ultimate consequences. Like Hume and Nietzsche, Macedonio practices philosophy by force, replacing reason, not with stone, but with the quicksand of negative specularity, whereby no subject can manifest itself without automatically being overthrown.

6

A Metaphysics That Only Begins: On Macedonio's Writing Passion

Julio Prieto

> ... chi pesca per lo vero e non ha l'arte.
> *Paradiso* XIII, 123

Macedonio's "Metafísica de la Afección" (Metaphysics of Affect)—or what he also calls "Nominalismo de la Afección" (Nominalism of Affect)—can be historically situated between two intellectual currents that were very active in the first decades of the twentieth century: what Bertrand Russell called "practical philosophies," which privilege action over knowledge, including Marx and the North American pragmatists, and what I would describe as "philosophies of flux," including such thinkers as Bergson, Whitehead, William James, and Uruguayan philosopher Carlos Vaz Ferreira, but also writers like Marcel Proust and Felisberto Hernández.[1] At the same time, Macedonio dialogues with a longstanding philosophical tradition: Russell's "philosophies of feeling," a tradition that includes Kierkegaard, Schopenhauer, Heidegger, among other influential thinkers. In Macedonio's major philosophical work, the unclassifiable *No toda es vigilia la de los ojos abiertos* (Not All Is Wakefulness in Open Eyes) (1928), he describes this as "metafísicos de la Afección-Subjetividad" (Metaphysicians of Affect-Subjectivity).[2] This tradition can be traced back to Spinoza's landmark treatise *Ethica ordine geometrico demonstrata* (1677) and continues to resonate in various ways in the work of late twentieth-century and present-day philosophers and scientists who in recent decades have been

---

[1] See Fernández, *NTV* (1990), 375 and 379. Also see Russell, *A History*, 792.
[2] See Russell, *A History*, 792. Also see Fernández, *NTV* (1990), 370.

rethinking the question of affect.³ What follows is an exploration of Macedonio's thought and literary practice regarding the key notion of passion, tracing its links with the "philosophies of feeling" tradition and its ramifications in contemporary affect theory.

The Style of Philosophy

A notable feature of Macedonio's metaphysics—and of his entire literary project—is what I would describe as his *post-philosophical* gesture: a paradoxical gesture through which philosophy is presented as a critique or "overcoming" of philosophy. This gesture is not unusual in modern philosophy—in fact, one could say it is one of its distinctive traits, given that thinkers as diverse and influential as Kierkegaard, Nietzsche, Heidegger, Carnap, Wittgenstein, and Derrida cultivated it in one way or another.⁴ Among these, it is perhaps with Kierkegaard that Macedonio has more in common, especially in the way they both deploy that gesture to develop idiosyncratic philosophical styles. Macedonio shares a number of remarkable inclinations with Kierkegaard that I can only outline here: the fragment as a favored form of writing and the fictionalization of philosophical discourse, the work with paratexts and philosophical heteronyms, or what Deleuze and Guattari call "conceptual personae," the centrality of affect and the importance given to humor and love in their metaphysical explorations, among other aspects.⁵

---

³ Philosophers such as Gilles Deleuze, Brian Massumi, Teresa Brennan, Franco Berardi, Antonio Negri, and Paolo Virno, as well as neuroscientist Antonio Damasio, sociologist Patricia Clough, political scientists Simon Thompson and Paul Hoggett, literary critics Eve Sedgwick and Lauren Berlant, and cultural geographer Nigel Thrift, to name but the most influential figures, all represent different approaches within the transdisciplinary constellation known as affect theory. On affect theory and the affective turn in the human and social sciences see *The Affective Turn* (2007), edited by P. Clough et al.

⁴ I examine this aspect of Macedonio's work in relation to modern philosophy in "(Con)fines de la filosofía" included in *De la sombrología* (2010).

⁵ Kierkegaard's *Philosophical Fragments and a Bit of Philosophy* (1844) or *From the Papers of One Still Living* (1838) are comparable in this sense to Macedonio's practice of writing (and occasionally publishing) scattered "papers": *PR* (1929), the "Arrangement of papers" of *NTV* (as he describes this work in the initial epigraph), or even the journal *Papeles de Buenos Aires* (1943–45) co-directed by his sons Jorge and Adolfo, containing many anonymous notes and articles written by him under pseudonyms like "Pensador Poco" ("Thinker Not Much") and "Impensador Mucho" ("Unthinker a Lot"). Macedonio's "Recienvenido," "Pensador Poco," "Deunamor, el No Existente Caballero" ("Newcomer," "Thinker Not Much," "Of-one-love, the Nonexistent Gentleman") are close relatives of Kierkegaard's "Anti-Climacus," "Johannes de Silentio," "Nicholas Notabene," or the "Seducer" of *Either/Or* (1843). On the notion of "conceptual personae," see Deleuze and Guattari, *What Is Philosophy?*, 197.

The post-philosophical writing of Macedonio and other philosophers of feeling like Kierkegaard could be described as different forms of *pathografeia*, to borrow the term coined by Argentine writer Héctor Libertella. In his essay book *Pathografeia* (1991), Libertella makes a distinction between literature and "pathography" in order to differentiate two modes of writing whose emblematic representatives in Argentina were, respectively, Jorge Luis Borges and Macedonio Fernández. As he puts it in another essay book, *Las sagradas escrituras* (The Sacred Scriptures) (1993), the difference between literature and pathography is between "an efficacy that in one case wants to be social, the search for public admiration, and in the other case familiar—the intimate search for affection."[6] One might point out that the Borges–Macedonio dichotomy—a favorite figure of Argentine literary criticism—has above all a propaedeutic function in Libertella's essays. Apart from the opposite stances these authors represent in Argentine letters, I would argue that both "efficacies" may very well coexist and are probably present to a greater or lesser extent in all writing and artistic practices.[7] Beyond this dichotomy (yet without completely abandoning it), I would like to propose a differently nuanced and somewhat broadened sense of the term in order to interrogate the relation between philosophy and pathography, which in turn may help us to better understand the productive interplay of literature and philosophy in these authors, as well as others.[8] "Pathography"—from the Ancient Greek *pathos* (feeling, emotion) and *graphein* (to write or inscribe)—is a useful notion, I would surmise, to designate a specific type of reflection on affect that adopts various forms in Macedonio, Kierkegaard, and other philosophers of feeling: a reflection that in Macedonio (and to some extent in Kierkegaard and Nietzsche) has the peculiarity of being a mode of thinking as much as— crucially—a *writing passion*.

Pathographeia as a way of thinking and writing affect is directly related to the question of *style*, essential for Macedonio, who says of his own metaphysics: "[s]ólo

---

[6] See Libertella, *Las sagradas*, 222. Here and throughout the essay all translations are mine unless otherwise indicated.
[7] Borges's influence on Argentine literature and elsewhere scarcely needs glossing; Macedonio's post-philosophical and an-aesthetic project, because of its opposite conception of style and its different articulation of philosophy and literature, forged in large measure in the intense dialogue with Borges in the 1920s and 1930s, initiated a specific "counter-Borgesian" tradition of undisciplined writing and "errant" poetics in Argentina and more generally in Latin America. See Montaldo, "Un argumento contraborgiano" and Prieto, *La escritura errante*.
[8] I have examined elsewhere how Borges and Macedonio competed in exploring that interplay in the Argentine cultural field of the 1920s and 1930s (Prieto, "Viajeras razones"). On the relation between philosophy and literature in Macedonio, see also Vecchio, *Egocidios* (2003); Monder, *Ficciones filosóficas* (2007); Cadús, *La obra de arte del pensar* (2007); and Attala, "Macedonio y el orden" (2009).

soy una manera de exponerla" (I am only a way of laying it out).[9] Macedonio's defense of "escribir mal y pobre" (ragged writing)—in notorious opposition to Borges's impeccable style—is the favored form of a "escribir pensando" (thinking through writing), a way of avoiding the discursive fixation of phenomenal mutability, its arrest within a logical-conceptual system.[10] In other words, it is a way to prevent the intensive modulations of experience, perception, and feeling from freezing into rigid patterns of knowledge and behavior. Macedonio's "urgent, blurred words" correspond thus to his metaphysical thesis of the lack of "profile" and "unity" of both consciousness and the world, which are not seen as opposed notions but as a continuity—what he calls "almismo ayoico" (selfless soulness)[11]:

> My theses, then:
> Neither Consciousness nor the World have *existence*.
> Neither Consciousness nor the World have *profile, unity*.
> Hence their immortality: We are individually immortal because *we don't exist*.
> […]
> (There it goes in blurred words, urgently scribbled before the world comes to an end—even though it doesn't exist.)[12]

Macedonio's "poor and bad" writing, with its frequent digressions and transdiscursive drifts where he leaps from metaphysics to fiction, poetry, humor, political theory, and so forth, is in that sense akin to what Brian Massumi, in his Deleuzian reflection on affect, calls "rig writing, unarresting," that is, a type of writing that is faithful to the dynamism of affect and at the same time capable of transmitting its "virtual" or "quasi-corporeal" dimension—its potential dimension as natural-cultural event.[13] Massumi's "incorporeal materialism" is thus not far from Macedonio's "Fenomenismo inubicado" (unlocated Phenomenism), insofar as they are both explorations of a writing/thinking that does not seek a finished form but rather, as Samuel Beckett would say, a way of "failing better": a fidelity to a doing, a process, a becoming—its goal not so much to "get things right" as to *get things moving*.[14]

---

[9] See Fernández, *NTV* (1990), 380.
[10] See Fernández, *Relato* (1987), 54.
[11] See Fernández, *NTV* (1990), 243.
[12] "Mis tesis, pues: / Ni la Conciencia ni el Mundo tienen *existencia*. / Ni la Conciencia ni el Mundo tienen *perfil, unidad*. / Por ello sus inmortalidades: Somos individualmente inmortales porque no *existimos*. / […] (Va urgente, borroneado, para antes que se acabe el mundo—aunque no existe—.)" (Fernández, *NTV* (1990), 373).
[13] See Massumi, *Parables for the Virtual* (2002), 67.
[14] See Massumi, *Parables for the Virtual*, 66; Fernández, *NTV* (1990), 59.

That philosophy should appeal to fiction or to poetry, as Macedonio and other philosophers like Nietzsche or Kierkegaard abundantly do, is perhaps not something anecdotal or exceptional but ultimately consistent with its most fundamental nature. Indeed, as counter-historical and purely speculative thought, philosophy is always a kind of "thought-fiction," a type of "virtual fable," to put in Massumi's terms: "Since philosophy only allows itself a virtual nonobject, it is an utterly *speculative* undertaking. Its moving against the grain of nature's cultural expression is a highly artificial movement of thought. It is an utterly contrived thought-fiction. Specifically, since its fiction concerns impossible objects, it is a *fable*."[15] In a way, what Heidegger disparagingly says of Descartes' *Metaphysical Meditations*—that they are at best a "bad novel"[16]— could be said of all philosophy, including his own. In fact, it has been said that philosophy is some kind of fiction—or, as Wittgenstein would have it, a "linguistic game"—which analytical philosopher Rudolf Carnap (1932) posited as the point of departure for his critique of metaphysics and Borges echoed in his famous statement: "metaphysics is a branch of fantastic literature."[17] This is at the origin of Borges's practice of a type of "philosophical fiction" in which philosophy is subordinated to literature.[18] Unlike Borges or Carnap, however, Macedonio never abandoned his core belief that metaphysics is a "science of happiness" and a way to achieve full understanding or "todo-conocibilidad" (all-knowingness)— what he also calls "Pure Vision."[19] Consequently, he explores a hybrid writing that draws on a symbiotic, non-hierarchical relation between philosophy and literature—and specifically, between metaphysics and the novel, as evidenced by *Museo de la Novela de la Eterna* (*The Museum of Eterna's Novel*), which he described as "primera novela buena" (the first good novel) precisely on account of its overtly metaphysical vocation. Thus, instead of giving us a metaphysics disguised as a (bad) novel (as Descartes did), or a belittled metaphysics as a branch of (fantastic) literature (as Borges did), he offers, purportedly for the first time in history (even though all claims of priority and the notion of "history" itself are profoundly ironic in Macedonio), a (good) novel that proclaims from

---

[15] Massumi, *Parables for the Virtual*, 241.
[16] Heidegger, *What Is a Thing?* (1967), 98.
[17] Borges, "Tlön, Uqbar, Orbis Tertius" (1989a), 436.
[18] See Monder, *Ficciones filosóficas* (2007).
[19] Macedonio, *NTV* (1990), 367. Macedonio defines metaphysics as a form of "crítico-mística," (mystical criticism) whose fundamental premise is: "Ciencia y Filosofía son Apercepción; Metafísica es Visión" (Science and Philosophy are Apperception; Metaphysics is Vision) (*NTV*, 63). In a 1930 fragment he states: "el 'ser' como Increación se da la plena Intelección: es la Claridad" ("Being" as Non-creation is available to full Intellection: it is Clarity) (*NTV* (1990), 354).

the outset its post-philosophical and anti-narrative intentions—an anti-novel as a proud branch of metaphysics, so to speak.

The lyrical opening and closing of Macedonio's *NTV* takes us back to the origins of philosophy.[20] Metaphysics began as a poem in Western culture in the writings of the pre-Socratic philosophers (Xenophanes, Parmenides, Empedocles) and is intimately linked with poetic speech in other traditions. The post-philosophical gesture of Macedonio's metaphysics, which profoundly disrupts the rhetoric and epistemic habitus of philosophy as modern discourse, lies not so much then in the appeal to poetry per se but in the fact that such an appeal is at the same time an appeal to fiction, to humor, to love, to utopian politics, and that is, in the decision to present his thought in a radically fragmentary and interruptive form that is deeply suspicious of any sedimentation of knowledge in a locus of epistemic privilege. Macedonio's digressive and simultaneous strategy of presenting a thinking *on the move* rather than a finished philosophical system, offering his thought as a puzzling mélange where all strands of his theoretical reflection and artistic practice continually coexist, is not therefore just a trait of style that would reflect a personal idiosyncrasy or a peculiar inclination of his character, but rather a textual disposition that is fundamentally in accord with his presentist ontology and with the ethical-political vocation of his epistemology, whereby knowledge must dissolve into action, metaphysics into passion. As he states in his posthumous "Crítica del dolor" (Critique of Pain): "I cannot stop being all that I am in all that I write; even if I wrote about Law or about Hygiene I cannot stop being jolly, mournful and metaphysical in each page."[21] This passage contains a sort of condensed manifesto on his writing strategy, a blueprint of the continuous intertwining of three major areas of his theoretical and artistic exploration: humor, fiction, and metaphysics or, to put it in his own terms, "Humorística Conceptual o Ilógica del Arte" (Conceptual Humor or the Art of Illogics), "Prosa del Personaje o Novela" (the Prose of Characters or the Art of the Novel, which has for him an essentially tragic dimension), and "Metafísica de la Afección" (the Metaphysics of Affect).[22]

---

[20] *NTV* opens with a puzzling epigraph presenting the text as an "arrangement of papers" made by a fictional character (1990, 229). This is followed by two pages of editorial considerations in verse ("Ediciones pro fantasía y expectación"), and various prefaces—one of them in the form of a fictional dialogue with Argentine writer Raúl Scalabrini Ortiz. Elsewhere he describes *NTV*, arguably his most important philosophical work, as "una lírica de doctrina" (a doctrinal lyric) (*MNE* (1993), 327).

[21] "No puedo dejar de ser todo lo que soy en todo lo que escribo; aunque escribiera sobre Derecho o Higiene no puedo dejar de ser risueño, doloroso y metafísico a cada página" (*T* (1997), 20).

[22] See Fernández, *T* (1997), 247–49 and *NTV* (1990), 375.

At a very basic level, the style of philosophy in Macedonio, in its digressive, interruptive, ever-beginning disposition, corresponds to the dream-like quality of all Being—what he calls "estilo de ensueño" (style of daydream)—and it is remarkable how the rhetorical notion of style seeps into even the most fundamental definition of his ontology.[23] In other words, the style of his writing (philosophical and otherwise) emulates the style of that continuous discontinuity which William James called "stream of consciousness,"[24] and was given literary form by a number of Macedonio's contemporaries, most notably by James Joyce in the long interior monologue that closes his landmark novel *Ulysses* (1922).

> Being, the world, all that exists, is the phenomenon, the internal-external state, merely the state, that is, what is felt and only what is presently felt. The style of daydream is the only possible way of Being, its only conceivable version. I call style of daydream all that presents itself as integral state of subjectivity, without pretensions of external counterparts, and so I call Being a selfless soulness.[25]

Conceptism and the Baroque Phrase

From another perspective, Macedonio's bizarre philosophical manner can be linked to the tradition of the Baroque, a mode of conceptual articulation that pervades Hispanic culture and Latin American modern literature in particular. Reflecting on the extravagance of the Baroque phrase cultivated by seventeenth-century writers, Morris Croll observes:

> Their purpose was to portray, not a thought but a mind thinking, or, in Pascal's words, *la peinture de la pensée*. They knew that an idea separated from the act of experiencing it is not the idea that was experienced. The ardor of its conception in the mind is a necessary part of its truth; and unless it can be conveyed to

---

[23] Just as he cultivates the "novel that does not begin"—its most accomplished example being *MNE*, a novel whose beginning is delayed by a seemingly endless sequence of prologues—there is also in Macedonio a metaphysics that *only* begins. Indeed, that is in his view all that metaphysics (and all being) can do: continually begin. In a posthumous fragment dated from 1931 he writes, "Metafísica—100° comienzo" (Metaphysics—100th Beginning) (*NTV* (1990), 354).

[24] James, *The Principles of Psychology* (1890), 239.

[25] "El Ser el mundo, todo cuanto es, es el fenómeno, el estado interno-externo, el estado meramente, es decir lo sentido, y únicamente lo sentido actualmente. El estilo de ensueño es la única forma posible del Ser, su única versión concebible. Llamo estilo de ensueño a todo lo que se presenta como estado íntegramente de la subjetividad, sin pretensiones de correlativos externos, y llamo por eso al Ser un almismo ayoico" (Fernández, *NTV* (1990), 243).

another mind in something of the form of its occurrence, either it has changed into some other idea or it has ceased to be an idea, to have any existence whatever except a verbal one.[26]

This Baroque decantation of the concept may be related to Deleuze and Guattari's observation of an absence of philosophical tradition in Spain and Italy (and in Portugal and Latin America, we might add). In these countries—so the argument goes—there were and will be philosophers (such as Macedonio Fernández) but there was no philosophy; instead, what emerged in these countries was *conceptism*.[27] In these nations, possibly because of the excessive social weight of Catholic counter-reformist ideology, what prevailed was a way of articulating the concept that excluded the creation of a plane of philosophical consistency—a "plane of immanence," according to Deleuze and Guattari.[28] In this sense, the contentious issue of whether or not Macedonio was a "true" philosopher, a discussion initiated by Macedonio himself with his frequent joking about his eccentric metaphysics and his adoption of self-deprecating authorial avatars ("Newcomer," "Thinker Not Much," etc.), should be approached differently.[29] The question is not whether Macedonio was a philosopher—in more than one sense he certainly was, precisely because of his penchant for presenting himself as something more or something less than one—but rather whether an Argentine (or, for that matter, Spanish or Latin American) philosophy ever existed.[30] As Horacio González succinctly puts it, "Macedonio Fernández is the philosopher of a country without philosophy."[31] It may very well be the case that, no matter how unique or profound a thinker he was, even if one were to claim that he had written, say, the South American equivalent of Kant's three critiques, the historical conditions of the cultural field in which he worked prevented

---

[26] Croll, *Attic and Baroque* (1969), 210.
[27] See Deleuze and Guattari, *What Is Philosophy?* (1994), 103.
[28] Deleuze and Guattari, *What Is Philosophy?* (1994), 35–60.
[29] In *NTV* he offers the following "philosophical" credentials: knowing how to whistle, being an expert on female cosmetics, having no rival as a guitarist among astronomers: "Diga que sé silbar y que soy entendido en procedimientos de belleza femenina, y que entre los astrónomos, aunque sean cordobeses, con toda la ventajita de sus ingentes aparatos, no me veo rival como guitarrista" (Tell them that I can whistle and that I am an expert on female beauty procedures, and have no rival as a guitarist among astronomers, even among those from the Argentine city of Cordoba, with all the advantages afforded by their gigantic instruments) (1990, 235).
[30] For Macedonio, being a philosopher—as with any kind of being—does not amount to a stable identity (professional, vocational, or otherwise) but at best to a passing state: whenever we have a feeling of perplexity of being, "we are, or have for a while the feeling of being, metaphysicians" ("somos, o estamos, metafísicos") (*NTV* (1990), 361), he says, accurately playing on the distinction the Spanish language makes between *ser* and *estar*, which, to put it in classical philosophical terms, is the distinction between essence (*essentia*) and existence (*ens, quidditas*).
[31] See González, *El filósofo cesante* (1995), 41. There is of course no scarcity of studies that trace the specific history of philosophy in Latin America. See Valdés, *Cien años de filosofía*, for example.

his philosophical figure from being recognized as such, given the absence of a "plane of consistency" on which that figure could stand—an absence he was keenly aware of, which may have been one of the reasons that triggered his frequent jesting and banter (upping the ante, so to speak) about his awkward, anachronistic, or "unoriginal" metaphysics.

Thus, in one of the prefaces to *NTV* he opposes the "ordered volumes of Kant or Schopenhauer" with what he describes as a mere exercise in "voice intonation"—not a philosophical "solution" but a "tone of solution" that foregoes and dismisses any claim to originality as hackneyed: "I just compose my voice; here I imitate all authors, abandoning my routine of innovation; [...] I do no present a solution—no reader believes in that any more—but a tone of solution [...] Who did create Originality, so that we all must have it now, by exhaustion of those authors?"[32] Needless to say, in his repudiation of originality Macedonio (very much like Borges, in texts like "Pierre Menard, author of *Don Quixote*") is quite original in the context of modern aesthetics, which values originality above all. But if the question of (un)originality has mainly a literary dimension in Borges and can be read as a critique of modernity's aesthetic ideology—and specifically of the cultural field of the historical avant-gardes of which he was a major actor in his youth—in Macedonio it also has a crucial philosophical dimension, insofar as it relates to his metaphysical critique of the subject and the Cartesian ego, whose existence he denies. His buffoonish posing as an "unoriginal" philosopher and literary author is thus a way of demonstrating his thesis of the insubstantiality of the ego—a comedic way of proving a philosophical argument by enacting it. Macedonio cannot be an original philosopher because, strictly speaking, there never was one. Any claim to originality—any attribution of an origin to a subject—cannot be but laughable, the notion of subject itself being a delusion fraught with inconsistencies in metaphysical terms, and especially in terms of his Metaphysics of Affect.

Actually, Macedonio *did* write the Argentine equivalent of Kant's three critiques, yet he did so in a post-philosophical way.[33] In that sense, I would

---

[32] "[C]ompongo la voz, nada más: aquí imito a todos los autores, dejo de lado mi rutina de innovar [...] no presento solución, ningún lector cree en tal cosa, sino tono de solución [...] ¿Quién comenzó la 'Originalidad' que ahora todos tenemos que tenerla, por exhaución de aquéllos? (*NTV* (1990), 231).

[33] Macedonio's bizarre and "unreadable" thinking-as-writing may also be viewed as typically philosophical, if we agree with Deleuze and Guattari when they claim that "becoming foreign" is the peculiar feature of philosophy: "Becoming stranger to oneself, to one's language and nation, is not this the peculiarity of the philosopher and philosophy, their 'style,' or what is called a philosophical gobbledygook?" (*What Is Philosophy?*, 110). As to the philosophical consistence of Macedonio's thought, notwithstanding its fragmentary form, see Attala, *Impensador mucho* (2007) and *Macedonio Fernández, "précurseur" de Borges* (2014); also see Aimino, *Apertura y clausura* (2010), and Muñoz, *Macedonio Fernández, filósofo* (2013).

suggest that Macedonio's post-philosophical manner, as well as his continued concern for the style of philosophy, beyond a technical question intrinsic to the articulation of philosophical discourse, is directly linked to a keen awareness of this cultural determination: to his awareness, that is, of being a "(non) philosopher on the edge" ("un no-filósofo en las orillas"), to paraphrase the title of Beatriz Sarlo's well-known essay on Borges, who shared with Macedonio a similar sense of cultural displacement, even if he negotiated it quite differently.[34] In order to appreciate the singularity of Macedonio's post-philosophical gesture, it is therefore necessary to understand it not only as a philosophical question but also as a matter of deterritorialization, as a unique intervention in the postcolonial dynamics of Latin American modernity.

In the end, what conspires the most against viewing Macedonio as a philosopher, apart from his own humorous recantations if not outright rejection of that label, is the fact that he was such a passionate polymath. Perhaps we would have no trouble with Macedonio as "philosopher" had he not been at the same time such a unique writer, such a memorable humorist, and such a rare poet.[35] Consider for a moment other versatile authors like Borges, Unamuno, Plato, or Nietzsche, who oscillated between different disciplines, between philosophy and literature, in particular. For all their wide-ranging talents, these authors ultimately concentrated their efforts on either literature or philosophy and succeeded in establishing themselves as prominent figures in one discipline or the other. Thus, there is no doubt about the status of Borges and Unamuno as accomplished literary authors, notwithstanding their remarkable philosophical preoccupations, just as Plato and Nietzsche are esteemed as philosophers above all, despite their evident talent as writers. In Macedonio's case, however, we would be hard put to tip the scale in one direction or the other. If we were to view him only as philosopher, something crucial would seem to be lacking, considering he was also the author of one the most radical avant-garde novels written in the twentieth century (*MNE*) not to mention a sublime humorist, perhaps the greatest the Spanish language has known since Cervantes. Conversely, something essential would be missing if we were to see him mainly as a literary author, as a

---

[34] See for instance Borges' essay "El escritor argentino y la tradición" (The Argentine Writer and Tradition) (1951). For a detailed analysis of the different strategies developed by Borges and Macedonio regarding this "being at the edge" (of philosophy, literature, Western culture), see Prieto, "La inquietante extrañeza de la autoría" (2007).

[35] In a letter to Ildefonso Pereda Valdés he claims, "Yo no soy filósofo ni hallo ningún sentido a la palabra Filosofía: soy metafísico, psicólogo o lógico, no simpatizo con el rótulo helado de Filosofía" (I am not a philosopher, nor do I find any meaning in the word Philosophy: I am a metaphysician, a psychologist or a logician, I do no sympathize with the frozen label of Philosophy" (Aimino, 16).

literato, a category he rejected as vehemently as that of philosopher, bearing in mind he is the author of one of the rarest works of modern metaphysics (*NTV*) and a prolific thinker who left behind a body of philosophical writing that is among the most illuminating and meaningful produced in the past century.

Perhaps a better comparison would be with polymaths such as Ramon Llull or Leonardo da Vinci, who mastered and cultivated various disciplines with equal passion. The difference is that while Leonardo and Llull excelled in disciplines that they significantly advanced or even contributed to creating, Macedonio was a great *undoer* of disciplines, someone who excelled as a non-philosopher as much as an anti-novelist and an ever "delayed" or "absent" humorist—a sort of Duchampian specialist in "minimums of being" ("mínimos del ser").[36] If Macedonio is always something less and something more than a philosopher and something less and something more than a writer, a humorist, and a poet, it is not least because he is an author in the strong sense of the term as defined by Foucault, i.e., because he is a begetter of discourses *at the threshold* (to borrow Ana María Camblong's felicitous expression) who inspired the many "undisciplined" explorations that followed in his footsteps. His originality lies in being an author without a discipline, a creator of a new vision that did not become an institutionalized practice such as Marxism or psychoanalysis, for example, in the case of Marx and Freud. A better comparison yet would be perhaps with someone like Walter Benjamin, another unorthodox thinker who, like Macedonio, engaged with various traditions of thought and contemporary artistic practices (most notably, with the historical avant-gardes) without committing to a school or movement, and yet managed to create a singular way of thinking-writing whose relevance in our present time would be difficult to overstate.

Macedonio's metaphysics is inseparable then from a writing passion, a passion *for* as much as *of* writing—a sort of metaphysical graphomania. His work is a good example of what Nigel Thrift calls a "non-representational" writing style:[37] a hybrid way of writing that projects arrhythmias and synchronicities with a world in constant change, a polymorphic writing that moves between art and science, between what is not yet a work and what has not yet abandoned life. In Macedonio's critique of the "Metaphysics of Representation"[38] the world is not

---

[36] Fernández, *NTV* (1990), 334. In his humorous authorial avatars and conceptual personae in *Papeles de Recienvenido* and *MNE*—as Newcomer or Continuator of Nothing, or as digressive or failed Novelist—he boasts of his expertise in minimalist, paradoxical, or impossible genres: the non-attending toast ("brindis inasistente"), the non-collaborating journal article ("un artículo que no colabora"), the speech without speaker ("brindis oral de faltante"), the novel that does not begin or does not continue, etc. See Fernández, *PR* (1989), 35, 57, 68.

[37] See Thrift, Non-Representational Theory: Space, Politics, Affect (2007).

[38] Fernández, *NTV* (1990), 370.

seen in Kant's manner as what lies beyond intellectual representation, but as pure immanence, as immediate stream of *affectedness*. Accordingly, he conceives a project of disorderly writing, a writing on the move that does not aspire so much to faithfully describe a "reality"—because reality, or Being, is "libre, sin ley" (free, without Law),[39] and thus inapprehensible—as to *re-create* it: to start it anew in its continuous potential for transformation, in its dynamic and affective becoming.

His "ragged" writing style and "trastornada sintaxis de mudanza" (unsettled moving syntax)[40] correspond to the world's fundamental lack of order, what he calls "the cosmic spectacle of reality's asymmetry and arrythmia,"[41] which demands a poetics of *descompás* and a radically "free and boundless" art, as he advocates in *MNE*: "Let art be free without limits, as well as everything related to it, its letters, its titles, the lives of its cultivators. [...] everything must ceaselessly play, overturn."[42] Hence his tongue-in-cheek invocation of "order" in the opening sentence of *NTV*: "If these papers are published, I will be the fortunate author of a book written in the most orderly manner; since the underlying idea in the word 'order' is: 'like Reality'—and this, Being, [is] free, without law."[43] As he puts it in the poem preceding this "prefatory note," "Being has no law, / everything is Possible. / A State, culture, art, science or book not made / to directly or indirectly serve Passion / have no justification."[44] These opening claims are intimately interrelated in that they connect Macedonio's ontology with his ethics and his aesthetics, bringing together his Metaphysics of Affect or "Crítico-Mística," his an-aesthetics or "Dudarte"—an "Art of Doubting" in disheveled writing ("escribir mal y pobre")[45]—and his Theory of Passion or "Altruistics," which seeks to convert the suffering of "being part" (to put it in Spinozian terms) into

---

[39] Fernández, *NTV* (1990), 231.
[40] Fernández, *Epistolario* (1991), 85.
[41] See his letter to Pedro Juan Vignale, published in 1933 in the journal *Poesía*: "Yo niego el compás en música, cuanto más en literatura. Ésta no debe tener ritmo. [...] El socorrido 'compás en el andar', simetría en las cosas, compás del latido del corazón, son hechos insignificantes en el universal espectáculo de descompás y asimetría de la realidad" (I reject the beat in music, even more so in literature. This must have no rhythm. [...] The convenient 'walking to the beat,' symmetry in things, rhythm of heartbeat, are insignificant facts compared to the cosmic spectacle of reality's asymmetry and arrhythmia) (*Epistolario* (1991), 131).
[42] "Libre sin límites sea el arte y todo lo que le sea anejo, sus letras, sus títulos, el vivir de sus cultores [...] todo debe incesantemente jugar, derogar" (*MNE* (1993), 47).
[43] "Si estos papeles se publican, seré el afortunado autor que presentará el libro más ordenado; pues en la palabra orden la idea es: 'como la Realidad', y ésta, el Ser, libre, sin ley" (*NTV* (1990), 231).
[44] "El Ser no tiene ley, / todo es Posible. / Un Estado, cultura, arte, ciencia o libro no hechos / para servir a la Pasión, directa o indirectamente, / no tienen explicación" (*NTV* (1990), 229–30).
[45] See Fernández, *Teorías* (1997), 235, and *Relato* (1987), 54.

the passion of *taking part*: moving, through love, towards another and towards the other, thus activating a principle of world transformation.

Macedonio with Spinoza: Affect and Ethics Under the Aspect of Eternity

Macedonio, like Spinoza, is a thinker committed to eradicating human "suffering." That "suffering" (*patimur*) to which the Sephardic-Dutch philosopher refers in Proposition II of Part IV of the *Ethics* ("Of Human Bondage, or the Power of the Affects,"), which claims, "We suffer, inasmuch as we are a part of Nature that cannot be conceived by itself and without the other parts."[46] This acknowledgment of a suffering common to all human beings and the philosophical will to remedy it lend a strong ethical orientation to Macedonio's metaphysical thinking, which he, like Spinoza, understands as a practice whose aim is to improve life, indeed as "Eudemonology," that is, as a "science of happiness" or, as Macedonio puts it, "tácticas para vivir" (tactics for living).[47]

In both Macedonio and Spinoza, then, the question of affect is central to the extent that it brings together ontology, ethics, and politics. But in Macedonio this entails something else: an aesthetic theory and practice, as well as a continued reflection on the form of philosophical expression. As I pointed out above, there is a fundamental agreement between Macedonio's three main areas of theoretical inquiry: metaphysics, ethics, and aesthetics, an agreement that only becomes clearer through the lens of Spinozian ethics. In the movement of passion from the suffering of "being part" to the joy of "taking part"—a joy directly linked to an awareness of a "power to act"—a new "distribution of the sensible" occurs.[48] Passion, as affecting action, releases a creative power that directly links Macedonio's metaphysics and ethics with an aesthetic, and political, dimension. This is why his thought adopts the form of a *theoretical practice* that simultaneously mobilizes ethical, metaphysical, aesthetic, and political strands, combining his various theories in different ways: the critique of pain, the theory

---

[46] See Spinoza, *Ethics*, 168. All quotes from Spinoza's *Ethics* refer to the original Latin edition (Amsterdam, 1677). I have also consulted the following editions: *Ética demostrada según el orden geométrico* (Madrid, Orbis, 1980) and *Ethics Demonstrated in Geometrical Order* (Early Modern Texts, 2004).

[47] Fernández, T (1997), 31.

[48] See Spinoza, *Ethics*, 137. On the notion "distribution of the sensible," see Rancière, *The Politics of Aesthetics*, 12.

of humor, the theory of the novel, the theory of the State, the theory of health, the theory of courage, and so forth.[49]

It should be said, however, that this theoretical practice achieves a clearer definition beginning in the 1920s. It is sharpened through his dialogue with the Buenos Aires artistic and literary avant-gardes and manifests itself especially in the texts published during those years or projected as concrete works at the time: in *NTV* (1928), in *Papeles de Recienvenido* (The Newcomer Papers) (1st ed. 1929; 2nd ed. 1944), and in the fictional diptych of the "last bad novel" and the "first good novel" (*Adriana Buenos Aires/MNE*), posthumously published in 1974 and 1967, respectively.[50] So we should distinguish at least two modes in Macedonio's writing: an external or public mode (his *modo éxtimo*), which adopts the form of a highly eclectic theoretical practice, combining to varying degrees fiction, humor, poetry, metaphysics, and aesthetic and political theory, and an intimate mode of writing "for oneself" or for a close circle of friends and family members (his *modo íntimo*).[51] This second mode is much less transdiscursive: philosophical writing (when the subject is philosophical, which is not always the case) usually adopts a more orthodox or monological form, and less attention is paid to questions of style. His early writings on issues of philosophy, psychology, and political theory, published in various journals between 1892 and 1907 and collected in volume I of his *Obras completas*, could be placed halfway between these two modes.[52] These texts partake of the external mode, in that they were conceived for publication, but tend to adopt a more "disciplined" form than the texts published (or conceived to be published) from the 1920s on, as they are still determined by a "horizon of scientificity" that will later be abandoned altogether.[53]

This second mode is, in a nutshell, what Libertella calls "pathography"[54] in order to distinguish Macedonio's ethics of writing from the worldly ambition of Borges's literary project. However, it is far from being the only mode in

[49] See Fernández, *T* (1997).
[50] On Macedonio's dialogue with the historical avant-gardes see Masiello, *Lenguaje e ideología*; Prieto, *Desencuadernados*; and Garth, *The Self*.
[51] In an article on Macedonio's unpublished writings, Adolfo de Obieta (his son and literary executor) describes this as "apuntes para algo así como 'uso privado' o 'uso interno' redactados no por una especie de placer solitario de anotar sino para confrontar la evolución de los propios puntos de vista" (notes for a sort of "private use" or "internal use" written not for some kind of solitary pleasure of jotting down but to confront the evolution of one's own views) (49–50).
[52] For a thorough study of this epoch of Macedonio's writing see Bueno, *Macedonio Fernández, un escritor de fin de siglo*. On Macedonio's writing modes see also Prieto, "(Con)fines de la filosofía," 32–5.
[53] See Aimino, *Apertura y clausura*, 71.
[54] See Libertella, *Pathografeia*, 222.

Macedonio's writing or even the most distinctive. Because his "literary" intent demands an endless practice of beginnings that indefinitely defer publication, we have to deal with texts in different states of unfinishedness (even in the case of those actually published during his lifetime), which further complicates a clear-cut distinction between these modes, often coexisting to different degrees in a single text. In fact, the best description of the "intimate" mode appears in *NTV*, a disparate "arrangement of papers" published in 1928, where otherwise the *modo éxtimo* prevails: "I speak and write here for myself, not because of any need of talking, or words, to think, but to stimulate myself and to keep signs of evocation, to think it again [...]. And I say this also for myself, to remind me later of the reason for jotting down and writing."[55] Conversely, a posthumous text like *El libro para sí mismo* (The Book for Oneself), whose title would seem to place it in the *modo íntimo* category, also presents notorious traits of the external or public mode.[56] Corresponding approximately to these two modes—*modo íntimo, modo éxtimo*—Macedonio's "escribir pensando" (thinking-as-writing) oscillates between two poles: a "thinking in plain view" ("pensar a la vista")[57]—a thinking "in progress" that we witness, so to speak, in the process of its coming into being—and the strategic deployment of a "calculated negligence."[58]

But let us return to Macedonio's dialogue with Spinoza's *Ethics*. Far from Spinoza's clockwork mechanism of axioms, propositions, demonstrations, and definitions,[59] in Macedonio's bizarre philosophical writing nothing is "proved": thought just happens, emerging amidst the turns and folds of wit with the brilliant flash of intuition or sudden revelation. Nothing here is demonstrated, everything is directly *shown*, because "to demonstrate is to show, to present and nothing else; all its efficacy and logical value humbly boils down to that."[60] In Macedonio there is no metaphysics in the sense of an organic and clearly structured system, but rather, as Borges put it in an early letter addressed to him

---

[55] "[...] hablo y escribo aquí para mí, no porque necesite hablar, palabras, para pensar, sino para estimularme y para guardar signos de evocación, para volver a pensarlo [...]. Y esto lo digo también para mí, para recordarme luego la razón de anotar y escribir" (*NTV* (1990), 315).
[56] See Fernández, *T* (1997), 104–11.
[57] Camblong, *Macedonio Fernández*, 182.
[58] Aimino, *Apertura y clausura*, 19.
[59] In *NTV* Macedonio regards Spinoza's modes of "expression and argumentation" with reservations, despite placing the Jewish philosopher among the few thinkers (together with Schopenhauer, Leibniz, Swedenborg, and Berkeley) who "fully penetrated Reality" (1990, 172).
[60] "Demostrar es mostrar, presentar y nada más; todo su valor lógico y eficacia es humildemente ése [...]" (*NTV* (1990), 73).

in 1923, "metafisiqueo" (metaphysicing).⁶¹ His philosophical arrhythmia occurs as an event of thinking-writing, although not in the sense of an spontaneity or an improvisation, at least in his most "public" and aesthetically self-conscious texts (what I called above his *modo éxtimo*), but rather in the sense of creating a style, carving out a gesture to do away with philosophical knowledge, to undo it and transform into something else—fiction, poetry, humor, politics—the key here being what Kierkegaard called the "passion of possibility," the invention of a way of thinking that is also a possibility of life.⁶²

And yet, and yet ... It is striking that the formidable edifice of Spinoza's *Ethics* should unravel in a "demonstration" through the evidence of what is seen and felt with the "eyes of the soul," that is, in a critical–mystical denouement, which is precisely where Macedonio's anarcho-metaphysics continually begins and ends. "We feel and experience that we are eternal," says Spinoza, and that unique consciousness of the now is felt by and through the body:

> Neither eternity can be defined by time, nor can it have any relation to it. But, nevertheless, we feel and experience that we are eternal. For the soul perceives no less the things conceived by understanding than those it has in memory. The eyes of the soul, through which it sees and observes things, are, in fact, the demonstrations themselves.⁶³

This is very close to Macedonio's critical–mystical dismissal of "demonstration" as a mere "decomposition" of vision: "There is no 'demonstration': there is decomposition of all the moments of formation of an image."⁶⁴ Indeed, Macedonio's post-philosophical project generally discredits logical argumentation and revolves around an almost single thesis (a repetitive mantra, rather than a postulate *sensu stricto*): the affirmation of the truth of pure immanence, the immediate "all-knowingness" of the sensible. Thus, he states, "A totally knowable Psychism is the truth of mystery. [...] Sensibility, Being, is one,

---

⁶¹ See C. García, *Correspondencia*, 5. As Macedonio states in one of his interventions as "Thinker Not Much" in the journal *Papeles de Buenos Aires*: "El amable y leve corto-saber debe cultivarse en su ágil variedad con la esperanza de generalizar un gusto por lo sustancial leve y un desalojo de sistema o de modalidad del saber pesante y no más seguro de los fanatismos del afirmar, opinar" (The light and gentle short-knowledge must be cultivated in its agile variety with the hope of generalizing a taste for substantial lightness and a system eviction that bans any form of the cumbersome and no more reliable knowledge of the fanaticisms of affirming, giving opinions) ("Del Pensador Poco" (2013), 64).
⁶² See Kierkegaard, *Either/Or. A Fragment of Life*, 41.
⁶³ Spinoza, *Ethics*, 252.
⁶⁴ "No hay 'demostración': hay descomposición de todos los momentos de formación de una imagen" (*Todo y nada* (1995), 204)

continuous, eternal, selfless and substantial and absolutely knowable: Being is because it is a Dream, that is, an immediate plenitude."[65]

The description of the "third kind of knowledge" in the last part of Spinoza's *Ethics*, what he also calls "intuitive science" (*scientia intuitiva*), the knowledge of the eternal Being in particular things, as set forth in Proposition XXIV, "The more we understand particular things (*res singulares*), the more we understand God"[66]—or as the Spanish mystic Teresa de Ávila would say, "seeing God amidst the pots and pans"—is indeed very similar to the pure intuition of Macedonio's *crítico-mística*. Both Spinoza's "geometrical" ethics and Macedonio's pulverized and ever-beginning metaphysics lead to a mystical outcome, a kind of secular *via mystica* of understanding, which in Macedonio, particularly in what he calls the Metaphysics of "Perfect Vision," is so immediate and ordinary that it is found in broad daylight walking down the street.[67] Likewise, the fundamental Proposition XXIII of Part V of the *Ethics*, in which Spinoza affirms the "eternal" of the soul— "The human soul cannot be destroyed absolutely with the body, but something eternal remains of it"[68]—is essentially in line with the critique of the categories of self, time, and space in Macedonio's "nominalism of affect," which reduces time, space, and subjective identity to an impersonal and continuous "present feeling" akin to a mystical state. "Futureless Feeling is the Mystical State,"[69] as he puts it in a posthumous fragment, or conversely, "All mystical experience is contained in this assertion: Being and Present are a single notion."[70] Indeed, Spinoza's intuition of the affective present of the body according to "a certain eternal necessity" is better understood in the light of Macedonio's "selfless soulness." For what would be such an intuition, what would be the idea of a present feeling "under the aspect of eternity," or better yet, what would be an

---

[65] "Un Psiquismo todo conocible es la verdad del misterio. [...] La Sensibilidad, el Ser, es única, continua, eterna, ayoica y substancial y de conocibilidad absoluta: el Ser es porque es un Sueño, es decir, una plenitud inmediata" (*NTV* (1990), 243–4).

[66] See Spinoza, *Ethics*, 253, 78.

[67] The goal of Macedonio's vernacular metaphysics is the suppression of the "feeling of infamiliarity" (*NTV*, 388), which he also calls "excessive apperception" ("super-apercepción o exceso de apercepción") (*NTV*, 65), an end so close to its beginning, so at hand that it is achieved daily by any common pedestrian. In a posthumous text entitled "Metaphysics" he claims, "The *mystical state*, which is the state of full truth [...] is possessed by all who never came to be metaphysicians and is regained by all metaphysicians who arrived to clarity" (*NTV* (1990), 405). For him, metaphysical clarity—"the mystical state"—is something so common and accessible to all that the driver of a car dodging another vehicle in traffic possesses it entirely and more perfectly than the philosopher in the solitude of his cabinet—since, after all, "la Vida no se funda en el Saber" (Life is not based on Knowledge) (*Todo y nada* (1995), 64).

[68] Spinoza, *Ethics*, 252.

[69] "Sentir sin Porvenir es Mística" (*Todo y nada* (1995), 211).

[70] "Toda la mística está en este aserto: Ser y Presente son una sola noción" (*NTV* (1990), 194).

intuition of the pure immanence of nature as infinite being, but *the only thing that exists* according to Macedonio, a "selfless soulness"?

Almismo ayoico is the name Macedonio gives to the sensible present *sub especie aeternitatis* (under the aspect of eternity). "Selfless soulness" is a notion that expresses the certainty that in the "todoconocibilidad y todoposibilidad" (all-knowingness and all-possibility) of the present "we feel and experience that we are eternal," and that this eternal feeling we are now is all there is for certain. This is what Spinoza expresses so memorably in Part V, Proposition XXIX of *Ethics*: "Nothing that the soul understands under the aspect of eternity is understood because it conceives the present and actual existence of the body, but because it conceives the essence of the body under the aspect of eternity."[71] Conversely, we can define Macedonio's "selfless soulness" in Spinozian terms, taking the explanation in Proposition XL for instance and substituting "Nature" or "Sensibility" for Spinoza's impersonal "God": "our soul, insofar as it understands, is an eternal way of thinking determined by another eternal way of thinking, and this in turn by another, and thus to infinity; so that all together constitute the eternal and infinite understanding of God."[72]

That is why Macedonio can assert, in a formula that condenses Spinoza's thesis of the continuity of the *res cogitans* and the *res extensa*, that "there is no border of Being to fall into not-being," because all that exists is the infinitude of present feeling: "For only what is felt *is*, and all that is felt in the world is what you are feeling now, and from that feeling one cannot fall, there is no border of Being to fall into not-being."[73] The soul, both Spinoza and Macedonio tell us, is not immortal in the sense of personal duration, as in that life beyond death in the Christian doctrine of reincarnation, but in the sense of the impersonality of the feeling-thinking body conceived "under the aspect of eternity," where the body—"the mystical-practical unit," as Macedonio would say[74]—partakes of the infinite and eternal being, as the way of being *now* of the infinite and eternal: the "thinking thing" or universal intelligence-with-sensibility (should we call it *todopsiquismo, res cogitans*, God, or Nature?) which is all that certainly exists.[75]

---

[71] Spinoza, *Ethics*, 254.
[72] Spinoza, *Ethics*, 262.
[73] "[S]ólo 'es' lo que se siente y sólo se siente en el mundo lo que tú sientes ahora, y de ese sentir no se puede caer, no hay ningún reborde del Ser por donde caer a la nada" (*NTV* (1990, 331).
[74] *NTV* (1990), 193.
[75] It is true that, along with the eternity of the "selfless soulness," Macedonio also conceives of a second type of immortality, one with a more "personal" inflection, envisioned by his Theory of Passion: the paradoxical immortality of "transposing the self" in love, "a contingent immortality of the encounter with an *other*" (Aimino, *Apertura y clausura*, 208).

Or, to say it with a metaphysical joke in Macedonio's manner, "para ser eternos no tenemos que esperar a morirnos" (to be eternal one must not wait until death). In this, Macedonio and Spinoza concur entirely[76]; if there is any eternity, it is not to be sought in the afterlife, in another world: we must find it—we are infinitely demanded to make it happen[77]—in this life, in the here and now.

---

[76] They also concur with what Alain Badiou calls "transitory ontology": "[…] everything is here, always here, and in the solidly perceived, firmly declared egalitarian banality, the recourse of thought is in what happens to us, here. Here is the place of the becoming of truth. Here we are infinite. Here is where nothing has been promised to us, except for the possibility of being faithful to what happens to us" (*Breve tratado* 20–22).

[77] On the "infinitely demanding" in an ethical as well as political sense, see Critchley, *Infinitely Demanding*.

7

Songs Without a Self: Macedonio's Anarchist Aesthetics

Luis Othoniel Rosa

Macedonio Fernández's anarchist aesthetics require a constant act of reappropriation on the part of his readers. As readers of Macedonio, many writers of the next generations understood this and appropriated him in different contexts, rewriting him, decontextualizing his anarchist aesthetics, and we might even say (re)inventing him as a precursor, following the logic of Jorge Luis Borges in his famous essay, "Kafka and his precursors."[1] And thus, in the works of Borges, Julio Cortázar, Ricardo Piglia, and Manuel Ramos Otero, to mention a few, the anarchist aesthetics of Macedonio are adapted to new contexts: they become a utopian nightmare of World War II ("Tlön, Uqbr, Orbis Tertuis"), an experimental self-critique of the counter-cultural intellectual life of the sixties (*Hopscotch*), a paranoid anti-capitalist machine at the beginning of the neoliberal age (*The Absent City*), and queer and feminist Puerto Rican ghosts of the past that take their revenge against their American colonizers in the present (*The Story of the Woman of the Sea* and *Blank Page and Staccato*).[2] His anarchist aesthetics can be downloaded, reprogrammed, and reused. It is almost as if Macedonio, the old anarchist teacher, was preparing us for the informational revolution of our present and future, in which the abundance of accessible information and knowledge challenges the modern conception of intellectual property and the capitalist dependence on scarcity.[3]

Even more acutely than his contemporary Walter Benjamin, who saw the advent of the information age as something that would destroy the art of

---

[1] See Borges, "Kafka y sus precursores," in *Otras Inquisiciones*.
[2] See Borges, "Tlön, Uqbr, Orbis Tertuis" (1940); Cortázar, *Rayuela* (*Hopscotch*) (1963); Piglia, *Ciudad ausente* (*The Absent City*) (1992); and Ramos Otero, *El cuento de la mujer del mar* (The Story of the Woman of the Sea) (1979) and *Página en blanco y staccato* (Blank Page and Staccato) (1988).
[3] One of the fundamental ideas in Paul Mason's *Postcapitalism* comes from Marx's "Fragment of machines" (see *The Grundrisse*, 690–712). Mason says that capitalism collapses under shared knowledge, and throughout the book he insists that capitalism's dependence on scarcity will make it obsolete as information becomes increasingly abundant and challenges the possibility of co-opting it by copyright. Macedonio Fernández is thinking about this much before the internet age.

storytelling,[4] Macedonio realized that technological advances in information, in fact, potentiated the capacity for collective storytelling. Plagiarism, appropriation, and falsification were and still are the key for this enterprise in his work. He justifies these acts by questioning intellectual property, which he saw as a form of theft from the community in terms not unlike those of contemporary cyber-anarchists who insist that all knowledge is what contemporary horizontalists and anarchists call a "commons," a communal possession that should be accessible to everyone.[5]

By freeing literature from the figure of the author as an owner, Macedonio envisioned a literary revolution. In this anarchist conception, his literary craft (literature) is a singular writing enterprise in which each generation corrects the drafts of their predecessors. Moreover, for Macedonio art and literature are the medium of liberation from our private selves, from Socrates's "idiot" or "private individual." Whereas Georg Lukacs and Benjamin understood the modern author, the novelist, as a confused figure who inhabits the present and is devoid of counsel (in contrast to the epic or the premodern storytellers who told the tales of a nation's distant past), Macedonio saw modern literature as a utopian projection towards the future. His literature, contrary to most modern writers, does not dwell on existential confusion. Quite the opposite, his writings are filled with counsel and with both quotidian and metaphysical wisdom. In this sense he more resembled Nietzsche, who, like Macedonio, did not seem to differentiate between everyday wisdom and the big metaphysical questions. Every reader of Macedonio has experienced this democratic plateau of knowledge in which a reflection about the nature of time is a followed by advice on the importance of drying off our feet before getting into bed.

The more than 50 prologues in his masterwork, the never-ending novel, *Museo de la novela de la Eterna* (*The Museum of Eterna's Novel*) (1967), as well as the titles of some of his other books, exemplify his insistence on projecting writing towards the future.[6] This differentiated Macedonio from his most famous disciple, Jorge Luis Borges, whose experimental writings were mostly projected towards the

---

[4] From our present it should be easy to prove that the Benjaminian binary of "information/storytelling" was wrong. Benjamin famously says that in Europe every person has become a writer, given the popularity of newspapers. Little did he know that the democratization that newspapers created would grow exponentially with social media. Benjamin laments this democratization, arguing that the revolution in the media kills the aura of the storyteller, by shortening distances in time and space, and that this revolution in information would privilege facts and demonstrable information rather than storytelling. I would argue the opposite. The democratization of writing that the internet revolution has produced actually goes against demonstrable information and privileges storytelling and speculative language, "fake news," conspiracy theories, echo chambers. What is the rise of fascism today if not the power of a compelling fiction over demonstrable facts and science?

[5] See Fernández, "El plagio y la literatura infinita" (1944), 5.

[6] *Una novela que comienza* (A Novel that Begins) or *Continuación de la nada* (The Continuation of Nothingness).

re-invention of the past.[7] By projecting literature towards the future, Macedonio's writings were decisively revolutionary, a term he did not shy away from. If we liberate literature from authorship, if we understand it as a collective enterprise projected towards the future, the existential confusion of the solitary individual dissipates. That is, the loneliness of the Cartesian cogito, the paranoid hero of modern novels in which the "I" in the present tense becomes the center of a chaotic world of illusions (for example, *Don Quijote*), becomes a piece of a much larger puzzle, a part of a potential "whole" that will find its cohesiveness in a future world.

It is precisely because of this that other novelists like Ricardo Piglia (or the author of these pages) understand that Macedonio's writings are a clinic on the future of literature. If the often repeated dictum of creative writing programs in the USA is "write what you know," Macedonio's would encourage the polar opposite, "write what we do not yet know," or "write the worlds that are yet to be," or even better, "write what ought to be in all its impossibility." In *MNE*, for example, Macedonio imagines the ultimate allegory of a direct democracy in which the entire city and all of its political institutions are connected to very specific affects of their citizens; when one citizen is in mourning for the death of his wife, this affect, through a telempathic literary device, disseminates throughout the entire city and reformulates it.

Benjamin or Lukacs could not find counsel in modern literature because they understood literature within the limits of the medium of the book and the historical context of the life of the author. For Macedonio, every modern book is just a draft to be rewritten in the future, a continuation in the river of time, with the certainty of a collective intelligence. Macedonio's writings truly part from the premise that the self is a modern fallacy. Because of this, many scholars read Macedonio through the lenses of post-structuralism, linking him to the deconstruction of subjectivity of later French philosophers like Levinas or Derrida. In *Comienzos para una estética anarquista: Borges con Macedonio*, I explain in depth how Macedonio's critique of subjectivity and the self is quite different from that of the post-structuralists: mainly because Macedonio's critique is anarchist in origin. Modern madness is an individualist disease; rampant depression, productivist anxiety, and political paranoia are all the consequence of that stubborn belief in the self. Similar to how Gilles Deleuze and Félix Guattari's *Anti-Oedipus* questions psychoanalysis and Freud's reduction of

---

[7] The most obvious example is "Tema del traidor y el héroe" (Theme of the Traitor and the Hero), but this is a constant of most of Borges's fictions, with the exception of two short stories that are inspired by Macedonio: "El Congreso" (The Congress) and "Utopía de un hombre que está cansado" (Utopia of a Tired Man).

trauma to the life of the bourgeois individual, Macedonio's writings part from the premise that trauma is always collective, that it should not be introjected by the self, and that it can only be cured collectively.

And yet, in Macedonio, there is something about art and literature, about aesthetics, that compels our subjectivity. He rejected the concept of expression when it came to aesthetics. Expression presupposes an original identity that codifies its unique inner self into an outer reality. Borges, who learned from Macedonio, would say that rather than expression he believes in allusion; that whenever we truly create a work of art we are not exteriorizing an inner emotion or idea, but rather, we are reconfiguring the emotions and ideas of others, we are alluding to others, to the fact that our interiority is made of others.

To explain this concept of a non-expressive art of allusion, Macedonio often refers to singing as a pedagogical example. Therefore, the only quotes by Macedonio that will be analyzed in this essay are two in which a recurring motive in his work emerges: the song without a self. The first quote belongs to one of the many prologues of his most important novel; the second to the ending of Macedonio's main philosophical book, *No toda es vigilia la de los ojos abiertos* (Not All Wakefulness Is with Open Eyes). By reading these two quotes, I will articulate the relevance of Macedonio's anti-capitalist and anarchist aesthetics to our historical present and to our future. What we learn from Macedonio in the present of the internet, the rebirth of white nationalism and fascism, the decadence of white supremacy, and the planetary destruction of capitalism is that by embracing our collective intelligence as a "commons" that belongs to anyone, we can take a peek at a post-capitalist world, at the wisdom that emerges in the time of the species and not the time of the individual.

Anarchist Aesthetics

Macedonio appropriated many of the main tenets of anarchism: the opposition to representative systems, either political or aesthetic, the postulation of property as theft, the idea that an individual is nothing but the "resultant" of mutual aid between collective forces, and the belief in direct action.[8] Nonetheless, his appropriation of these ideas often results in intellectually obscure, metaphysical, and experimental writings that would seem unrecognizable to most anarchists of his time.

---

[8] For the anarchist idea of the individual as a resultant of collective forces and for the concept of direct action see the entries on "direct action" and "resultant" in the now famous *Little Philosophical Lexicon of Anarchism from Proudhon to Deleuze* by the French anarchist philosopher Daniel Colson.

Similar to the way in which Deleuze and Guattari also appropriated anarchism decades later, Macedonio takes the anarchist tenets as a stem from which to make a critique of reality, present language as a vast organ of creative plagiarism, and theorize the production of subjectivities. In his work, Macedonio translates the three fundamental anarchist tenets from politics into aesthetics: (1) participation against representation, (2) collective possession against private property, and (3) selflessness and mutual aid against individualism and meritocracy. Without a doubt, the most polemical of the three with respect to Macedonio is the anarchist understanding of the individual as a resultant of collective forces due to the frequent Spencerian and liberal interpretations of Macedonio's politics that show a serious misreading of "poor individualism."[9]

We cannot ignore the coherence in Macedonio's oeuvre; if the main goal of his aesthetics and metaphysics is to dissolve the self in an extra-subjective Sensibility, to finally put an end to the superstition of the individual, how can we understand his political thought as a liberal defense of what he so patiently proved to be the fallacy of the self over five decades of writing? Moreover, the use of Spencer and the liberal tradition from Locke, Hume, Berkeley, the social Darwinists, and even William James was a very common tactic that anarchist philosophers used against their statist counterparts on the left, the same way they would use Proudhon and Marx against the liberals. This is exactly what Macedonio (and later Borges) would do. Philosophically speaking, the influence of liberal philosophers (and here I am including Berkeley and Hume) in the thought of Macedonio and Borges is a thorny one. If it is true that they devote an astonishing number of pages to these philosophers, there is always that brutal critique of the concept of the self and its continuity in time that they consistently bring up every time they quote these liberal thinkers.

For instance, if for Berkeley *esse est percipi* (to be is to be perceived), Macedonio and Borges take that principle a step further, replying to the liberal tradition that the same must apply to the perceiver; that is, the self, the individual, is also just a perception and not a *cogito*. Moreover, the misreading of Macedonio's texts ignores the many pages in which he (more than Borges) deconstructs another of liberalism's principle tenets: private property. From his very first published text, "La desherencia" (The Disinheritance) (1897) to his final pages before dying,[10] and spanning the entire volume that his son and editor Adolfo de Obieta titled

---

[9] See the essay by Borges of the same title, "Nuestro pobre individualismo."
[10] See Fernández, "El plagio y la literatura infinita" (1944).

"Teoría del estado" (Theory of State), Macedonio systematically lambastes the concept of private property with Proudhon's same anarchist arguments (namely, that property is theft). The reason for this constant return to the destruction of private property in Macedonio is very much tied to the coherence of his critique of the self. If there is no self, no individual, then there is no private property and no intellectual property. Everything we write has been written before. When we write we are effectively "suffocating the self" in the heat of intertextuality.

Creation Is Repetition

The first quote of Macedonio with the recurring motive of the song without a self says:

> When the world hadn't yet been created and there was only nothingness, God heard it said: it's all been written, it's all been said, it's all been done. "Maybe that's already been said, too," he perhaps replied out of the ancient, yawning Void. And he began.
>
> A Romanian woman once sang me a phrase of folk music and I have since found it tens of times in different works from different composers of the past four hundred years. Indubitably: things do not begin; or they don't begin when they are created. Or the world was created old.[11]

Something aesthetically powerful happens once we accept the premise that there is no originality, that the self is just an agglomerate of influences—"a subjectivity influenced by other subjectivities," that creation is always an act of repetition.[12] And yet, there is no anxiety of influence in this quote, no creative block, no stuttering; the Creator in this quote dismisses what is obvious ("that's already been said") and simply starts to create ("and he began"). Here Macedonio solves a fundamental problem with our conception of art as we begin the decadence of the capitalist world system, which Macedonio called "La Santa Cleptomanía" (Blessed Kleptomania).[13] Modern Western aesthetics have made us think

---

[11] Schwartz, *The Museum of Eterna's Novel*, 7. "Todo se ha escrito, todo se ha dicho, todo se ha hecho, oyó Dios que le decían y aún no había creado el mundo, todavía no había nada. También eso ya me lo han dicho, repuso quizá desde la vieja, hendida Nada. Y comenzó. / Una frase de música del pueblo me cantó una rumana y luego la he hallado diez veces en distintas obras y autores de los últimos cuatrocientos años. Es indudable que las cosas no comienzan; o no comienzan cuando se las inventa. O el mundo fue inventado antiguo" (*MNE* (2014), 13).

[12] "una subjetividad influida por otras subjetividades" (*NTV* (2015), 246).

[13] Fernández, "La Santa Cleptomanía," in *Relatos*, *OC*, vol. 7, 82–4.

that beauty is the result of the virtuosity of an original soul, that the greatest works of art are those that showcase their uniqueness. In other words, Modern Western art is tautological: it only seeks to validate itself and its creator. Reading Macedonio, we believe, helps us to solve a significant contradiction in our conception of art in the age of capitalism, a contradiction that, for the sake of brevity, we see most striking in the works of Walter Benjamin, one of the most influential cultural theorists of the last decades. On the one hand, how can a piece of art or craftsmanship or storytelling retain its uniqueness, its aura, in the age of mechanical reproduction, an age in which anyone can falsify, print, or create a machine that will rival the skill of any artisan? On the other hand, Benjamin would ask us, how can art and storytelling retain its pre-modern power of reproducibility by the collective in the age of the cult of the genius, the cult of the artist and the author? We seem to separate mechanical reproduction in capitalism from the reproducible nature of pre-modern craftsmanship and, at the same time, we seem to equate what Benjamin calls "aura" with the cult of the genius self.

Macedonio, however, is starting to theorize a post-capitalist art in which reproducibility by either technique (craftsmanship) or technology (machines) is the value to seek (not uniqueness), in which the aura is only achievable by removing the self from the work of art. This last point is fundamental for understanding Macedonio's project against death itself, because for him only art ("Belarte") can emancipate us from death. When we remove uniqueness and the self from the work of art and open it to its infinite repetitions, reproductions, allusions, plagiarisms, and falsifications, only then as creators can we access what he deems our Eternity, the state of the "almismo ayoico" (selfless soul), in which we finally see our life as a variation of so many others, extended both in time and in space. By understanding our lives as a simple derivative of an eternal struggle, we emancipate ourselves from death.

Macedonio's *Belarte* is a pure form of direct action through which we rid ourselves of the modern capitalist values of productivity, meritocracy, and individuality, as well as the fundamental philosophical constructs of Time, Self, and Death. The most impacting artistic forms for Macedonio are the ones that bind us to the collective, to a Sensibility that was there before we were born and will persist after we die. The song of the Romanian singer in the quote above illustrates this: Macedonio listens to her sing in the present, only to later find out that the song has been sung for over four hundred years. When the Romanian singer sings, her voice no longer belongs to the fragile temporality of her body, and it becomes part of something that endures in the time of the species. In Macedonio's literature, the characters and poetic voices are not as concerned with the individual's present, but rather with the forms that extend from centuries past towards an unknown future. It is not an epic temporality, but it consumes it and then extends towards the future. Macedonio's literature is written within an immanent utopian temporality. That is what we call "the time of the species," a temporality in which both dead and unborn generations enter into dialogue.

In our present (and our future), as we continue to create increasingly more intense ways to connect our brains to the digital hive mind, understanding creation as an act of repetition and reproducibility becomes more exciting than the solitary understanding of creation as the work of an individual genius.

The World as Affection and Representation

Macedonio says that our world is shaped by affections and representations, and that, whereas representations are more or less agreed-upon "imaginería" (illusions/imaginations), affections are much more complex and determinant in our collective consciousness. Rather than a plurality of selves, Macedonio sees our world as one collective Sensibility (with a capital S), which he sometimes calls an "almismo ayoico." Emotions and affects are not anchored in the self; the sadness or happiness that "I" might feel is more like a virus, a contagion, a flux that is transmitted from one apparent individuality to the other. The things we feel are not *ours*. The emotion or affect creates a particular person in a particular moment only to then disappear and create another, but all within the Sensibility. Yet, we have generated certain representations (the self, time, space, death, the State, the Nation, God, etc.), certain tricks of the imagination (illusions of separation) in order to conceive ourselves as entities separate from the Sensibility.

This is perhaps the central plot of *MNE*, in which a writer is writing a novel about the defeat of death, filled with a plurality of characters who are also writing similar novels and who finally collaborate to produce contagious stories, contagious sensibilities that will take over the city so we can see the city as one Sensibility, a federation of affects without subjects. The ending of the novel, "Al que quiera escribir esta novela" (To Whoever Wants to Write This Novel),[14] redoubles the stakes of the main plot when it invites the reader to take part in that

---

[14] *MNE* (2014), 265.

collective conquest of the city (and also of death). Many authors in subsequent generations will attempt to rewrite "this novel."

The second quote with the motive of the song without a self appears towards the end of the metaphysical treatise, *NTV*:

> This mother of divine sacrifice (there is only divine: the transferal of the self) for her children and who now lives long-sufferingly, sang at length a popular song about the sorrow of motherhood, and at no point did she consider that she was that sorrowful mother to whom the composing village had accorded rhythmical and rhyming words in that verse or song meant to cradle (*"to express" is too much to hope for*) her situation, but the verse that she decided to sing *was not chosen by her*: she found it because someone nearby was humming it, a boy. *Chance* filled her mouth with words that were as personal for her as they were ridiculous for a young boy. She was the only one to say what should be said, and the only one who didn't think the verse was speaking to her. She did not hear it; what's more: I think that as she sang it, she thought about her mother and thought about herself as a daughter; she felt herself to be the daughter who torments her mother; and she was a martyred mother.
>
> I find this to be enormous, heartening, this ghost of the Spirit in the vicissitudes of these Words that casually arrive to rest upon the lips of the person who needs them, *that do not emerge from within, that say everything about that soul, and that soul does not hear them in their exact meaning* (italics added).[15]

The mother who sacrifices herself for her children hears a child humming a song she remembered, which is about a mother who sacrifices for her children, and she begins to sing it, but when listening to the lyrics, instead of seeing herself in the song, the mother thinks of her own mother and her own childhood. She sees the very affect that identifies her (the suffering mother) projected onto others and expressed by others. In this song we find Macedonio's aesthetic principles; art is neither a mirror of the self nor of reality, but rather it is a conduit, a relation;

---

[15] "Esta madre de divino (divino sólo hay: la traslación del yo) sacrificio por sus hijos y que al presente vive muy sufriente, cantó largamente un tema popular de dolor de madre, y en ningún momento recapacitó que ella era la madre dolorosa a quien el pueblo versificador había dado palabras acompasadas y rimadas en ese verso o canto para mecer *('expresar' es mucho pretender)* su situación, pero el verso que dio en cantar *no fue elegido por ella*: lo tomó porque alguien lo tarareaba por ahí, un chico. *La casualidad* llenó su boca de las palabras que eran tan íntimas en ella, como grotescas en un chico. Sólo ella dijo lo que debía decir, y sólo ella no pensó que el verso le estaba hablando. Ella no lo oyó; aún más: creo que mientras lo cantaba pensó en su madre y pensó en sí misma como hija; se sintió niña que mortifica a su madre; y era una madre mártir. A mí me parece inmenso, alentante, *el fantasismo de Espíritu* que hay en la vicisitud de estas Palabras que vienen casualmente a posarse en los labios que las necesitaban, *que no salen de dentro, que dicen todo lo de esa alma y esa alma no las oye, en su acepción*" (*NTV* (2015), 342–3).

it neither represents nor expresses; it simply alludes to an infinite web of affects and sensibilities in which our self is just a variation and a repetition. A selfless song emerges when what identifies me comes from a series of others, as in the mother who, without knowing it, sings an old popular song that ends up being about her. Sensibility, like nothing else, tells our singular ways of being, and at the same time, shows that "I" am nothing but a superstition, a quote, connected to a hive mind, to a collective sensibility.

A Theory of Imitation

In one of the central passages of *A Thousand Plateaus: Capitalism and Schizophrenia*, Deleuze and Guattari appropriate or, perhaps, imitate an idea by the "microsociologist" Gabriel Tarde to explain their theory of micropolitics and segmentarity, of a world consisting of molar structures and molecular series. That chapter is crucial for understanding contemporary anarchist philosophy. Deleuze and Guattari argue that sociology is often too preoccupied with the big collective representations in a society to grasp the multiplicity of small desires and beliefs, the infinitesimal, the little imitations, apparitions, and inventions that lie in the subrepresentative matter of society. There are microimitations among individuals that become viral, that produce a flow, and thus end up explaining what the big collective representations cannot. Later in that chapter Deleuze and Guattari give a concrete example of the power of microimitations versus molar representations in the rise of fascism in Germany. We tend to think about the rise of the Third Reich as a molar change in the field of collective representations, yet we often ignore the power of the little imitations, of the internalized microfascists among all sorts of people within that historical context. Molecular flows of desires and beliefs better explain the rise of fascism than do the discourses of the Fuhrer, or more precisely, the molecular flows are what made the Fuhrer "desirable." What better way of understanding the current rise of white nationalism and fascism than by the viral microimitations facilitated by social media across the decadent white world that feels their supremacy threatened? That fear of losing power operates at the microsociological level, as affectation.

Macedonio Fernández was of the same generation as Gabriel Tarde and was also influenced by anarchism to the point that he shows in his fictions what we now call molecular flows or micropolitics. For example, Macedonio's humoristic campaign for president consisted of making very small changes in the daily routines of the people of Argentina: changing the weight of coins, alternating the height of steps, and other minor nonsense acts. In the less-humoristic *MNE* those molecular changes consist of very strong affects like the city falling in love or mourning a dead poet. Macedonio shows us that the little forms of imitation that make us who we are can take over the world as they become viral, like the small *zapallo* (pumpkin) in his story "El zapallo que se hizo cosmos" (The Pumpkin that Became the Cosmos), his own version of Deleuze and Guattari's "rhizome."

Perhaps that song about the suffering mother is also another example of one of those molecular flows imitated from one person to the other and yet so specific, so singular, so accessible. Ricardo Piglia, in his great novel *The Absent City*, fictionalizes Macedonio as a sort of proto-malware capable of infiltrating the information networks with a very particular affect (the loss of a loved one) in order to reconfigure capitalism from within. In many parts of the world today in which fascism is on the rise, especially in the USA, we complain about how rational scientific argumentation (the denial of climate change being one obvious example, but also "fake news," the post-truth era, and the conspiracy theories surrounding COVID-19) is incapable of countering our self-destructive paths. Fascism is immune to logic, to rationality as the West has imposed it. Fascism and the capitalist death drive (necrocapitalism) to dominate life and nature are disseminated through emotions. Trump's slogan, "Make America Great Again" is not a rational statement (the past it alludes to never existed), it is an emotional one and it "convinces" through the power of white nostalgia for a fictional past of white supremacy.

Macedonio understood very well how under liberal rule and holy capitalism, fascism would encounter a fertile ground in which to disseminate virally.[16] The rationalism behind the liberal and capitalist project operates on the world of representations and it is completely vulnerable to affectation. Fascism conjures an emotion in the molecular world of affectations in order to take over the molar representative structures of power. Macedonio, like many anarchist and anti-capitalists of the last century, codified direct action projects that, like fascism, would conjure emotions in the molecular world of affectations, but not in order to take over the representative structures of power; rather, to do the opposite, to dissolve them.

---

[16] See Fernández, "Brindis a Marinetti" (Toast to Marinetti), in *PRC* (2007), 60–3.

Walter Benjamin says in the enigmatic ending to his famous "The Work of Art in the Age of Mechanical Reproduction" (1935) that fascism is the aesthetization of politics, that aesthetics allowed fascism to maintain the structures of power and private property intact throughout the capitalist crises by aestheticizing war, as did the Futurists. He then offers a counter without explaining it; communism, he says, is the politization of aesthetics. Benjamin falls victim here to a binary imagination. Macedonio's anarchist aesthetics offers a step beyond Benjamin. Aesthetics, like the fascists cleverly proved, is a powerful weapon against the "cold calculation" of the capitalist modern project. Macedonio, rather than arguing for a politization of aesthetics, rather than attempting to domesticate and control the power of aesthetics, focuses on how all forms of art in their viral reproducibility are capable of destroying the private self, the "I," the very root of private property and power in our modern capitalist world. Isn't fascism, even in Benjamin's thought, exactly this? That is, isn't fascism a way of manipulating aesthetics as a medium and a weapon? Art and literature are a virus, a good pandemic, imitations and microimitations that become contagious and create subjectivities, a virus that cannot be controlled by the macrostructures of representations. Contrary to the Marxist or Messianic paradigm in which art is determined by historical materialism, for Macedonio there is something fundamentally unruly about art and literature. It is there that he finds a true emancipation from historical determinism. The clue, for Macedonio, is allowing art to operate outside of our modern attempts to control it, to let art liberate us from our transcendental modern representations (the Individual, Death, Time, etc.) in order to open our worlds to the immanent anarchist world of the "selfless soul." Therefore, the true act of courage in modernity is not to dominate aesthetics, but rather, to let aesthetics emancipate us from the self and to cease to exist as separate entities. The true emancipation from the forces of capitalism and fascism appears through acts of direct action that suffocate the self so we can finally breath as a collective in the time of the species. Aesthetics, for Macedonio, is (or should be) these acts of collective direct action.

The Self as a Fractal

The reason why Deleuze and Guattari's work seems so close to Macedonio's conception of the world as affection and representation is not because Macedonio was a prophetic genius who anticipated philosophical systems decades prior.

Their fractal division of the world in which the microscopic is able to take over macrostructures, in which representation is an authoritarian simplification of society, in which the self is as fragmented as the society it inhabits, have their common origin in anarchism. From the very first anarchist text by Proudhon in the 1840s, *What is Property?*, the individual is not understood as an entity but as a resultant of collective forces. The individual is, in fact, divisible into millions of small faculties often in conflict. The individual is a crossroads of many flows at each particular point in time that create a subjectivity, a singularity only to be rapidly reconfigured into something else depending on the flows that transverse it.

It is in this sense that Macedonio's desire for a "minimum of state and a maximum of individual," a phrase that is repeated many times in his oeuvre, should be understood. He is not making a liberal individualist argument. He is referring to the fractal nature of the self as the resultant of collective forces, which the State and our forms of representation interrupt. The anarchist philosopher and biologist Pyotr Kropotkin—who famously argued against the social Darwinists that collaboration is a more determinant factor of evolution than the survival of the fittest, that the most successful living forms on Earth are the ones that collaborate in more complex ways—contended that our self is nothing but the resultant of the different modes of help and aid we have received from others.[17] Quite different from Thomas Hobbes's autonomous individual who has agency only in order to eventually surrender it to the Leviathan, in anarchism the self is fundamentally vulnerable, porous, and completely dependent upon others. The genealogy of biopolitics and micropolitics is fundamentally anarchist.

The following quote from Kropotkin may shed new light on Macedonio's *MNE*, in which the author's self is fragmented into many different characters who are also authors writing about their own characters (who are also authors), in a fractal pattern:

> And when a physiologist speaks now of the life of a plant or of an animal, he sees rather an agglomeration, a colony of millions of separate individuals than a personality, one and indivisible. He speaks of a federation of digestive, sensual, nervous organs, all very intimately connected with one another, each feeling the consequence of the well-being or indisposition of each, but each living its own life.

---

[17] See Kropotkin, *Mutual Aid: A Factor of Evolution* (1905).

Each organ, each part of an organ in its turn is composed of independent cellules which associate to struggle against conditions unfavorable to their existence. The individual is quite a world of federations, a whole universe in himself.

[...] More than that: in each microscopic cell he discovers today a world of autonomous organisms, each of which lives its own life, looks for well-being for itself and attains it by grouping and associating itself with others. In short, each individual is a cosmos of organs, each organ is a cosmos of cells, each cell is a cosmos of infinitely small ones; and in this complex world, the well-being of the whole depends entirely on the sum of well-being enjoyed by each of the least microscopic particles of organized matter. A whole revolution is thus produced in the philosophy of life.

[...] Taken as a whole, man is nothing but a resultant, always changeable, of all his diverse faculties, of all his autonomous tendencies, of brain cells and nerve centers.[18]

Kropotkin breaks down in continually fractal ways all the infinitesimal particles that conform the individual. Every person is a multitude of fluxes, a federation of organs, that communicate beyond the self. That is why in anarchism the revolution must be consistent on all scales, from the macrostructures of the State and the Market, to the immediate, mundane, and bodily affects of daily life. The term "fractal" did not exist when Kropotkin, Macedonio, or Deleuze and Guattari were writing. It is a term coined for the first time by the Polish mathematician Benoit Mandelbrot in the 1980s, and it refers to a geometrical form found in nature in a recursive set; a snow flake, a cauliflower, a galaxy, and the coast of England are all fractals because they have recursive forms that repeat at many scales; with a microscope or a telescope, one can zoom in or out, and the pattern keeps repeating in messy variations.

The formula for fractals (the Mandelbrot set) is quite simple and consists of basic arithmetic (Mandelbrot considered algebra to be overrated), and yet, we could not figure it out before because the sequence is so long that a computer is needed to help us see it. Similarly, we believe that our digital revolution, rather than a way of escaping a so-called "natural reality," allows us to see ourselves in more complex ways, just as Kropotkin and Macedonio were trying to show. The self is a multitude, a recursive set that repeats patterns at any scale. What people used to called meta-fiction or meta-literature to describe the works of Macedonio and Borges is a fractal geometry that through the lenses of literature and art can zoom in or out on the self in order to finally destroy the arbitrary border we have created between our selves and the collective.

[18] Kropotkin, "Anarchism: Its Philosophy and Ideal," 118–19.

Collaboration and Mutual Aid as Experimental Aesthetics

In one of his most explicit texts, the previously mentioned "El plagio y la literatura infinita," Macedonio says that just as anarchism seeks to liberate us from the tyranny of private property, a similar revolution ought to happen in literature to free us from intellectual property. Yet, as tends to happen with revolutions, its simple postulation makes us wonder if that revolution has not already happened a million times; isn't literature already that which Macedonio postulates as a revolution? That is, what are *Don Quijote*, *Frankenstein*, or *El Aleph*, for that matter, if not great works of intergenerational mutual aid? When thinking about literature in these terms, completely detached from the figure of the singular author as proprietor, literature seems to be something more than an artistic medium. Literature seems to be a unique technological device that allows us to expand the modes of collaboration keeping us alive in the present to include beings who are long dead and others who have not yet been born. Defined like this, the Internet could be understood as the daughter of literature that speeds up the collaborative process of language by breaking up distances in real time, sustaining previously impossible conversations between millions of people. Literature is a mode of collaboration among the species set in a different temporality than that of our functional language. Music, of course, is also another mode of collaboration with the dead and the not yet born. It responds, however, to a faster temporality than literature, or to an even slower one. When measuring the speed of collaborative flows, the fast and the slow become confused depending on the intensities with which the microimitations or "plagiarisms" are taking place. Why does Macedonio often present a song as being the medium of our selfless liberation?

The Aesthetics of Direct Action

As stated earlier, in order to comprehend Macedonio's work we must decontextualize his writings, appropriate him, and change him. His work can help us in our cultural present where the battle between Capital and Life is being fought not just in macrostructures but in our daily lives, a cultural present in which we are looking for an aesthetic and theoretical opposition to Capital that is not sedimented in the State but in our bodies. It is our responsibility to reinvent the work of Macedonio and even to brutally forget his name while making use of his philosophy (namely, the postulation of a Sensibility without subjects and the idea that art can be a form of the molecular's direct action over the molar) to make it better so it can continue to speak to us. For instance, it is worth considering how to combine Macedonio with the current radical feminist groups that have become the symbol of a new resistance against neoliberalism; or with the current decolonial, indigenous, and black resistances around the world that question the whiteness of "human rights" and the often forgotten relation between capital and slavery; or with current indigenous groups today who are postulating the effectiveness and efficiency of localized revolutions in the small communities that seem so close to Macedonio's utopias. The reason for this is that Macedonio's metaphysics is a fundamentally anti-modern philosophy. Thus, he can be a powerful ally when thinking about an effective form of art or a form of writing to counter the pervasive way in which Capitalism presently organizes thought and even academia. Collaboration, plagiarism, rejection of individuality and private property, and a revalorization of the Sensible: these are the tools in Macedonio's toolbox that can help us continue singing a selfless song today.

8

The Thought of Macedonio Fernández: A Dictionary*

Daniel Attala

In 1952, standing before the tomb of Macedonio Fernández, Jorge Luis Borges confessed that in his youth he had imitated Fernández "to the point of transcription, to the point of devout and passionate plagiarism."[1] This sentence assumes that what he imitated had been the maestro's texts, which the adult Borges, the sentence's author, in fact no longer admired. In any case, he did not admire them as much as he did Fernández's personality, a personality he never stopped admiring: not the writer, not the poet, not the novelist, but rather the thinker, the philosopher. When the young writers of Argentina rediscovered Fernández's work in the 1970s, they were largely driven by their need for a liberator who could counterbalance the suffocating paramountcy that Borges held in Argentinian culture. The apotheosized Borges's predilection for Macedonio *the thinker* was understood to be a veiled criticism of Macedonio the writer. Whether it was intended as a criticism or not, what is certain is that, contrary to Borges's judgment, the younger generation almost exclusively preferred Macedonio *the writer*: the anarchic humorist, the marginal novelist, the passionate poet. His thought, when not scorned, was considered minor and undeserving of study or, at the very least, just another way of creating literature (among them were disciples of Borges himself, who liked to repeat that metaphysics was a branch of fantastic literature). Several years ago, a new movement was launched that sought to countermand this reception by giving greater attention to Macedonio's philosophical writings and reevaluating his entire body of work with the help of this newly garnered perspective.[2] The following essay is part of this movement.

---

* Translated from the Spanish by Sean Manning.
[1] "Yo por aquellos años lo imité, hasta la transcripción, hasta el apasionado y devoto plagio" (Borges, "Macedonio Fernández (1874–1952)," 306).
[2] In addition to my previous work on Macedonio, also included in this movement are Marisa Muñoz, *Macedonio Fernández, filósofo* (2013); Gabriel Sada, *Macedonio Fernández. Confrontaciones filosóficas* (2011); Dante Aimino, *Apertura y clausura* (2010); Samuel Monder, *Ficciones filosóficas* (2007).

It is true that Macedonio's philosophical texts rarely prescind from literary devices. Within a series of definitions, inferences, and conclusions, he intersperses characters, allegories, metaphors, irony, lyrical expressions, narrations, and even fiction and fabulations. And vice versa, almost all his literary texts, including poetry, tend to contain entire arguments for or against certain theories or doctrines. *No toda es vigilia la de los ojos abiertos* (Not All Wakefulness Is with Open Eyes), published in 1928, offers philosophy interwoven with numerous literary devices. In *Museo de la novela de la Eterna* (*The Museum of Eterna's Novel*), a posthumous novel published in 1967 by his executor, there is not a single page without some trace of a rational argument. In the first of these two books—defined in its prologue as a philosophy of *afección* (affection) in the face of the current "grueling intellectualism"[3]—philosophical aspects take precedence; however, literary criticism, driven, at its best, by a profusion of literary considerations (and at its worst, by intellectual laziness plain and simple), ignored it altogether, when not actively excluding it from the field of philosophy. In contrast, several clearly theoretical passages in *MNE* have succeeded in having their novelistic fiction be read by some as an exponent of a theory or philosophy of the novel rather than as a novel itself.

Based on the critical reception of Fernández's work, it would seem as if the blending of literature and philosophy had not in fact existed since the beginning of the history of Western thought or as if throughout this history, occurrences of such blending had only been exceptions. As if Plato, who according to Nietzsche was the originator of the novel, had not systematically utilized myth at critical points in his thought.[4] As if Parmenides, Empedocles, or Lucretius had not expressed their ideas in verse and shaped their philosophical discourse into poetic fiction or, like Heraclitus, into a series of metaphors. As if Descartes in his *Meditations on First Philosophy* had not inscribed his reasoning inside a highly literary tale. As if the majority of German Romantics (from Friedrich Schlegel or Novalis to Hölderlin or Schiller) had not blended theory and literature, similar to Voltaire, Diderot, or Rousseau, for the creation of a deliberate method first to consider and then to study conceptual problems, if not to resolve them altogether. And despite his harsh criticism of these Romantic thinkers, we see the same in Hegel's *The Phenomenology of the Spirit*, as well as in various works by Kierkegaard and Nietzsche, and in others by Camus or Sartre after them. In each of these examples, critics have consistently studied and justified the blending of

---

[3] "intelectualismo extenuante" (*NTV* (1990), 232).
[4] See Nietzsche, *The Birth of Tragedy*, 48–51.

genres. Rarely has this been used as an excuse to spare themselves the trouble of understanding these texts as components of a philosophy and not just literature.

Macedonio's works, on the other hand, have not enjoyed the same consideration. Whether as a form of praise or of criticism, his hybridity or generic blending was used to explain against their argumentative value and in favor of their literary nature. There have undoubtedly been other factors that have contributed to this: the fragmentary aspect of the texts, their dispersed publication, or the fact that many of them have still to this day not been properly edited, and in some cases not edited at all—in short, the peculiar context of their production and reception, always unaffiliated with academic institutions.[5] As I have already mentioned, for the last several years some critics have been attempting to dispel the error of those who fail to find anything but literature (if not dreadful confusion and total chaos) in Fernández's philosophical work—again, whether they consider this to be a virtue or a defect. From my point of view, one of the primary obstacles impeding such a rectification is a deficient understanding of his terminology and of the fact that, even when this terminology is seemingly inadequate, the author's effort to achieve the greatest degree of precision possible is clearly visible, even against the very nature of things. What I offer here is a selection of this terminology as well as an explanation of the essential lines of thought that are formulated with it.

The alphabetical order of this brief dictionary, according to Fernández's terms in Spanish, should not conceal the logic governing the set of concepts. There are hierarchies among them concerning generalities, logical priorities, values, etc. With regard to the concepts themselves, the majority originate in a particular tradition. In most cases that tradition is nineteenth-century naturalistic psychology, namely that of Herbert Spencer, "that incredibly beautiful mental and moral character," whose only shortcoming, as with "all Englishmen," was the lack of a "metaphysical" calling.[6] Several other authors from the same school, English as well as German and French, also appear in Fernández's works. He

---

[5] These are some of the most important titles of Fernández's philosophical works, followed by their year of publication: included in *PA* (1981), "Psicología atomística (Quasi-Fantasía)" (1896); in *NTV* (1990),"Ensayo de una nueva teoría de la psiquis. Metafísica preliminar. Psicología psicológica" (1907), "La metafísica, crítica del conocimiento. La mística, crítica del ser" (1924), "Descripciometafísica: el Todo pensado como no-ser, como un 'todo' de 'no-ser'" (1942), "Verdades pedantes frías y verdades calientes" (1944), "Una imposibilidad de creer" (1949); *NTV* (1928); *NTV y otros escritos metafísicos* (1967); eight unedited texts included in *Impensador mucho* (collaborative edition directed by Attala, 2007).

[6] "aquella bellísima naturaleza mental y moral (a la que faltó sólo, como faltó siempre a todo inglés, la solicitación metafísica" (Fernández, "Diario de vida e ideas," in *T* (1990), 95).

read them in English, Spanish, and, most of all, in French.[7] The underlying idea or thesis—his philosophy of affection—comes from Schopenhauer, whose metaphysical perspective allowed him to correct the fundamental limitation of naturalistic psychology.

Although the conceptual framework is based on Spencer's classic works, the terminology itself takes its origin from the French branch of that variety of psychology. It is likely that Fernández read Spencer's *The Principles of Psychology* in Epinas and Ribot's French translation, published in 1892: his expression *estado de conciencia* (state of consciousness) (or *estado psíquico* (psychic state) or *de la psiquis* (of the psyche)) voices the French expression *état de conscience*, which is generally equated with the English word "feeling." In accordance with English empiricism, Spencer categorized the mind's immediate components into "feelings" and "relations between feelings."[8] The relations are real, which means that the feelings are real as well. The difference between these two components lies in the divisibility (in terms of time and space) of the feelings themselves and in the unanalyzable unity of the relations. Feelings are distinguished from one another according to their origin: if they are centrally initiated, they are referred to as "emotions"; if they are peripherally initiated, then they are called "sensations." The former are more complex than the latter.[9] Sensations are subsequently divided into two classes: those which are caused by outer agents (with respect to the body) and those which are caused by inner agents. Feelings, from the point of view of the agents involved in their production, are classified into real (or primary) and ideal (or secondary). The distinction is determined according to their intensity, where the degree is higher in the first and lower in the second. Primary feelings suggest the presence of an agent, unlike secondary ones. Lastly, buried at the end of the more than one hundred pages of this classification, Spencer initiates one more, hardly a paragraph in length and only for the sake of completeness: the division of all feelings into pleasures and pains.[10] In the wake of Théodule Ribot's psychophysiology and inspired, like Ribot, by the philosophy of Schopenhauer, Fernández attempts to invert the prioritization

---

[7] In addition to Herbert Spencer and a countless number of disseminators, Fernández read Stuart Mill, Théodule Ribot, Wilhelm Wundt, Alexander Bain, James Sully, Johann Herbart, Gustav Fechner, Jean-Marie Guyau, Ernst Mach, Henri Bergson, and William James. In turn, the terminology used by these authors, as is the case with the concept of emotion, has its roots in earlier philosophies from René Descartes, whose work *Passions of the Soul* is a distant precursor of nineteenth-century psychophysiology.

[8] *The Principles of Psychology*, § 65, 163 sq.

[9] Spencer, *The Principles of Psychology*, § 66, 165 sq.

[10] Spencer, *The Principles of Psychology*, §§ 122–9, 272–88.

of representation over affection that occurs in Spencer's psychology and in the majority of psychology prior to Schopenhauer. Hence the importance he places in his work on the difference between both types of psychic phenomena and the search for its dissolution by reducing the entirety of the mind's contents to affection. Before opening the dictionary, let us consider the word that lies at the heart of this endeavor.

0. *Terminología* (Terminology). In a project for a work that Fernández intended to title *El libro para sí mismo* (Book for Its Own Sake)—likely inspired by an essay from *Society and Solitude* by Emerson, whom he greatly admired—he dedicates the following paragraph to philosophical terminology:

> The great works, Kant and Schopenhauer, with their one or two thousand pages, are infinite repetitions of two or three affirmations or demonstrations that could be contained in five pages; this is essential so that the reader can have a good command of the vocabulary and their acceptations as intended by the author because words lack constancy of meaning; the word "sensitivity" has a thousand acceptations, related but always different depending on whether it is Plato, Aristotle, Leibniz, Hume, Kant, Schopenhauer, Herbart, Lotze, Mill, Spencer, Berkeley, etc., etc., who is using it, and the entire task of the book is consumed by the process of establishing agreed-upon meanings of certain words, between author and reader. For this reason, a great work is an incessant repetition. Once the lexical acceptations have been set, an entire Metaphysics, a thinker's entire theory, can be communicated in five pages. In the same fashion, every work by Chopin, Beethoven or Wagner is the repeated expression of eight or ten artistic ideas at most.[11]

---

[11] "Los grandes libros, Kant o Schopenhauer, obras de mil o dos mil páginas, son repeticiones infinitas de dos o tres afirmaciones y demostraciones, que cabrían en cinco páginas; ello es indispensable para que el lector domine el vocabulario y acepciones del autor porque las palabras carecen de toda fijeza de significación; la palabra sensibilidad tiene mil acepciones aproximadas pero diferentes siempre según que la emplee Platón, Aristóteles, Leibniz, Hume, Kant, Schopenhauer, Herbart, Lotze, Mill, Spencer, Berkeley, etc., etc., y toda la tarea de un libro es absorbida casi por el trabajo de tasar convencionalmente el sentido de ciertas palabras, entre autor y lector. Por eso un gran libro es una incesante repetición. Después de fijadas las acepciones verbales, toda una Metafísica, toda la teoría de un pensador puede transmitirse en cinco páginas. Del mismo modo todas las obras de Chopin, Beethoven o Wagner son la enunciación repetida de ocho o diez ideas artísticas a lo sumo" (*Teorías* (1990), 107). Also see Emerson, "Society and Solitude" (1870), in *Emerson's Complete Works*. The project titled "El libro para sí mismo" overlaps and becomes confused with another whose title is "Diario de vida e ideas" (Diary of Life and Ideas), written around 1918. In these texts, Fernández appears to be answering Emerson's call for "some charitable soul" who might serve as a guide to future readers by indicating which books, among so many useless ones that they have read, "have been bridges or ships to carry him safely over dark morasses and barren oceans, into the heart of sacred cities, into palace and temples" (in *T* (1990), 184). In his essay, Emerson offers the same advice that Borges credited to his father: "Never read any but what you like" (p. 188). Jorge Guillermo Borges, Jorge Luis's father, was an avid reader of Emerson, like his friend Macedonio Fernández.

Whoever reads this passage has every right to ask why, if he was aware of the problem, the author did not write his own treatise of "one or two thousand pages" so that his terminological acceptations and the handful of ideas to which "a thinker's entire theory" can be reduced were also made clear. The answer lies in the ironic character of this passage. Someone familiar with the works of any one of the philosophers mentioned will agree that, by virtue of repeating and varying the perspectives on a single problem, they all attempt to transform ordinary language, polysemic and vague by nature, into a technical language as unambiguous and precise as possible, capable of transmitting those four or five essential ideas on which their philosophy is based. Every now and then, those four or five ideas can even be reduced to one single thought. According to Fernández, Schopenhauer himself was aware of this.[12] The irony here is that if only a few definitions succeeded in clarifying the meanings of primitive words, then it would not be necessary to write a great treatise and every philosophy could be contained in four or five pages. This explains (if we put aside some of Fernández's character traits like laziness, periodic discouragement, and a lack of self-confidence) the brevity of this author's philosophical texts; this explains why on not just a few occasions he attempted to concentrate the entire nucleus of his thought into the simplest of formulations possible; this also explains why he attempted time and time again to define his key terms; in short, this explains why a large amount of his philosophical exposition assumes the form of a definition.

In fact, *Terminología* is the title he gave to a brief set of definitions, published posthumously in 2007. It opens with the following sentence: "There are a few terms in need of clarification regarding some imprecision or serious discrepancy in acceptation."[13] And indeed, what Fernández is interested in is clarifying vagueness and polysemy, the two basic causes of philosophical errors in the tradition inspired by Book III of John Locke's *An Essay Concerning Human Understanding* (1690). It seems that Fernández did not read Locke except through successors like John Stuart Mill. And for Mill, just as for Locke, vagueness and polysemy are the primary causes of error and misunderstanding

---

[12] See Fernández, *Teorías* (1990), 105. Fernández is undoubtedly thinking of the prologue to the first edition of *Die Welt als Wille und Vorstellung*, in which Schopenhauer explains to the reader how his work should be read. It is in this same prologue where Schopenhauer also declares that all his work is nothing more than the development of *one single thought* (*ein einziger Gedanke*).

[13] "Pocos términos necesitaré despejar de alguna vaguedad o de fuerte discrepancia de acepción" (Attala, ed., *Impensador mucho*, 297).

in the philosophical community.¹⁴ Fernández refers to this type of defect as *verbalismo* (verbalism). He believes that a large amount of philosophy, to the extent that it is a discipline conceived as a theory of definitive reality, can be reduced to pure verbalism.¹⁵ And this is due to the simple reason that language is a useless tool when expressing metaphysical theories. In Fernández's days, the fiercest inheritors of this empirical criticism of language were the philosophers of the Vienna Circle, inheritors of Ludwig Wittgenstein's early work and defenders of the so-called empirical theory of meaning according to which a statement's meaning is the method for its verification.¹⁶ Notice the similarity between this school's critique and the following passage from Fernández:

> Classical and modern metaphysical literature is marked by profusion, an overabundance of statements without images, without representations, without conception, in short, without formulated thought. There are three elements at play: the belief one is thinking and the belief one is speaking, which both benefit from the most fascinating of the three: the belief one is understanding, all three of which feed and project a vast illusion of "believed–thought–understood." Multiple examples: a meticulous investigation would afford the opportunity to discuss them all, but for now I'll refer to the greatest and most valuable case: three

---

[14] From John Stuart Mill, see *A System of a Logic, Ratiocinative and Inductive* (1843), Book 6, Chap. 4, "Of the Requisites of a Philosophical Language, and the Principles of Definition." In his reading notes, Fernández praises Francis Bacon's *Essays* (*Teorías* (1990), 96–7), which supports the idea that he could have also had in mind the third class of *idola* proposed in *Novum Organum* (1620), *idola fori*, relating precisely to words, as it deals with the importance of philosophical terminology.

[15] Such disqualification does not apply, however, to ancient authors beyond the reach of our criticism as well as our comprehension. Fernández believes that unlike humankind itself, which changes very little if at all throughout the ages, their language changes so much that after only a few centuries, it becomes incomprehensible: "Me parece temerario fiar en entender el lenguaje de Hipócrates, Platón, Galeno, Petrarca, Dante" (It seems very reckless to trust that we understand the language of Hippocrates, Plato, Galen, Petrarch, Dante) (*Teorías* (1990), 109). He was also skeptical about the possibility of understanding texts belonging to cultures that are far removed from one's own, as Borges mentions in the prologue to his anthology of Macedonio Fernández's writings (1961): "La esencia onírica del Ser era uno de los temas preferidos de Macedonio, pero cuando yo me atreví a referirle que un chino había soñado que era una mariposa y no sabía, al despertar, si era un hombre que había soñado ser una mariposa o una mariposa que ahora soñaba ser un hombre, Macedonio no se reconoció en ese antiguo espejo y se limitó a preguntarme la fecha del texto que yo citaba. Le hablé del siglo quinto antes de la era cristiana y Macedonio observó que el idioma chino había cambiado tanto desde aquella fecha lejana que de todas las palabras del cuento la palabra mariposa sería la única de sentido no incierto" ("The oneiric essence of Being was one of Macedonio's preferred subjects, but when I dared to tell him that a Chinese man had once dreamt that he was a butterfly and when he awoke, he did not know if he was a man who had dreamt that he was a butterfly or a butterfly that was now dreaming that he was a man, Macedonio did not recognize himself in that ancient mirror and only asked me for the date of the text that I was citing. I told him the fifth century before the Christian Era, and Macedonio noted that the Chinese language had changed so much since that distant time that of all the words in the story, the word 'butterfly' was likely the only one whose meaning was not to be doubted") (11).

[16] See Rudolf Carnap, *Der logische Aufbau der Welt*, § 179.

thousand years of syllogisms reveal how a missing thought is substituted with a hidden figuration of words, of a set of empty spaces or contents, in a complacency abstracted by imagining the "extensions" of the lexical acceptation, comparing them quantitatively[17]; the syllogism is probably the most authentic Emptiness to ever be produced, even though the "demonstration," the "application," etcetera, everything that is not merely a modest display, is also empty.

In short, I want to say that everything is what it seems and this is enough and even comprehensive; and it is irresponsibly capricious to think that there is something more than what appears in consciousness, as if states of consciousness were just a mockery or a falsification, when in fact they are a totality, and a totality that no imagination can surpass in the intensity of its effectiveness, even to the point of frequently overwhelming and exasperating us.[18]

Even in his earliest publications, Fernández tends to initiate the exposition of his ideas by declaring the acceptance of certain words. This is the case in his first philosophically themed article "Psicología atomística (Quasi-Fantasía)" (Atomistic Psychology (Quasi una fantasia)), published in 1896: "I will begin by establishing the meaning of some of the terms that I will be utilizing most frequently, as the ideas that they express constitute the fundamental nuclei of my thought,"[19] which is then followed by a series of definitions (of the terms *conciencia* (consciousness), *substractum físico de la conciencia* (physical substratum of

---

[17] I assume that here Fernández is alluding to the idea of extension and set theory in judgment and syllogistic logic.

[18] "Hay en la literatura metafísica antigua y moderna, pues, profusión, superabundancia de enunciaciones sin imágenes, sin representaciones, sin concepción, en suma, sin pensamiento enunciado. Hay todo el triple juego: del creer pensar y el creer decir, favorecidos por el más curioso de todos: el creer entender, que entretienen y fingen una vasta ilusión del 'creído-pensamiento-entendido'. Múltiples ejemplos: una investigación minuciosa daría oportunidad de señalar, pero ahora indico el caso máximo y generador, casi: tres mil años de silogismo muestran cómo se produce la sustitución de un pensamiento ausente por una figuración oculta de palabras, de un juego de áreas o contenidos planos, en una complacencia abstraída en figurar las 'extensiones' de la acepción verbal, comparándolas cuantitativamente; el silogismo es probablemente el más auténtico Vacío que se ha dado, aun cuando la 'demostración', la 'aplicación', etcétera, todo lo que no es meramente una humilde mostración, también es vacío. / En fin, quiero decir que todo es lo que parece y esto es ya bastante y hasta total; y que es un antojo irresponsable que haya algo más que el aparecerse a la conciencia, como si los estados de la conciencia fueran una mera burla o falsificación, cuando son el todo y un todo que ninguna imaginación puede superar en su intensidad de efectividad, hasta el punto de abrumarnos y desesperarnos frecuentemente" (*NTV* (1990), 196–7). I have already alluded to Fernández's fragmentary and scattered publication of his writings (see p. 159), implicit in the last quotation. Now, I would like to draw attention to how this quotation shows that the edition is also not entirely accurate. The editor places this text at the end of an article published in Issue 2 of the journal *Proa*; in reality, the passage was not a part of the original edition. Was it added later by the author himself? In what year? Is it a passage that was a part of the original at some moment and then omitted by the editors at *Proa*? There is no indication by the editor that the text differs from the original. Other small differences suggest that the second explanation is the correct one.

[19] "Empezaré por determinar el significado de algunos de los términos que con más frecuencia voy a emplear, pues las ideas que ellos expresan constituyen los núcleos primordiales de mi pensamiento" (*NTV* (1990), 23).

consciousness), *materia* (matter), *sensación* (sensation), *imagen* (image) or *recuerdo* (memory), and *emoción* (emotion). A seminal text in his intellectual trajectory is "Ensayo de una nueva teoría de la psiquis. Metafísica preliminar. Psicología psicológica" (Essay on a New Theory of the Psyche. Preliminary Metaphysics. Psychological Psychology) from 1907. While it does not include definitions, its central argument concerns a problem of nomenclature in contemporary psychology: the unbridled proliferation of phenomena categories and the resulting need for their reduction or rigorous simplification. The essay's thesis takes the form of a definition: "the secret nature of consciousness," he writes in this article, is *afección* (affection), which in the end is nothing more than *placer-dolor* (pleasure-pain).[20] Fernández did not publish anything else until the 1920s, when his exchanges with the young avant-garde writers, led by Jorge Luis Borges, inspired him to resume his philosophical and literary production. In 1924 he published an essay titled "La metafísica, crítica del conocimiento. La mística, crítica del ser" (Metaphysics, Critique of Knowledge. Mysticism, Critique of Being), whose opening sentence reads: "In this concise introduction to Mysticism, I will use assertions and provisional, unreliable terms; without this, the reader and I would not share a language."[21] The rest of the article is nothing more than a series of brief definitions of key terms such as *hombre* (man), *mística* (mysticism), *práctica* (practice), *ser* (being), *pasado* (past), *presente* (present), and *futuro* (future). This is the way in which the author generally approaches philosophical problems. For this reason, in conclusion, it is essential to know the sense he regularly assigns in his texts to a series of basic ideas like the ones explained below.

1. *Afección* (Affection). A non-representative state of consciousness consisting only of a certain degree of what Fernández, following Schopenhauer, calls *placer–dolor* (pleasure–pain) and what we might describe as pure subjectivity if the notion of subject did not also suggest the notion of object.[22] According to

---

[20] Fernández, *NTV* (1990), 37. "Ensayo de una nueva teoría de la psiquis" was published, according to the editor of his *Obras completas*, in the journal *La universidad popular* 2, no. 10–12, January–February–March in 1907. I am not familiar with its first edition or with any study comparing the first edition to the one included in the *Obras completas*. The way in which these have been edited casts doubt on the text's accuracy; it is possible that the editor, one of the author's sons, could have inserted later passages by Fernández, as he has done on other occasions.

[21] "En esta sucinta introducción a la Mística usaré asertos y términos provisionales, infieles; sin ello no tendría idioma con el lector" (*NTV* (1990), 193). Language's unreliability is a result, as has been pointed out, of its inadequacy for Metaphysics. Its objective is completely different, even contrary, to that of Metaphysics: the human animal's fight for existence.

[22] "However [Schopenhauer writes], we are quite wrong in calling pain and pleasure representations, for they are not these at all, but immediate affections of the will in its phenomenon, the body; an enforced, instantaneous willing or not-willing of the impression undergone by the body" (*The World as Will and Representation*, vol. 1, 101).

Fernández's artistic metaphysics, affection creates its object and even its world without ceasing to be pure subjectivity, though the act itself a mystery. An affective state can arise from a cause exterior to the consciousness, in which case it is assimilated as a *sensación* (sensation), or from the consciousness itself, in which case it is referred to as an *emoción* (emotion). In contrast to representative states of consciousness, affective states lack objects. It matters not whether the pain arises from fire or from intense freezing and whether it is classified as heat or as cold; it matters not whether we feel fear when facing a real tiger or one that we have dreamt: the fear is the only thing that is truly (metaphysically) real in both cases. A large amount of Fernández's early thought can be characterized as a metaphysics of affection that, like Schopenhauer, argues against those philosophies that designated intellect and representation as the determining region of the psyche. Spencer writes, "the phenomena of Pleasure and Pain are perhaps the most obscure and involved which Psychology includes."[23] Is this obscurity the reason for the scant amount of attention Spencer's work dedicated to its study? Following Schopenhauer, but without abandoning a naturalistic psychology framework, Ribot (1839–1916) attempted to alter this hierarchy by placing greater emphasis on affection. The excerpt below from *La Psychologie des sentiments* (1896) explains this point of view and mentions the philosophical sources on which it is based:

> The term *feeling* is applied to two distinct groups of psychic manifestations, originally confounded—the affective and the representative states. So far, in employing this term we have taken account of the affective states only, because they and the movements are the sole primary constituents of character. They form the lower stratum, which is the first to make its appearance: the intellectual dispositions form a second layer, superimposed on the first. What is fundamental in the character is the instincts, tendencies, impulses, desires, and feelings; all these, and nothing else. This fact is so easily verified, and so obvious, that there would be no need to insist on it if the majority of psychologists had not confused the question by their incurable intellectualist prejudices—i.e., by their efforts to connect everything with intelligence and explain everything by means of it, to lay it down as the irreducible type of mental life. This view is quite untenable, for just as, physiologically, the vegetative life precedes the animal life based on it, so, psychologically, the affective precedes the intellectual life, which is based on it. The groundwork of every animal is "appetite" in Spinoza's sense, "will" in Schopenhauer's—i.e., feeling and acting, not thinking. I do not wish to insist on

[23] Spencer, *The Principles of Psychology*, 273.

this point, which would require to be developed at great length; I forbear, not on account of the scarcity, but of the superabundance of proof.[24]

Fernández would certainly endorse this paragraph. However, for him, as for Schopenhauer, this point of view is only of interest and justified if it grants access to a deeper knowledge of existence. Fernández calls such knowledge *experiencia mística* (mystical experience).

2. *Anonimia* (**Theory of Anonymity**). Fernández develops this concept in "Ensayo de una nueva teoría de la psiquis" (Essay on a New Theory of Psyche) (1907), in which he claims to have discussed it in his correspondence with the revered William James.[25] Subsequent writings often refer to it. It is the radicalization of one of the fundamental operations of modern idealism: the negation of certain qualities. The theory of anonymity is the negation of all qualities, or in other words, of all representation: visual, auditory, tactile, olfactory, or gustatory; these are nothing more than derivative or extrinsic values of one irreducible value that is affection. Fernández calls this *anonimia* because it supposes that the quality or specificity of representative states of consciousness (image or sensation) are the psychic equivalent of nouns. By denying that these qualities exist, it also denies that they can be named; that is, they are denied any substantial character, which is the ontological equivalent of nouns. What are qualities really? They are affective states, adjectival variations of the affection-subject which is the only thing that is real. Saying that the world is anonymous means that it is a fluid with no fixed intrinsic form, that nothing is substantial except for affection. With this theory, Fernández abandons subjective idealism, where the world is regarded as the reference of representation (thus the name idealism), and approaches the philosophies of Schopenhauer, Nietzsche, Bergson, and William James, where something more profound than the idea exists and is in a constant state of ebullition, referred to as Will (Schopenhauer), Dionysus (Nietzsche), duration (Bergson), or stream of thought (James).

3. *Apercepción* (**Apperception**). An associative activity that links states of consciousness (affective or otherwise) to one another and establishes an order between them that *a posteriori* is the very world we all know, with its distinct orders. The associative links established by apperception are not grounded in

---

[24] Ribot, *The Psychology of the Emotions*, 390–1.
[25] All attempts, even those made by this chapter's author, to locate such correspondence have been unsuccessful. I have explained elsewhere why those who believe that this amounts to one of Fernández's inventions are incorrect. See Attala (2014), *Macedonio Fernández, "précurseur" de Borges*.

knowledge but rather in utility, ultimately in the struggle for life driven by an impulse that Fernández calls *longevismo* (longevitism). Apperceptive activity does not obey the interests of consciousness but rather those of the organism to which the consciousness is subservient; the order of the world is not originary, but adventitious.[26] The idealist tradition underlying this notion reappears, through Schopenhauer, in nineteenth-century naturalistic philosophy in the works of Friedrich Herbart (1176–1841), Gustav Fechner (1801–87), Hermann Lotze (1817–81), Herbert Spencer (1820–1903), Wilhelm Wundt (1832–1920), and Ernst Mach (1838–1916) with his *Analysis of Sensations* (1897).[27] Fernández also proposes an analysis of sensations and, although more closely related to the tradition of Berkeley's and Condillac's philosophical idealism, like Mach he also rejects the scientific legitimacy of metaphysical doctrines that pretend to know the world's ultimate reality (realism, idealism, etc.). Nevertheless, his objective is not the same as physiological psychology and differs greatly from Mach's objective, which remains aligned with that of his predecessors: to pave the way for positive investigation. The analysis that Fernández undertakes is part of a metaphysics. But this metaphysics, rather than a theory, is a technique of asceticism that leads to the mystical experience.

4. *Arte* (Art). Like metaphysics, this is also a technique except that its method is not conceptual, nor does it operate in a sincere and direct fashion. The art that Fernández proposes is an indirect technique; it should operate outside of the recipient's field of vision. It is a sort of trap conceived by the artist-thinker to liberate the human being from the alienation in which they live. Such art induces deception similar in nature to a white lie bearing a noble purpose. Fernández develops two primary forms: humor and the novel. Each one sets out to free the human being from one of its two main forms of alienation: reason and death.

---

[26] This idea is not only related to Spencer's evolutionism. It is also at the heart of the philosophy of Schopenhauer, for whom knowledge, both in animals and in human beings (although not always and not in every human being), is nothing more than "a means for preserving the individual and the species" (*The World*, Book 2, § 27, vol. 1, 152).

[27] For the final author in this list, highly influential on the philosophy of the early twentieth century and whom Fernández knew and mentioned in his writings, see Mach, *Beiträge zur Analyse der Empfindungen*; there one can read the following: "In this investigation we must not allow ourselves to be impeded by such intellectual abridgments and delimitations as body, ego, matter, mind, etc., *which have been formed for special, practical purposes and with wholly provisional and limited ends in view*" [emphasis added] (*Contributions to the Analysis of the Sensations*, 23–4). In 1900, Mach greatly modified this work, including the title; however, as regards this matter, his idea remains consistent: "As soon as we have perceived that the supposed unities 'body' and 'ego' are only makeshifts, designed for provisional orientation and for definite practical ends (so that we may take hold of bodies, protect ourselves against pain, and so forth), we find ourselves obliged, in many more advanced scientific investigations, to abandon them as insufficient and inappropriate" (*Contributions to the Analysis of Sensations*, 13–14).

While they are very useful in the struggle for survival, reason and death are illusions concealing deception. Humor and the novel can help the individual to become aware of this. Humor (conceptual, not realist), allows for the individual to momentarily comprehend the incomprehensible: consciousness frees itself from reason's grip. The novel (those with fictional characters—not realistic novels) attempts to make readers believe themselves to be characters in the novel, that is, inexistent, so that they might discover, even for that brief moment of virtual inexistence, that it is possible for them not to exist: consciousness frees itself from death's prison. The novel offers readers the same thing that the dream offers Romeo in Act V, Scene 1: "I dreamt my lady came and found me dead— / Strange dream, that gives a dead man leave to think!— / And breathed such life with kisses in my lips, / That I revived, and was emperor." If the readers are successful at convincing themselves that they are nothing more than characters, they will first discover that they can be dead and conscious at the same time, which is to say, they will then realize that they cannot be dead given that they are conscious. Here Fernández puts a new twist on the Cartesian *cogito*. Shakespeare also provides an example of conceptual humor: two beings that devour one another. This is an impossible and illogical act, and nevertheless the listener or reader of the joke, for a brief moment, believes to comprehend it. In *Macbeth*, Ross recounts the sudden disobedience of Duncan's horses; Old Man says: "'Tis said they eat each other," to which Ross replies: "They did so, to th' amazement of mine eyes" (Act II, Scene 4). This "amazement" is the emotion that conceptual humor hopes to provoke. It is the psychic miracle that corresponds to the impossible act of two horses (two lions in Schopenhauer's version) devouring each other and then disappearing.[28]

5. *Emoción* (Emotion). An affective state of consciousness, i.e., non-representative or of pleasure–pain, whose origin, contrary to that of the sensation, is centrally, not peripherally, located. Emotion is born within consciousness, it does not impose itself upon it from the outside, it is not a brute or animal like the sensation and implies a certain degree of freedom. Feelings (pride, happiness, sadness, love, indignation), movements of the soul that since Descartes have been referred to as passions, are for Fernández a type of

---

[28] This act is a sort of miracle, as Thersites responds in *Troilus and Cressida* after Hector, being convinced that the other is nothing more than a rascal, spares his life: "God-a-mercy, that thou wilt believe me; but a plague break thy neck for frightening me! What's become of the wenching rogues? I think they have swallowed one another. I would laugh at that miracle; yet, in a sort, lechery eats itself" (Act 5, Scene 4). Schopenhauer's version appears in Chapter 8 of the *Supplements* in *The World as Will and Representation*, 97.

emotion. There are emotions whose affective value is neutral: these are emotions in the strict sense. Among these there exists one that, like Descartes, Fernández calls "pure" or "intellectual" emotion, in which consciousness seems to be free of all subjection.[29] If it is related to the realm of metaphysics (knowledge, truth), this pure emotion is called an impression; in art (taste, beauty), it is an aesthetic emotion; in ethics (the charitable act, kindness), it is a Passion (capitalized so as to distinguish it from ordinary passions or feelings, which, while they can be considered emotions, are attached to the living mechanism or organism). Impression, aesthetic emotion, and Passion are pure emotions, affective movements or states originating inside consciousness and realized against the living mechanism in which consciousness ordinarily unfolds. They are what is properly human in the human being because they are free: they are not controlled by an individual's animal or brutish qualities. This theory bears a certain resemblance to Schopenhauer's denial of the Will, which is also divided into three classes: science, art, ethics. But unlike Schopenhauer, Fernández does not presume to affirm that such a pure emotion truly exists. In this sense, Fernández is more Kantian, more critical than Schopenhauer. If this emotion exists, Fernández argues, then the Human also exists.[30] Otherwise, the individual is simply pure animality and their spirit is a confusion of savage sensations subject to the bloodthirsty laws of the evolution of the species. Given the hypothetical and utopian nature of this concept of pure emotion, Macedonio calls his theory a doctrine. By doing so, he suggests that it is impossible to verify and exists as a dogma or hypothesis that can only be believed, or disbelieved, which is what occurs with sensitive people when they realize that the world has long resembled a simple slaughterhouse.[31]

6. *Idealismo* (Idealism). Idealism is the philosophical answer to the question regarding the intrinsic difference between representative states of consciousness. Idealism rejects that there are any fundamental differences between them. Sensation, image, perception do not differ from one another. After comparing them, it is impossible to know which ones represent something exterior and which ones do not. Those we experience while awake are no different from those we experience while asleep. We only establish a difference based on the set of relationships produced during the task of practical life, that is, with the help of apperception. Thus, the difference is not the result of metaphysical knowledge,

---

[29] See Descartes, *Les Passions de l'âme*, Articles 91 and 147.
[30] See Fernández, for example, *NTV* (1990), 223.
[31] *NTV* (1990), 350.

but rather of practical knowledge.[32] From a metaphysical point of view, idealism is inescapable. From a practical point of view (where knowledge is measured not by truth but by effectiveness), idealism is not the final word. Therefore, metaphysics should not be conceived as a science but as a technique or therapy. Then, the final word belongs to the metaphysics of affection, which is strictly speaking not idealism.

7. *Imagen* (Image). Essentially identical to the sensation, the image differs only in its vigor or intensity, a difference that the human being generally explains by postulating an exterior object in the case of the sensation and denying the existence of one in the case of the image. That hypothesis is unwarranted; there is no intrinsic difference between sensation and image. This lack of difference is the main thesis of idealists like Berkeley and Condillac. It is likely that Fernández would add contemporary authors like Mach and Husserl to this list.[33]

8. *Inmortalidad* (Immortality). This is a topic of great importance and yet critics have given it little attention. One of the objectives of the novel is to assist the reader in gaining an awareness of their immortality, in realizing that death is inconceivable, a mere verbalism that the human being cannot comprehend without falsifying the object of such comprehension. As a fiction, however, death has allowed poets to express one of the greatest glories imaginable: Passion. In one of his most profound and heartbreaking poems, *Elena Bellamuerte*, written after the death of his wife Elena de Obieta in 1920, the deceased beloved and her surviving lover are compared to the hider and the seeker in the children's game. Another text that is equally heartbreaking is "Una imposibilidad de creer" (An Impossibility of Believing), published in Issue 22 of the journal *Davar* in Buenos Aires in 1949. It develops an unusual argument not so much against death as it is against the loss of faith in the goodness of existence: the reality of moral outrage is inconceivable. In the fable developed in the text, the author reveals himself to be incapable of believing that a child could die thinking that his father, facing imminent danger, had abandoned him. The act is so horrible that it represents a logical contradiction for Fernández's reasoning: it is as impossible as two plus two being five. It is perhaps no coincidence that the text was published in a journal from the Argentinian Hebraic Society and at a time when the world was fully aware of the magnitude of the Nazi massacre: the biblical reference—from

---

[32] Descartes had already established this distinction in *Objections et Réponses* to his *Méditations Métaphysiques*; see Attala, "Condiciones y sentido de la duda cartesiana," 9 sq.

[33] See his "Metafísica de 'estatua de Condillac' adicionada de 'asombro de ser'. Veinte comienzos para una Metafísica sin Principios," in Attala, *Impensador mucho*, 300–3.

Psalm 22:1 to Matthew 27:46, Maccabees 15:34, and Luke 23:46—should be obvious to the journal's readers.[34] Fernández, like his mentor Schopenhauer, rejects the ontological consistency of the human individual. He therefore also rejects the Christian idea of personal immortality. Nevertheless, his poetics of love, which at times interferes with his metaphysical texts, makes an exception to this rule: love desires the immortality of an individual, the whole person of the beloved. Apparent in these themes is the influence of another American great: Edgar Allen Poe, of whom Fernández suggests he once believed himself to be the reincarnation.[35]

9. *Metafísica* (Metaphysics). This is not a science and it is not strictly knowledge, although it occurs through knowledge. It does not operate with the intention of affirming the human being in its fight for survival, or even of elaborating a theory concerning ultimate reality. Metaphysics is a theoretical or conceptual technique whose objective is to liberate the mystical dimension of the human being, the inherent inclination of the consciousness that Fernández calls *hedonismo* (hedonism) and that during everyday life is trapped inside the corporal mechanism's fight for survival. The symptoms of such alienation are numerous. One is the feeling of anxiety concerning death; even the richest and most well-adapted individuals experience it. Another is astonishment and doubt concerning existence. In order to navigate this alienation, the metaphysician must conceptually dismantle the errors that have led them to fall prey to it until convincing themselves of their alienation. Success should result in a pure emotion or impression: a sort of ataraxy, spiritual tranquility, or mystical union whereby all struggle ceases along with any anxiety, astonishment, or doubt. Clearly underlying this procedure is the influence of Book IV in Schopenhauer's *The World as Will and Representation*: the intense fight for existence by those beings who are the embodiment of Will in the phenomenal world, the subjugation of intelligence to the designs of that Will, and finally, albeit rarely, the liberation from that subjugation as a result of a certain form of knowledge.

10. *Metafísica de la afección* (Metaphysics of Affection). If we accept the logic imposed by philosophies of representation during the modern age subsequent to the work of Descartes, the answer to every question is ultimately, according to Fernández, idealism. Once the logic of representation

---

[34] *NTV* (1990), 381–3.
[35] "Prólogo a mi persona de autor" ("A New Prologue to My Authorial Persona") (*MNE*, 35; Schwartz, 30).

is overcome, with the help of Schopenhauer, the ultimate answer is what Fernández refers to as metaphysics of affection. In order to move from idealism to this metaphysics, one must abandon the correspondence theory of truth (*veritas est adaequatio rei et intellectus*) and instead adopt a pragmatic criterion of truth (effectiveness); one must abandon the correspondence between a representation and its object as the criterion for truth and instead adopt effectiveness. We move, then, from Aristotle to William James, the third great American influence on the work of Fernández (the others, as has been mentioned, were Emerson and Poe). It no longer matters what elements of consciousness correctly represent the world but rather what elements of consciousness are the most important or have the greatest value: "the order of affectivity, a Being's only worth."[36] Either as a result of an analysis of consciousness (in texts from 1907 to 1908), or the adoption of a pragmatist criterion for truth (in *NTV*, for example), Fernández's answer to the question concerning value has always reverted to affection. With it, metaphysics ceases to be knowledge and becomes an attitude, an ascetic technique, a therapy. Oddly enough, the Austrian philosopher Ludwig Wittgenstein, also an avid reader of William James, particularly of his writings on the religious experience, proposed something similar around the same time period.

11. *Metafísica artística* (Artistic Metaphysics). When Fernández understands metaphysics as knowledge, he calls it *descriptiva* (descriptive). In this way it resembles phenomenology in that it does not set out to explain phenomena but only to describe them exactly as they appear in consciousness. Fernández despises explanation: it obscures the object, disregards it, and forgets it to instead go in search of its cause. Once an explanation finds it, it abandons it to go in search of another, and then another, and so on, never resting. Metaphysics, if it hopes to adequately comprehend a phenomenon, should limit itself to describing it exactly as it is. However, to the extent that a phenomenon presents itself to consciousness via representative states, descriptive metaphysics works with substitute, derivative, secondary material. We have already mentioned that

---

[36] "el orden de la afectividad, única valía del Ser"(*NTV* (1990), 267-8). The following is a general formulation of the same idea: "En la concepción mística repugna admitir la existencia en el Ser de estados absolutamente inafectivos, pues el placer–dolor es lo único que importa en el Ser, en la Vida y en el Arte, y las Representaciones, tan principalmente estudiadas por los metafísicos, sólo valen quizá como signos de la presencia o inminencia del placer y del dolor" ("In the mystical conception, admitting the existence of entirely nonaffective states within a Being is repellent, because pleasure–pain is the only thing that matters in a Being, in Life and in Art; and Representations, so fundamentally studied by metaphysicians, only serve perhaps as indications of the presence or imminence of pleasure or pain") (*NTV* (1990), 285).

Fernández counters the metaphysics of representation with a metaphysics of affection, even more radical because affection precedes representation. And if the first corresponds to descriptive metaphysics, then metaphysics of affection corresponds to artistic metaphysics, which occurs when affection has been liberated from representation. If affection is determined by images during everyday life (my pleasure comes after having seen my beloved, my pain comes after having learned of her death), artistic metaphysics is the attitude wherein affection is independent and produces its own world or object: it is my pleasure and my pain that conceive the beloved or deny the fact of her death. The title *NTV* (Not All Wakefulness Is with Open Eyes) attempts to capture such artistic metaphysics: there is a wakefulness more awake than normal wakefulness, one that occurs when affection is operative, like during our dreams, producing its own world. Berkeley is replaced by Fichte, Kant by Schopenhauer, and Schopenhauer by a philosophy of love that has no equivalent in modern philosophy, only in literature: Dante, Petrarch, Goethe (*Faust*), Poe.

12. *Pasión* (Passion). One of the pure emotions. It is the movement through which one person places themselves at the service of another. However, establishing its purity is a difficult task because life, in order to affirm itself, seeks to reproduce and therefore requires a link with other individuals in the species. Fernández believes that in these cases there is no authentic Passion. Passion is completely unrelated to sex, an inclination that resides in the human being's animality, not in its humanity. Passion is the movement through which consciousness, whose suffering and pleasure emerge naturally from its own body, chooses to suffer and enjoy what happens to another body. In this idea, also present in the work of Schopenhauer (*The World as Will and Representation*, Book 4), we find a radicalization of the thought of the Apostle Paul (Ephesians 5:28–33): Passion is a new birth in which consciousness chooses a body for itself that is different from the one it was shackled to at its first birth. It is the clearest image of a pure emotion: Passion violates natural law and establishes the kingdom of consciousness. Fernández employs the terms *Altruística* (Altruistics) and *Traslación* (Transferal) as synonyms for Passion: in Passion, consciousness abandons its own body (whose rigor subsequently lessens or softens), and moves into another body, whose rigor will no longer be a source of torment because it is a body that has been freely elected. It will also not experience the ultimate rigor, death, because once the consciousness has been transferred, it frees itself of everything that might befall its body and, in fact, everything that might befall any body. Through Passion, and through any pure emotion, the human animal becomes truly Human and approaches or achieves immortality.[37] It is no longer slave to the interests of its body—because every body wants to live the longest amount of time possible: *longevismo* (longevitism)—but rather to that of the person with whom it has freely decided to associate itself.

13. *Percepción* (**Perception**). The collection of sensations and images associated through an act of consciousness called *apercepción* (apperception) and that refers to a (supposedly) exterior object.

14. *Psiquis* (**Psyche**). A synonym for *espíritu* (spirit) and even of *conciencia* (consciousness) in his early writings (dated by the editor at around 1907 and 1908). It is the opposite of *materia* (matter) and is the realm, the only realm, of which the individual has direct or immediate knowledge. Given that metaphysics operates through direct or immediate knowledge, psyche,

---

[37] I would like to take the opportunity here to quote from a previously unpublished text in which Macedonio Fernández attempts to define what it is he understands by Passion: "Pasión o Altruística llamo a todos los grados de la simpatía, e. d. del hacer propio, del dolor o placer de otro; no se trata de una sola representación del sentir ajeno, pues esa representación la tiene el odio, la envidia tan netamente como el amor, sino de representar con emoción participante en el estado ajeno. Enfáticamente llamo Pasión a la opción máxima del altruismo, al todoamor y no doy interacción alguna a las apetencias sexuales, que no revisten calidad alguna ética, estética ni metafísica. Amor es todo situar en el placer o dolor manifestado por otro cuerpo (por sus gestos, sus acentos ...) nuestro placer y dolor, porque lo que tiene de metafísico la altruística es la ruptura interesante, embellecedora del lazo cuerpo mío sentir mío, y esta disolución disuelve la noción de muerte porque es un experimento de la autonomía de la Sensibilidad respecto de un cuerpo, de que uno no sigue el destino del otro. En la mera sensualidad sexual no hay esta graciosa, metafísica Traslación; al contrario, separación [ilegible] de los 'yos'—La fina Traslación sería total sin la precisión de la Noticia, e. d. sentimos lo nuestro, *sin dato*; para sentir lo de otro (e. d. sentir igual a otro, pues lo insinuado por Kant 'intuir' el estado (sentido) de otro es infantil; se infiere (causalmente), se 'conoce' como diría [William] James, y basta esto para promover el mecanismo emocional, la simpatía) necesitamos el dato[,] un rostro sonriente o lloroso, la inflexión de voz; noticia del sentir, del 'presente' de una sensibilidad, es necesario al amor, y no al egoísmo; el misterio de la separación de la Pluralidad, que trataremos de resolver" ("Passion or 'Altruistics' is what I call all degrees of sympathy, i.e., taking possession of another's pain or pleasure; this is not one single representation of another's feelings, because hatred and envy have that representation just as clearly as does love, but rather about representing the state of another through participating emotions. I use Passion to emphatically refer to the highest option of altruism, to *todoamor* ['totalove' in Schwartz' translation], and I do not allow for any intervention from sexual desires, which bear no ethical, aesthetic or metaphysical value. Love is fully positioning our pleasure and pain inside the pleasure or pain expressed by another body (by its movements, its intonations ...), because the metaphysical nature of Altruistics lies in its interesting, embellishing rupture of the *my body-my feeling* bond; and this dissolution dissolves the concept of death because it is an experiment in autonomous Sensitivity with respect to a body, where one is not tied to the destiny of the other. In basic sexual sensuality this gracious, metaphysical *Traslación* (Transferal) does not occur; on the contrary, separation [ilegible] of the selves—This delicate Transferal would be absolute were it not for the preciseness of the *Noticia* (Notification), i.e., we feel what is ours, *without information*; in order to feel what is another's (i.e., feel the same as another, Kant suggests that 'intuiting' the state (feelings) of another is naïve; one infers (causally), one 'knows' as [W.] James would say, and this is sufficient to advance the emotional mechanism, sympathy) we need information[,] a smiling or crying face, the inflection of a voice; love, not egoism, needs a notification of feeling, of a sensitivity's 'present'; the mystery of the division of Plurality, which we will attempt to resolve"). I am grateful to the *Fundación San Telmo* in Buenos Aires and its director Nicolás Helft for their permission to use this text.

consciousness, or spiritual nature all fall within the field of metaphysics (similar to the phenomenon in phenomenology). This is indicated by the term's very etymology: beyond the physical, that is, beyond matter. The foundational text of Fernández's philosophy, "*Ensayo de una nueva teoría de la psiquis*" (Essay on a New Theory of Psyche) (1907), clarifies this with its subtitles "*Metafísica preliminar*" (Preliminary Metaphysics) and "*Psicología psicológica*" (Psychological Psychology), the latter standing in contrast to physiological psychology from Ribot's experimental school. Regarding the former, "*Metafísica preliminar*" echoes Kant's opuscule *Prolegomena to Any Future Metaphysics*. Here, Fernández carries out a sort of phenomenological reduction: he seeks the essential element of "Spiritual Nature," exactly as it is accessed, directly and immediately, that is, independent of "concomitances, physiological precedents and consequents."[38] His answer is well known by now: that essential element is *afección* (affection). From an anthropological standpoint—as a component of an organic compound—the psyche naturally seeks pleasure and avoids pain; Fernández calls this basic tendency *hedonismo* (hedonism).

15. *Representación* **(Representation).** The nature of those psychic states that are characterized by having an object. It can be a *sensación* (sensation), *imagen* (image), or *percepción* (perception). They are said to "represent" because the object they possess forces a subject to confront the problem of discovering whether or not it corresponds to that entity which lies outside of the representation: reality. The thought of Fernández is an effort to liberate the subject from this problem. His most radical answer affirms the derivative nature of the representation, which in truth or in the end is nothing more than *afección* (affection) in disguise. No one can live in perpetual agreement with this philosophy because, in order to live, people need representations. But one does not live on bread alone; one often feels the need to cure life's malaise. How can this be achieved? Contrary to Schopenhauer, who proposes a denial of the Will, Fernández believes that in order to gain access to the mystical state, one must deny the representation. And this denial can be reached, as has already been stated, by metaphysical, artistic, or ethical means.

16. *Sensación* **(Sensation).** A sensation is a state of consciousness originating in its periphery. The sensation imposes itself upon consciousness. For this reason, Fernández uses the adjective *bruta* (brute) to describe it, which he understands as savage and even animal (as the word "brute" is synonymous

---

[38] "las concomitancias, precedentes y consecuentes fisiológicos" (*NTV* (1990), 34).

with animals). Sensations arise in the periphery of consciousness, that is, in the body, the animal component of the human being. They are usually classified according to their quality or specificity: visual, auditory, tactile, gustatory, olfactory. Inasmuch as a quality or specificity can be distinguished within them, the sensation is a *representative* state of consciousness: it has an object, the core—the *quid*—of the sensation (a sensation of heat, of cold, of redness, of seriousness, of brightness, etc.). From a metaphysical perspective, however, sensations are perhaps nothing more than *afección* (affection). This is what he argues in his theory of anonymity.

17. Ser humano (Human Being). Fernández's anthropology takes its inspiration from Spencer.[39] In the past it was believed that the individual was a unity of body and spirit. Fernández prefers function concepts, not substance concepts. For him, the human being is a *"unidad místico-práctica"* (mystical–practical unity). The "mystical" and the "practical" oppose one another. The mystical is the present certainty of being and of being without distinction regarding another thing. The practical is the lack of any such certainty and the individual system's fight for survival inside a hostile world.[40] The life of the human being occurs immersed within the practical, that is, within a means-end logic that is well described by the evolutionist philosophies of Spencer and Schopenhauer. But the mystical can, and perhaps does, occur more often than philosophers, like *Hamlet*'s Horacio, seem to believe. In some texts, Fernández uses *conciencia* (consciousness) in place of *místico* (mystical), and *organismo* (organism) in place of *práctico* (practical). He also attributes the tendency, following Spencer, that he calls *hedonismo* (hedonism) (the search for pleasure and the flight from pain) to consciousness and the tendency, following Spencer and especially Schopenhauer, that he calls *longevismo* (longetivism) (living, regardless of how painful it might be) to the organism. What is certain is that in everyday life these opposing tendencies are interlaced inside one intricate unity, albeit undoubtedly in discordance. The most frequent unity is that which occurs from *hedonismo* submitting to *longevismo*, consciousness submitting to the organism, the mystical submitting to the practical. Certain symptoms remind us that these natural marriages display characteristics of alienation. One of these symptoms is the same that Plato and Aristotle placed at the root of philosophy: admiration, astonishment, to the extent that these emotions reveal ignorance, a

---

[39] See Spencer, *The Principles of Ethics*, 203–7.
[40] See Fernández, "La metafísica, crítica del conocimiento. La mística, crítica del ser," *NTV* (1990), 193.

lack of familiarity with Being. How can these symptoms be cured? There is not just one variety of therapy. Some will accept this alienation, and even accentuate it by adopting a hygienic method: all life is subjected to the rule of health. Others will seek to liberate the consciousness by placing everything under the rule of *hedonismo*, even if this causes the individual to lose their health and indeed their life. Metaphysics, art, and ethics are distinct paths that lead the human being to the mystical experience.

Part Three

Metaphysics on the Move

Notes on Macedonio in a Diary*

Ricardo Piglia

5. VI.62

Out of the blue, Carlos Heras brought up Macedonio Fernández in a seminar on anarchism in the 1920s. He'd met him in Misiones when Macedonio was a prosecutor for the Court in Posadas. "Someone needs to look into Macedonio's arguments and charges as a prosecutor," said Heras. "None of the defendants he accused were ever found guilty." He recalled the case of a man who had murdered his two daughters with a knife, first one and then, two hours later, the other, who was at that point of course almost unconscious with fear. He then buried them deep inside a church because it was sacred ground. "Macedonio managed to put together charges that made sentencing almost unnecessary." According to Heras, Macedonio's argument was that the man had killed his two daughters, ages twelve and fourteen, because he didn't want to see them destined to the same fate as their mother, who had gone insane, or that of their older sister, Elisa Barrios, a well-known popular singer. The man had planned to kill himself afterwards but either didn't have the courage or was unsuccessful, despite, according to Macedonio, having tried to hang himself with barbed wire. The fact that he had used barbed wire became a key element in Macedonio's prosecution. Professor Heras couldn't remember the exact details of his reasoning, but he clearly pictured, he said, the courtroom and Macedonio's pale, lean figure standing before a skeptical audience that had gone to hear him. The professor was almost certain the daughters' murderer had been exonerated or had only received a symbolic sentence. Heras very elegantly connected Macedonio's work as a prosecutor with the problems of double legality that had arisen in Buenos Aires during the Day of the Three Governors.

---

* Translated from the Spanish by Sean Manning.

12. VI.62

"Macedonio," Professor Heras says to me as we're leaving the building and heading down 7th Street towards the train station, "liked to avoid unwanted contact. He preferred to keep his distance. I don't think he liked shaking hands." But it also seems he thought about his body more than most intellectuals of his day. "Even so," said the professor, "women gave themselves to him with amazing ease, without putting up the least bit of resistance. Well, instead of *even so*," said Professor Heras, "I should say *because of this*." Macedonio didn't like to make plans for the future or for people to point out nature's beauty to him. "It's already hard enough," he would say, "to capture those truly critical moments." As the train enters the station and people swarm to board, the professor suggests I look for the copy of *Una novela que comienza* (A Novel That Begins) in the university library because it has handwritten notes from Macedonio Fernández himself.

14. VI.62

The copy of *Una novela que comienza* was donated by someone, maybe Virasoro. Inside there's an inscription ("To Benjamín Virasoro, Porteño and metaphysician, with all my friendship," Macedonio Fernández), and on the last page the following notes in his usual microscopic handwriting:

They are small men (physically: fragile) (crossed out and written above: scrawny), like Raskolnikov, who weighed 58 kilos, or Kant (1.60m), or that Japanese jockey I saw one afternoon at the tracks in Lobos, who possess a special drive due in part to their intensity, in part to their apathy. When it comes to social relations, they are perfectly devoid of any interest. They are generally exceedingly calm—elegant and calm—and of course they cannot accomplish anything in one sitting. One must, they would say, know how to be slow, how to be quiet. Valéry, for example, stayed silent for twenty years, Rilke didn't write so much as a poem for fourteen years, then the *Duino Elegies* appeared.

Below and off to the side:

Nothing. The artist is alone, abandoned to silence and ridicule. They are responsible for themselves. They begin their projects and they carry them out. They obey an inner voice that no one else hears. They work alone, the poets; the poet always works alone, because in every decade there are always only just a few great poets (no more than three or four) spread throughout the different nations, writing poetry in various languages, usually unaware of each other: these *phares*, lighthouses as the French call them, those figures who illuminate the plains, the fields, for a long period of time while they themselves remain in the shadows. (This is an expression from Gottfried Benn.)

They grow old. Knut Hamsun lived to be ninety-three but spent the end of his life in hospice care. Also interesting is the case of Ricardo Husch, who lived to be ninety-one and then committed suicide. (Lagerlöf 82, Voltaire 84). Old people are dangerous: completely indifferent to the future. The twilight years. Those twilight years! Most of them are poor, coughing, hunched over, drug addicts, drunks, some are even criminals, almost all of them are unmarried, almost all without children, almost all in hospice care, almost all blind, almost all impersonators and frauds.

On another page:

"When the contrabandist Oskar Van-Velde jumped off Barracas Bridge (or was it the Alea Building?), he left behind a mysterious message: At 7,300 meters above sea level, this is the edge of death, one more kilometer and we will be there. The traveler looks downward. Good news, if you ask me (writes Macedonio), neither up, nor down, the center ruins everything, the magnetic needle and compass rose, out of the question, but conformism grows stronger and stronger. To avoid being infected by this dying society consumed with greed for money and recognition, we must isolate ourselves from mainstream trends and ignore them: refuse to understand why the dominant beliefs are what they are."

(Macedonio wrote these notes seemingly *before* giving the book to Virasoro.)

6. VI.65

Last night at *Los 36 billares* [Pool Hall], a discussion about Macedonio's style. It's an oral style even though it seems to be the antithesis. It's a form of private orality, which assumes a circle of very familiar interlocutors who are able to appreciate all the understood implications. The real presence of the listener decides the tone and the ellipses. Proof that orality is first and foremost musical and tends toward illegibility. Analyzing Macedonio's speeches at the dinners held by the journal *Martín Fierro*: the setting for his style. Within that space, neologisms, allusions, philosophical slang, the baroque pleasure of trivialities intermingle. I'll also say that last night the writer most similar to Macedonio Fernández was

Father Castañeda: the pamphlet and the diatribe, a taste for scandal, the satirical violence of controversy, Macedonio transforms all this into an intimate style, into chamber music.

In Macedonio orality is never lexical, it operates inside the syntax and the rhythm of the sentence. Macedonio is the best writer of the spoken word since José Hernández.

2. XI.67

Negative thought in Macedonio Fernández. Nothingness: every variant of negation (paradox, nonsense; antinovel, antirealism). Most of all, linguistic negativity: hermetic pleasure. The idiolect, an encoded personal language. The creation of a new language as the ultimate utopia. Macedonio's phrasing, verbs in the infinitive, hyperbaton. The archaic syntax found in popular speech. "An oneiric grammar," says Renzi. "In that sense, he resembles Gadda. *Criollo* speech as a pastiche. The philosophical *payada*.[1] A guitarist. "He was a guitarist," says Renzi. "This is why he was always having pictures taken of himself with a guitar, not because he knew how to play it, but because he discreetly wanted to say that he was only interested in being an Argentine guitarist. Don't you think?" says Renzi. "Yes. What could be better? A folk singer and guitarist, and proud of it."

12. II.68

One of Macedonio's ambitions was to go unpublished. To erase his tracks, to be read as one reads someone who is an unknown, without any prior knowledge. He insinuated on several occasions that he was writing a book and that no one would ever see a single page of it. In his will, he stated that the book should be published secretly, around 1980. No one should know that the book was his. At first, he had considered having it published anonymously. Later he thought that it should be published under the name of a well-known writer. Credit his book to someone else: reverse plagiarism. To be read as if he were that writer. In the

---

[1] Translator's Note: "PAYADA. An Argentinean song or ballad, generally anonymous, in simple meter, sung by popular poets who wandered the pampas. These mod. troubadours were called *payadores*, and their improvisations were generally accompanied by the guitar" (Cushman et al., eds., *The Princeton Encyclopedia of Poetry and Poetics*, 1014).

end, he decided to use a pseudonym that no one would recognize. The book should be published in secret. He liked the idea of working on a book designed to go unnoticed. A book lost in a sea of future books. The voluntarily unknown masterpiece. Encrypted and concealed in the future, like a riddle cast into history.

True legibility is always posthumous.

14. VIII.68

I'm rereading *Diario escrito en la Estancia* (Diary Written at the Ranch). Macedonio wrote it between January and March in 1938, at *La Suficiente* [Ranch] in Pilar [outside Buenos Aires]. Absolutely exceptional everyday remarks mixed with his reading of Schopenhauer. "I am the one who has best sensed the amazing helplessness of his language in his interactions with thought. Indeed, I get lost in my thinking like someone dreaming, like someone bursting in on their thoughts. I am one who knows the delights of loss." In this *Diary* we understand why the writer has no other choice but to keep a diary of the work he is not writing.

2. V.71

The poetics of the novel. Macedonio's implicit quarrel with Manuel Gálvez. They represent the two traditions of the Argentine novel. Gálvez is his perfect antithesis: the diligent "social" writer, successful and mediocre, who relies on literary common sense.

Until Witold Gombrowicz came to Argentina, we could say that Macedonio had no one to talk to about the art of making novels. *Transatlántico* (*Trans-Atlantyk*), an Argentine novel, is part of the Macedonian tradition (not to mention *Ferdydurke*). With Gombrowicz, we can begin to read Macedonio. Or rather, Gombrowicz allows us to read Macedonio.

4. V.71

In 1938, he decides "to publish the novel as a serial, primarily in the newspaper *Crítica* or in *La Nación*." A typical avant-garde act: isolation, a break with the market combined with fantasies of accessing mass media. To study this (always unsuccessful) strategy is to understand the internal tension of the form in his novel (the didactic prologues). The avant-garde is a genre. Macedonio was well aware of this. He used to say that an arriviste writer is one who has not yet arrived. But isn't it extraordinary that he envisioned *Museo de la novela de la Eterna* (*The Museum of Eterna's Novel*) as a serial?

Macedonio starts writing *Museo* in 1904 and works on the book until his death. For almost fifty years he methodically buries himself inside this enormous work. The example of Musil's *The Man Without Qualities*, a book whose very conception excludes the possibility of giving it an ending. The infinite novel that includes every variation and every detour; the novel that lasts the length of the life of the person who writes it.

9. VII.71

In Gombrowicz's *Diario argentino* (Argentine Diary), I come across a note about Macedonio that now I am unable to find again (as if it had never really existed). "There is a certain stutter particular to the Argentine language that fills me with a strange feeling of elation. It is a rhythm that goes more or less like this: da, da, do, da, da, which is inside the words themselves and not just occurring between one word and the next. One letter collides with another like pebbles in a tin can. Macedonio Fernández is the only one who has been able to capture this toctoc, toctoc, toctoc, this *criollo* gallop, in his style. That Mr. Fernández, I tell my friend Mastronardi, that Mr. Fernández sure knew, ahem, how to write, ahem, he had, how can I put it? a sense of rhythm, or am I wrong? Yes, definitely, of course, answers Mastronardi, certainly, indeed, without a doubt, that's right. Would you like another cup of tea?"

6. VII.73

Love as a narrative cliché. In *Museo*, the story of Eterna, of the woman lost, triggers a philosophical frenzy. Complex constructions and alternative worlds are created. The same happens in Borges's "El Aleph," which resembles a microscopic version of *Museo*. The magical object inside which the entire universe is concentrated takes the place of the woman who has been lost. Strangely enough, several of the best Argentine novels recount the same thing. In *Adán Buenosayres* (*Adam Buenosayres*), in *Rayuela* (*Hopscotch*), in *Los siete locos* (*The Seven Madmen*), in

Museo de la novel de la Eterna (*The Museum of Eterna's Novel*), the loss of the woman (whether her name is Solveig, La Maga, Elsa, Eterna, or Beatriz Viterbo) is the necessary condition for the metaphysical experience. The hero begins to see reality for what it really is and learns its secrets. The entire universe is concentrated inside that fantastic and philosophical "museum."

This is in fact the tradition of the tango. The man, having lost the woman, looks at the world with a metaphysical and extremely lucid gaze. The loss of the woman is the necessary condition for the tango's hero to acquire that perspective that distances him from the world and allows him to philosophize on memory, time, the past, forgotten purity, the meaning of life. The heartbroken man can, at long last, see reality for what it is and discover its secrets. One need only consider [Enrique Santos] Discépolo's heroes. The man, betrayed, skeptical, faithlessly moralistic, finally sees the truth. In this sense, Discépolo's "Cambalache" is the "El Aleph" of the poor.

5. V.74

Macedonian reading: scattered, incomplete, interrupted, abandoned. His texts produce interruptions on a microscopic level: they are serials in miniature installments. By this I mean they utilize the technique of the newspaper serial to suspend the action but extremely atomized and condensed and repeated several times within the same page.

30. IX.78

Macedonio worked with disparate fragments of language taken from law or philosophy, from the Entre Ríos Province, Golden Age Spanish, neighborhood slang, committees, or translated German, and he treated each one as if it were a different language. In this way he resembles the Joyce of *Finnegan's Wake*.

13. XI.78

A long conversation with Renzi about Macedonio Fernández. "Of course he was the one who wrote Hipólito Yrigoyen's speeches. He put his baroque hermeticism into presidential language," he says. They met through Clara Anselmi. Yrigoyen first hires him when he has his dispute with Leopoldo Melo and Pedro Molina in the year 1912; a fraction of his party had organized in opposition to the extended abstention. Macedonio writes the entire debate for him. From that point on, he lends his style to the Cause. During those years Macedonio doesn't publish anything. When he distances himself from Yrigoyen in 1922, he starts to publish again. But then, the one who goes silent is Yrigoyen. "Along those lines," says Renzi, "someone should examine the impact of politics on the language of the time." Besides, it's a national tradition. For example, when Juárez Celman assumes the presidency, Eduardo Wilde writes his acceptance speech for him, and later, Ramón Cárcano writes his resignation speech. "Also," said Renzi, "it was then that Macedonio started to become fixated on the President and made him a central character in *Museo*."

9. X.80

"But there's another matter," says Renzi. "What is the main concern of Macedonio's art? The relationship between thought and literature." Thinking, Macedonio would say, is something that can be narrated like one narrates a trip or a love story, but not in the same way. In his view, it is possible to use the novel to express thoughts that are just as difficult and just as abstract as those found in a work of philosophy, provided they appear to be false. "That illusion of falsity," said Renzi, "is literature itself."

10

What Is Believing?*

Horacio González

It was a matter of obsession for Macedonio Fernández. Nowhere in any of his reflections was there a moment in which the irrepressible flow of reality paused long enough for one to be able to declare "I believe" without being immediately swept away by the current. We use this everyday verb to insouciantly begin our sentences, aware that all human interaction involves tolerating uncertainty. Macedonio's writing never rests on the belief that it can be read by an external eye perceiving a natural binary order and differentiating between the skills of the writer and those of the reader. In his thought and texts, this distinction does not exist and, as a result, the belief in an encounter with the reader, in an intersection between his writing and its reading, is shaken. The possibility of such a belief arises largely by not doubting that the readerly act itself possesses some faint objectivity, which while not appearing to offer a sufficiently stable foundation on which to raise a belief, it does assist him or her during the necessary task of reading a text that lies in an as yet unfamiliar world. "Do not read so hurriedly, my dear reader; my writing cannot keep up with your reading," pleads Macedonio as he reveals an operative premise in his metaphysics of belief.[1]

In the reality of the written text there is something more, an excess, that the writer was never able to reach, but which is indeed within the grasp of the reader. One would then suspect that, like writing, belief must also possess a later instant in which it can be confirmed. And what should that other instance, that other belief, be? Macedonio seems to suggest that one must believe in belief. Hence, the first spontaneous act of the believer's consciousness should be guarded by an element that is also a belief but positioned at a different or superior level, as if some god had offered up a piece of its own flesh to create another figure in its

---

* Translated from the Spanish by Sean Manning.
[1] "No lea tan ligero, mi lector, que no alcanzo con mi escritura adonde está usted leyendo" (Fernández, *Papeles de recienvenido* (1989), 29).

likeness. One would thus reach a belief in belief through a never-ending chasmic game, like the prologues of *Museo de la novela de la Eterna* (*The Museum of Eterna's Novel*), through a return to an uncertain origin toward the nothingness of believing, an absolute disbelief, a world devoid of any orienting here or there, which is precisely writing's unreachable destination.

Believing in the belief yields the supplement that duplicates it, producing a second belief to sustain the first. This is what is generally necessary for human existence regarding whether or not it is possible to believe. It is possible provided that one takes a step back and fashions a guarantee, a foothold, from the same language as the belief, a guarantee that shares its same name, and that, ultimately, certifies the belief—unless it is in need of further duplication ad infinitum. This is the Macedonian problem par excellence and what leads him to the question of the impossibility of believing, which is precisely the title of one of Macedonio's most prophetic tales: "Una imposibilidad de creer" (An Impossibility of Believing) (1949).[2] The essay consists of a short introduction followed by an unexpected exemplification in the form of a bible-like story. A father and son set out on a walk, which Macedonio depicts using deliberately heart-rending details that would be unnecessary if he were not preparing an emotional atmosphere for everything he will later attempt to express. Thus, the illustrative story becomes indispensable to the rest of the essay:

> A father and a twelve-year-old boy are out walking along the edge of the sea. They begin to feel tired and decide that it is time to turn back, at which point the boy, reaching out to catch a butterfly, breaks free of his father's hand and slips, falling into the water. The father leaps in after him and manages to grab hold of the boy by the hair but, being a very poor swimmer and weighed down by his clothing, he soon grows exhausted and sinks, drowning as he lets go of the boy's hair. They both perish.[3]

In this moving tale, recounted with seemingly superfluous (the butterfly) or violent (grabbing the boy by the hair) description, Macedonio wants to investigate the idea that belief surpasses knowledge, which corresponds to memory and the present. However, this proposition is merely a hypothesis, given the difficulty in accepting that a belief is not a component of knowledge. Macedonio resolves to

---

[2] See Fernández, "Una imposibilidad de creer," in *NTV* (1990), 381–3.
[3] "Un padre y un niño de doce años caminan paseándose por una ribera de mar. Cuando ya algo cansados habían de abandonar su paseo, en un impulso del niño por alcanzar una mariposa se desprende de la mano del padre y resbala al mar. El padre se lanza al agua y logra asir al niño por los cabellos y retenerlo, pero muy poco nadador y molestado por la ropa pronto está extenuado y húndese, se ahoga y suelta los cabellos del niño. Perecen los dos" (Fernández, NTV (1990), 381–2).

reshape this situation, but we will not call his reshaping a hypothesis, rather an inquiry into the very being of belief. Is believing possible? To ask this question is to challenge those who believe. Macedonio writes that "[sometimes] it is not possible for me to believe in what is evident in the present and the past."[4] Such a declaration is not surprising from someone who so often experimented with *esse est percipi* [to be is to be perceived]. But he affirms this—now that he has free rein—in order to say that, on the other hand, it is possible for him to believe in what is denied in the present and the past. For this it is sufficient to believe in one's own practices of critiquing and negating historical evidence. The impossibility of believing, however, is an ambiguous formulation considering what it wishes to express. For Macedonio the answer to this statement means engaging with an act of profound suffering, the result of a death, to which a reparation might be offered. It would include an afterlife that follows the tragic destiny whose knell has tolled. What Macedonio is not capable of believing in then is that there is not a continuance posterior to death containing some sort of emendatory life wherein one can realize what was not able to be said while living. What would that moment be? Without a doubt, a form of life within death and a form of death within life.

It could be formulated in the following way: for me it is impossible to believe that there is not some sort of immortality that does not last forever, that does not span a perhaps inconceivable eternity, but is instead an immortal reparative segment in which one can speak specific words whose expression was impeded by a sudden death that caused a certain amount of confusion. The son might have believed that his father was careless in his attempt to save him, when, in fact, his father was the first to die. Impossibility is so evident in this story that there is clear intent to render this question of the impossibility of believing both possible and extraordinary. It involves a desire. The title of the text is misleading. It was not about there simply being impossibilities that interfere with believing, or that believing is impossible, but rather the contrary. What exists is the desire to believe that there is a span of time governed by a provisional but necessary immortality in which to reinstate a truth that could not be expressed due to a real death. This belief, therefore, negates death in order to create an eternity lasting a few additional seconds, minutes, whatever exceptional sliver of time is needed to resolve the enigma of responsibilities that tragedy had left behind.

Macedonio addresses the readers with a challenge. Would they not feel the same as he does? Would they not also think that belief is always at the center

---

[4] "[a veces] experimento la imposibilidad de creer en lo evidente actual y pasado" (Fernández, NTV (1990), 381).

of knowledge? But then embrace the same impossibility of believing that there is not something more than knowledge? And what would that be? Knowledge expropriated from every rung of the act of knowing and then extended—until exhausting itself as knowledge—to a mystical form of believing. This belief exists because the idea that a Son could lose confidence in his Father as a result of a situation such as the one evoked in the biblical tale is intolerable. Macedonio writes:

> And you too, reader, if caringly and meticulously imagining the agony of these beings, are unable to believe that between the two of them there was not some communication, an explanation that resolves and compensates for the bitterness of their feelings, the desperate pain of the boy losing faith in his father during the final moment of his existence; the father in his final moment foreseeing his son's devastation as his filial faith dissipates.[5]

However, he explains that it is not a question of not being able to believe in the circumstances of this tragic event, rather the impossibility of believing that *Reality* denied these two beings an auxiliary instant of life to afford them a mutual explanation and a restitution of their faith, illuminating uncertainties and freeing them from "such darkness in their souls."[6]

Is the problem suitably well defined? In the story, it is clear that the son was an anxious child, if perhaps an imprudent butterfly hunter. What else would we expect of a twelve-year-old? On the one hand, this makes the expectation that they be conceded one more minute of eternity appear extremely demanding. But, on the other hand, it reveals that true love has a limit and that the lives it had at its disposition were not sufficient for it to express itself. And now love requests—and Macedonio grants—a moment of life beyond death in which it can truly materialize.

As we have said, Macedonio posed the questions. He directed them at the reader and then presents his own meditation. Nevertheless, the same declaration persists: "I cannot believe it."[7] Is this another way of alluding to the impossibility of believing? Time and time again the title is ambiguous. Not only is believing not impossible, but one can also believe in an impossibility. What Macedonio cannot believe is that one cannot believe. "I cannot not believe," he says at another point

---

[5] "Y usted también, lector, si se representa cariñosa, detalladamente el martirio des esos seres, no puede creer que entre ellos no hubiera nunca comunicación, una explicación que aclare y compense la amargura del sentimiento, de la punzada desesperada de perder la fe en el padre el niño, como momento último de su existir; de adivinar el padre en su último momento esta abrumación del hijo con ese desmayo de su fe filial" (Fernández, NTV (1990), 382).

[6] "tal negrura en el alma" (Fernández, NTV (1990), 382).

[7] "No lo puedo creer" (Fernández, NTV (1990), 382).

using a different formula, an entreaty directed at himself.[8] He wonders whether in the minute immediately subsequent to the story or somewhere in the future, a dialogue might not have occurred: "'My dear father, why did your hand let go of me? Did you no longer love me?'; and the father says: 'I died before you and it was my dead hand that let you go.'"[9] Could we not then eliminate once and for all the possibility that the father was never able to explain himself to the boy who may have experienced the horror of thinking he had been abandoned? It was necessary to envision a situation, envision it as an impossible but necessary belief, in order to prevent the boy's sadness and the father's suffering. We assume that these bodiless feelings live only inside the interrogative statements in which they are pronounced. If the body no longer lives, then language's soul does.

Concerning the fact that a more realistic way of thinking would discount these possibilities, Macedonio writes, "I cannot not believe." This double negation calls our attention to the difficulty of believing. Belief imposes itself through this double negation. It possesses a somewhat mystical dimension that we are forced to accept. However, it is not the mysticism of a prophet or preacher, but that of the mystic who requires him or herself to take on this role at a particular moment. It is precisely in death that these questions of love emerge because there is a scientific contention for "a *final* psychism."[10] To protect his affirmations, Macedonio must reject the idea of "the cessation of the individual psychic progression" as a consequence of death.[11] For those steeped in scientific knowledge, however, matter is what would be immortal while the psyche would not inherit this quality. However, Macedonio would argue that there are effects without effects because the word "matter" is used to suggest a "certain family of psyches (color, tactility, resistance, muscularity)."[12] Here he reveals whom he had always spectrally wished to be: a disciple of William James. Matter is nothing more than this, a name we can bestow with assorted immaterial attributes that cannot be resolved through intuition. The impossibility of believing is a difficulty overcome by affirming that one can believe, first and foremost, in what is not evident and what has not been perceived.

At the end of his essay, Macedonio asserts that this is how it has been in his own experience, which is both the weakest and most convincing piece

---

[8] "No puedo no creer" (Fernández, NTV (1990), 382).
[9] "—Padre mío, ¿cómo me soltaste de la mano? ¿Es que ya no me querías?; y el padre le diga:—Yo morí antes que tú y mi mano muerta te soltó" (Fernández, NTV (1990), 382).
[10] "un *último* psiquismo" (Fernández, NTV (1990), 383).
[11] "la cesación de la serie psíquica individual" (Fernández, NTV (1990), 383).
[12] "cierta familia de psiquismos (color, tactilidad, resistencia, muscularidad)" (Fernández, NTV (1990), 383).

of evidence to support his argument. This is what happens to him, these are the dreams of a subjectless dreamer, or as he used to say, "a dream without a dreamer."[13] Therefore, a temporary inhabitant of eternity only thinks when visited by those fortunate and reparatory moments of immortality sent by dreams into the emptiness that Macedonio fills with his earthly writing, which asks the reader to continue reading amid nothingness what will eventually be a text. His allegation consists of little more than a personal attempt to create the possibility of that impossibility. With respect to his "[b]elief in a psychic non-death," he writes, "I am unable, with all my analytical might, to drive it from my consciousness. Not believing in experience is sometimes a fact of experience. At least that is what is happening to me now."[14] This "now" clarifies everything. The text is the analysis of a dream whose author is unknown to us. William James, in his lectures compiled in *Pragmatism* (1907), wrote, "[Pragmatism] will count mystical experiences if they have practical consequences."[15] In *The Will to Believe* (1897) James says, "There are passional tendencies and volitions which run before and others which come after belief."[16] Macedonio was undoubtedly inspired by this, but rather than employ clever comparisons, examples, and allusions to the dictums of another thinker, he chooses to go beyond James by proposing these death gambits about which he writes and the eternity of the reader who reads them.

---

[13] "un sueño sin soñador" (Fernández, "La metafísica, crítica del conocimiento; la mística, crítica del ser," 194).
[14] "Creencia en la no muerte psíquica [...] no puedo, con toda mi fuerza de análisis, expulsarla de mi conciencia. Es un hecho de experiencia el no creer en la experiencia a veces. Al menos a mí me ocurre ahora" (Fernández, "Una imposibilidad de creer," 383).
[15] James, "Lecture II: What Pragmatism Means," 80.
[16] James, *The Will to Believe*, 11.

No hay proa sin popa / There Is No Bow without the Stern*

Liliana Weinberg

I have here the beginning and the ending of my essay: the bow and the stern of a text that will grow and expand like the metaphysical holes through which Macedonio Fernández summoned everything out of nothing. As a newcomer to this collective work on the verge of completion, I played no part in its conception or development, but it is my responsibility to bring it to a close. The bow and stern of a ship are unmistakable allusions to the powerful forces that drove the avant-garde: a fascination with machines, the possibility of uniting distant objects, and the temptation to "set sail for untouched waters." In this case the ship is a symbol of novelty and discovery, a self-sustaining mechanism, transit between seas and continents. The ship also represents a new way to organize meaning, an ocean crossing aboard a vessel of tremendous draft, and an appeal to metaphor in all its senses, starting with the first, which is itself pure transport, but also novelty, revelation, a link between diverse realities that produces a new meaningful entity: the metaphor is "the spell with which we disordered the rigid universe," writes Borges, to which he adds:

> The metaphor, linking distant things, shatters that dual rigidity. […] But I do not want us to rely on it and I hope that by forgetting it our art can set sail for untouched waters, like the adventurous night sails toward the day's beaches. […] Adding provinces to Being, imagining cities and spaces in the collective reality, is a heroic adventure. Buenos Aires has not yet claimed its poetic immortalization.[1]

---

* Translated from the Spanish by Sean Manning.
[1] "El conjuro mediante el cual desordenamos el universo rígido. […] La metáfora, vinculando cosas lejanas, quiebra esa doble rigidez. […] Pero no quiero que descansemos en ella y ojalá nuestro arte olvidándola pueda zarpar a intactos mares, como zarpa la noche aventurera de las playas del día. […] Añadir provincias al Ser, alucinar ciudades y espacios en la conjunta realidad, es aventura heroica. Buenos Aires no ha recabado su inmortalización poética" (Borges, "Después de las imágenes" (After Images), (1924) 22–3). All translations are by Sean Manning.

In this passage announcing the Borgesian plan for the literary and mythical refounding of Buenos Aires, one of the possible "fabulatory efforts" that will carry the city to its glorious destiny will be none other than "Macedonio Fernández's brilliant and enigmatic Newcomer."[2]

M. F.

The tempting invitation to return to Macedonio Fernández was too much for me to resist; as many authors have said on many occasions, including Borges himself, Macedonio *is* literature. This is borne out by fate: his initials coincide with those of *Martín Fierro*, a foundational work in Argentinian literature whose name we also associate with one of the foremost journals of the Río de la Plata avant-garde. M. F. are initials in a strong and inceptive sense: person, character, song, story, foundation, counterpoint, and refoundation of Argentinian literature. In every one of these cases literature looks at itself looking at reality and reality looks at itself through literature.

In order to read M. F. we must deploy an extensive toolbox that contains everything, but which cannot contain itself: contradiction, irony, paradox, oxymoron, dilemma, loops, and many other artifices, like humor and caricature made solemn and solemnity tenaciously put to the test in the tension between literal and figurative senses, between the arrival at a possible real world and the infinite game of meanings that causes us to break with the conventions of time and leads us to the text itself. Once the box has been opened and the tools laid out before us, we feel that they are not enough: the mystery of Macedonio's genius is still there, and every text is a perfect mechanism that we cannot deactivate without it all being destroyed. M. F. is literature.

Macedonio and *Proa*

If we examine Macedonio's texts published in the first and second iterations of the literary journal *Proa*, we will discover that his inclusion was programmatic,

---

[2] "El genial y soslayado Reciénvenido de Macedonio Fernández" (Borges, 1924, 23).

strategic, and essential.³ In these avant-garde journals spurred by Borges and other young writers associated with the *ultraísmo* and *criollismo* movements and with a general atmosphere of renewal, the inclusion of Macedonio's texts, so vital that they reach beyond their own boundaries and so disruptive that they enable the launching of new imaginary and infinite dimensions, is without a doubt an element heavily endowed with the inchoative nature typical of all inaugurations. Likewise is the place accorded to his figure, complemented and endorsed by Borges's many mentions of him, to the reproduction of some of his letters, to his nods to other authors, or to Dardo Salguero's "Arquicaricatura" (Archicaricature), which together constitute much more than just a message given that it involved the staging, destabilizing inclusion, and antisolemn deployment of an avant-garde program of disruption for which the editorial note that appeared in the first issue was but a starting point.⁴ Macedonio's texts, the Newcomer's pioneering incursions into a city that would become a capital of literary renovation, paved the way for an upheaval whose epicenter would now be Buenos Aires.

Literature and Caricature

A reflection on Macedonio's "archicaricature" reveals certain fundamental keys to understanding some of the mechanics of his writing. As Riccardo Boglione notes in "Dardo vanguardista" (2017) with regard to Salguero's work, these synthetic caricatures, cubist and futurist in nature, rid themselves of political commentary in order to develop as an artistic form. Considering such qualities as instantaneity, essentiality, the mathematical reduction of characteristic traits, and synthetism (the predominance of the structural over the accessorial in the constant effort to move from the living portrait to the abstraction and

---

[3] The initial *Proa* ("bow" in English) released three issues, which included three texts written by Macedonio: "Desperezo en blanco" (Blank Pandiculation), "Macedonerías. Confesiones de un recién llegado al mundo literario" (Macedonioisms. Confessions of a New Arrival to the Literary World), and "El Recién venido" (The Newcomer) as well as "Una epístola del maestro" (An Epistle from the Maestro), written for Borges and signed by Macedonio, and "Versos confesionales" (Confessional Verses), an article signed under the pseudonym Santiago Juárez. The second *Proa* spanned fifteen issues between August 1924 and January 1926 and published four more texts by Macedonio: "La Metafísica, Crítica del Conocimiento; La Mística, Crítica del Ser" (Metaphysics, Critique of Knowledge; Mysticism, Critique of Being), "El 'Capítulo siguiente' de la autobiografía de Recienvenido. De autor ignorado y que no se sabe si es bueno" (The "Next Chapter" from the Autobiography of a Newcomer. By an Ignored Author Who May or May Not Be Good), "Evar Méndez," and "El capítulo siguiente" (The Next Chapter), along with a letter written to Ricardo Güiraldes.
[4] Salguero Dela-Hanty, "Caricatura," 29.

transformation of minute elements) also helps to better understand Macedonio's work between perceived experience and abstraction in a continual exercise to liberate the circumstantial.

Macedonio's pages in *Proa* are fundamental in my opinion when distinguishing between the idea of an accommodation of the European avant-garde and the much more radical undertaking of founding the same avant-garde on this side of the Atlantic. In this sense that Macedonio is an essential figure. In Macedonio's initiatory, antisolemn acts (his literary undertakings and language games) Borges saw the possibility to make Río de la Plata speech the basis for creating the inaugural language and foundational aesthetic of a new literary tradition. There is no *Proa* without Macedonio. Against all solemnity, this precursor who abhorred statues becomes a founder-cum-newcomer, an originator whose actions can be understood as those of one who invites you to stop or to continue on, and who uses literary operations or "artifices" as a starting point as well as a point of flight.

In addition to their programs, nods, gestures, and manifestos, few avant-garde journals were able to include the living and active author himself contributing to the foundation of that proposed new aesthetic. Few journals invited Macedonio to their pages, as *Proa* did, publishing, interpreting, reading, and quoting him while simultaneously constructing their own aesthetic. The constant games through which the hardened figures of author, editor, and reader become disrupted are all part of that foundational aesthetic. Thus, Macedonio Fernández's dual presence, one tangible and one virtual: the texts coexist with the moment of their writing. Macedonio is outside and inside the journal, he makes his appearance while also slinking away, disordering again and again, and hiding, perhaps because, as Carlos García says in his "Arqueología de 'Papeles de Recienvenido' (1929)" (Archaeology of "The Newcomer Papers" (1929)) (2016), he wishes to respect the lack of conclusiveness in his own texts, which we can regard as that eternal pure beginning, that act of enunciation offering itself as the constructive birth of a story, that playful act of naming its own beginning, that celebration of a work-in-progress evincing and revising itself in the actuality of the enunciation.

Pure inception, a foundational act in the discourse of a *criollo* reader of Sterne and Mark Twain, of Schopenhauer and William James, and whom a handful of young writers choose as the inaugural voice for a new avant-garde literature, their ne plus ultra. During those years of *Proa* when Argentina was experiencing a period of political stability and cultural splendor, when publications, innovations, proposals, and theories circulated in abundance, Macedonio also realizes discoveries in the field of logic that he then applies to language: master of recursion and incompleteness, integrator of paradox and irony, creator of parts that are greater than the whole, adept wayfarer of the various levels of meaning, Macedonio makes literature adjoin metaphysics at the horizon of the unsayable and explores the great aesthetic potential of logical enigmas and the traces of the unsayable in everyday life. Paradox returns revitalized to the world of literature and philosophy. Around this same time, Kurt Gödel turns to paradox to study the logical inconsistencies of certain systems and the inconsistencies of a reasoning that is without a resolution while also demonstrating that there can exist a system that is simultaneously inconsistent and complete, or a system that is simultaneously consistent and incomplete. In both cases, these topics are also, by way of the Macedonian conspiracy, relevant to literature. Many are Macedonio's nods to Gómez de la Serna's *greguerías*, but many more are his connections to the Borgesian universe.

Proa, "doing justice to its name" as Borges would, is a declaration in and of itself of an entire program to construct a new aesthetic based on the exploration of the potentialities of the Argentinian language. In *Proa*, beginning with Macedonio's "Desperezo en blanco" (Blank Pandiculation), we witness the *criollo* refoundation of universal literature. Language and reality: naming in absence, naming in presence. The mythical foundation of a literature can arise out of any point in a language, from that inaugural stretching, from the performative act found between dreaming and wakefulness and from which everything emerges. That initial act, that beginning of beginnings, can occur at a time and place as valid as any other: a place in time that we know and, at the same time, do not know, because it is outside our experience, and can thus shroud itself in the solemnity of all beginnings and the anti-solemnity of a witticism. This is how the language of the Argentinians carves out a place for itself in the universal language. And this is how the game of designations escalates, taking on an increasingly greater role: the hair the barber parts down the middle can be the line that slices in two, that divides, as well as the line that duplicates conversations. The eternal singularity that forever condemns boots to be an item in pairs is but another leap, a curl, a loop, through which the very appellative act is forced to confront itself. The language that is able to name holes—a recurrent figure in Macedonio—can also slip through them, transforming them into something bigger and capable of devouring that which names them. "I maintain that nothing is empty and occupiable; extension and time are nothing; everything that is, is something, and, as such, nothing can occupy it," he writes in "La Metafísica, Crítica del Conocimiento; La Mística, Crítica del Ser" (Metaphysics, Critique of Knowledge; Mysticism, Critique of Being), in which he devotes his attention to the problem of representation: "A being contains nothing occupiable. Neither does it readily lend itself to so-called representations; everything is a substantial, full, present state. Any state that claims to be the representation of another is a mere verbalism."[5] A barber's conversation flows and spills out onto the sidewalk where it enters the jurisdiction of the shoemakers: opposite ends meet while also diverging. The world of the senses—the only world we know—becomes an intelligible entity and immerses itself in a new life.

The things, characters, and customs of a city: scissors and barbers, boots and shoemakers, police officers and telegrams, inhabit the street, literature, and language simultaneously. Shaped into figures with a life of their own through the skill of a painter and caricaturist, they become that which demands to be designated in language as well as that to which language refers: nouns achieve a new existence, they become things once again; verbs explore landscapes founded by their own enunciation, like the figures that slip into the paintings of Xul Solar, in order to sketch a new geography detached from Buenos Aires, its things, and its people. Each of Macedonio's texts is the new foundation of a city and language conjoined, and far from being offshoots of another world, they become a new constellation that orbits itself: they become the center. The language and the metaphysical landscape of the Argentinians determine each other, they name themselves, they converse with one another, like hair with a part combed down the middle.

The texts that appear in *Proa* provide us with another of Macedonio's great contributions: the concern for communicating the present of an enunciation, that moment of crisis for the materialized figures of the author, editor, reader, and literary characters who, called into action, reveal their perceptible side on the one hand and their metaphysical side on the other: "It is the reader who is difficult to keep hold of: where might they have wandered off to now?"[6] Language flows into the book that names it. The writer invents the figure of an editor who preexists him and who also names him. The Newcomer himself,

---

[5] "Sostengo que nada hay vacío y ocupable; la extensión y el tiempo nada son; todo lo que es, es algo, y, si tal, nada puede ocuparlo. El ser nada contiene ocupable. Y tampoco se presta a las llamadas representaciones; todo es estado sustancial, pleno, presente. Un estado que sea representación de otro es mero verbalismo" (Fernández 1924, on *Proa*, no. 2, 33–4).

[6] "Lo que es difícil de retener es al lector: ¿por dónde andará ahora?" (Fernández, "El Recién venido," 1923, 4).

who has just arrived at an experience that testifies to his sensitive existence, is not a new arrival to a reality that predates him, but rather a newcomer to a world that only consists of the here and now that anchors him to that sensory experience.

Metaphysics and Literature

The inclusion of one of Macedonio's own texts on metaphysics, a subject that *Proa* would begin to broach in a variety of ways, is significant:

> *Being* and *Present* are one notion in the same. [...] Mere practicalities like causality, time, space, the self, matter, they send their ghost into the mystic soul and generate perplexities like the one contained in this question or pseudo-question. How was reality caused? How did it start? The amazement of being, that something exists, is the result of this conflux and the critique of knowledge or metaphysics revives it with its only assertion: time, space, causality, matter, and the self are nothing, neither forms of judgment, nor intuitions. The world, being, reality, everything, is a dream without a dreamer; one single dream, only a dream and one's own dream only, and thus, no one's dream; the more real it seems, the more it is entirely a dream. [...] The dream is everything; what is not the dream, is not. Matter, what pre-exists and post-exists us is nothing, neither substance nor appearance.[7]

Following these metaphysical reflections would come some of the most memorable texts from Macedonio's Newcomer, where infinite games transpire between the figure of the author, the mobilization of the figure of the reader, and the protagonistic appearance of the editor.

One of those texts is "El capítulo siguiente" (The Next Chapter), in which we observe the extraordinary game of language tenses and levels that result from the Newcomer's birthday: "One might say: But Newcomer, again a year older!

---

[7] "*Ser* y *Presente* son una sola noción. [...] Meras practicidades como son la causalidad, el tiempo, el espacio, el yo, la materia, echan su fantasma en el alma mística y engendran perplejidades como la envuelta en esta pregunta o seudo-pregunta. ¿Cómo fué causada la realidad? ¿Cómo empezó? El asombro de ser, de que algo sea es obra de esta confluxión y la crítica del conocimiento o metafísica, la remueve, con su aserto único: tiempo, espacio, causalidad, materia y yo nada son, ni formas de juicio, ni intuiciones. El mundo, el ser, la realidad, todo, es un sueño sin soñador; un sólo sueño, sólo un sueño y el sueño de uno solo, por tanto el sueño de nadie, tanto más real cuanto más es enteramente un sueño. [...] Todo lo es el sueño; lo que no es sueño, no es. La materia, lo que nos pre-existe y nos pos-existe nada es, ni sustancia ni apariencia" (Macedonio's italics) (Fernández, "La Metafísica," 1924, 31–2).

You never learn; this experience is of no use to you! Another year at your age!"[8] And the struggle between life, customs, and institutions begins: "It's true, I would certainly not do this among friends. But in biographies there is nothing more necessary. [...] In short, the truth [is] I have never aged so many years in a single day."[9] Again, we see the transit between literal and figurative senses.

Movable and Immovable Property

For those of us who were born in Buenos Aires many years ago—and despite the fact that as descendants of immigrants only at very few points could our paths cross with those of the pure-bred criollos, as Macedonio insisted on referring to himself—there is an enormous set of implements whose great practicality is rendered merely aesthetic: matches, canes, hats, urban landscapes occupied by statues and "cordones de la vereda" (sidewalk curbs), by streets and trolleys and trains, by pastry shops and family residences where respectable women toast to their birthdays together with men who live in boarding houses and cheap hotels—a cartography that leads to a Xul Solar painting. Hence, his note in *Papeles de Recienvenido* (The Newcomer Papers) in which he refers to the city where one is "once a newcomer, always a newcomer," where "one must quickly rid oneself of that late newcomerness, that air of having just arrived, the indecorum of not having been born there that is written all over one's face."[10] This is a nod to Ramón Gómez de la Serna and Guillermo de Torre, and a criticism of Ortega y Gasset, who had visited Argentina for the first time in 1916 and remarked on the "grain and livestock heroism" of the Argentinians.[11] Perhaps Macedonio's work, brilliantly anti-heroic and anti-rhetorical, can also be read as a skillful reply to Ortega's preconceptions.

The language games, the changes in discursive levels, the inclusion of voices and figures, the wordplay, the incorporation of characteristically Argentinian objects and references constitute the assertion of a prerogative to exist and to write in the

---

[8] "Alguien dirá: ¡Pero Recienvenido, otra vez de cumpleaños! ¡Ud. no se corrige; la experiencia no le sirve de nada! ¡A su edad cumpliendo años!" (Fernández, 1925, 7).
[9] "Yo efectivamente entre amigos no lo haría. Mas en las biografías nada más exigido. [...] En fin lo cierto [es] que nunca he cumplido tantos años en un solo día" (Fernández, 1925, 7).
[10] "La recienvenidez, de solo una vez, no se la saca uno nunca [...] hay que sacarse pronto la recienvenidez tardía, todo el primera vez llegado, que conoce en los semblantes el mal gusto del no haber nacido en ella" (Fernández PRC (1996), 15).
[11] "heroísmo cereal y ganadero" (Ortega y Gasset, *José Ortega y Gasset*, 48).

register of Buenos Aires Spanish. Objects enter into the discourse that includes them, forcing it to accompany them in their insubordination. Socks, boots, glasses, suitcases, barbers, shoemakers, knives, and scissors participate in this general movement: "If [barbers] used their conversation parted down the middle like that incomparable hairstyle, they would have enough for two customers at once;" in this way, the placement of the city's objects, spaces, and customs into circulation contributes to feeding this apperceptive vision of reality.[12]

Even texts by other writers can be read through the lens of Macedonian disobedience, which exerts pressure on the basic distinctions between genres and mocks the formalities of letters and speeches, of the Book and the Novel, with capital letters. Like in our author's first contribution published in *Proa*, text emerges from an enormous "desperezo en blanco" (blank pandiculation), the naming word is born of gratuitousness and freedom, qualities that in turn merge with humor, like the entire world that, according to Auerbach's timely expression, could be contained in Pantagruel's mouth. Thus, Macedonio's initial act makes it so that everything can be read as Macedonian, including Borges's own text on "La nadería de la personalidad" (The Nothingness of Personality) and his look at the figure of the self, that trap set by language to capture experience.

On Navigations

It was not without reason that *Proa*'s editors would later say, in a letter reprinted in issue 11 in 1925, that "from the very beginning we wanted *Proa*, doing justice to its name, to be a concentrated struggle, more for the work than for the controversy. We work on the freest and sturdiest part of the ship, while literature's bourgeois are asleep in their cabins."[13] And there are many other writers who also looked to the powerful image of the ship, the bow, and navigation, such as Alfonso Reyes, who wrote "in order to reclaim my place atop *Proa*'s figurehead," in the part of the ship most exposed to the wind and the sea[14]; or the works of Xul Solar that appeared in every issue: a ship navigating the time and space of the plastic arts.

---

[12] "Si usasen [peluqueros] la conversación partida al medio como el inimitable peinado, tendrían para dos clientes a la vez" (Fernández, "Desperezo en blanco," 3).
[13] "Hemos querido, desde el principio, que *Proa*, haciendo justicia a su nombre, fuera una concentración de lucha, más por la obra que por la polémica. Trabajamos en el sitio más libre y más duro del barco, mientras en los camarotes duermen los burgueses de la literatura" (Borges et al., "Cartas," 47).
[14] "Para reclamar mi puesto encima del mascarón de *Proa*" (Reyes, "Carta," 51).

I have been saving this passage from Macedonio's "El capítulo siguiente" (The Next Chapter) for the end:

> For this reason, I take great pains to stop here and here I switch myself off as well, for it is late, and even later than now; and it is out of courtesy that the reader deems the conclusion be awakened and that I desire to sink alongside those with whom I sail, rather than be on another ship; likewise I avoid being present at the close of my writings, which is why before that can happen, I end them.[15]

Therefore, reader, I will end my chapter before reaching the stern: we must refrain from being present at the close of our writings, we must risk sinking alongside those with whom we sail, we must elude conclusions before they reach us. I will continue my voyage at the bow: there is no stern without *Proa* / *no hay popa sin Proa*.

---

[15] "Por eso me esmero aquí en cesar y aquí apago yo también que ya es tarde, y aun más tarde que ahora; y es fineza que el lector estima madrugar el concluir y yo gusto de naufragar con quien navego y no yo en otro barco; asimismo huyo de asistir al final de mis escritos, por lo que antes de ello los termino" (Fernández, "El capítulo siguiente," 1925 9).

Contributors

Gonzalo S. Aguirre is a professor at the Law School at the University of Buenos Aires. His research focuses on Aesthetics of Law, Philosophy of the Law, and Literature. He has published several articles in peer-reviewed journals. In his more recent work published in *Philosophy Today* and *Revista ARS de São Paulo* (2019), he reflects through Gilbert Simondon's thought on the formation process of legal norms. He has published a book *Analítica de la crueldad* (Analytics of Cruelty) (Hekht, 2017) and co-edited *Juicio, proceso, drama* (Judgment, Process, Drama) (Aldina, 2018).

Daniel Attala is a professor of Spanish and Latin American literature at the Université de Bretagne-Sud. He holds two PhDs in Humanities and in Spanish and Latin American literature from Pompeu Fabra University. In addition to several articles on literature and philosophy, he has published the following books: *Impensador Mucho. Ensayos sobre Macedonio Fernández* (Corregidor, 2007), *Macedonio Fernández, lector del Quijote* (Paradiso, 2009), and *Macedonio Fernández, "précurseur" de Borges* (Rennes, 2014). He is also the co-author of *Cuando los anarquistas citaban la Biblia. Entre mesianismo y propaganda* (Catarata, 2014), *La Biblia en la literatura hispanoamericana* (Trotta, 2016), and *Chute et rédemption dans la littérature* (Rennes, 2017).

Mónica Bueno is a professor of Argentinean Literature at the University of Mar del Plata and a researcher at the Center of Hispano-American Literatures (CELEHIS). She also directs the research group "Culture and Politics in Argentina" at this center. Her research has mainly focused on the Argentinean avant-garde and on Macedonio Fernández. Among several articles and books, she has published in *Diccionario sobre la novela de Macedonio Fernández* edited by R. Piglia, the book *Macedonio Fernández: un escritor de Fin de siglo* (Corregidor Award, 2001), and co-edited with Piglia and N. Jitrik *Conversaciones imposibles con Macedonio Fernández* (Corregidor, 2002). She has recently published with T. S. Garth the *Tríptico. Alfonsina Storni* (Eudem, 2019).

Ana Camblong is an Emeritus Professor at the National University of Misiones, and specializes in semiotics. She developed and published with Adolfo de

Obieta the first genetic criticism and the UNESCO archive edition of *MNE* in 1993. She has also published several articles in international peer-reviewed journals, book chapters, and the books *Macedonio. Retórica y política de los discursos paradójicos* (Eudeba, 2003) and *Ensayos macedonianos* (Corregidor, 2006), among others.

Federico Fridman is a Visiting Scholar at The Center of Latin American and Caribbean Studies and a Lecturer of Spanish at the University of Michigan, Ann Arbor, where he has taught advanced courses in the Spanish program. He holds a Ph.D. in Romance Studies from Cornell University and a BA in Political Science from the University of Buenos Aires. Although his research has primarily focused on Latin American Studies, his interdisciplinary approach draws upon literary theory, comparative literature, cultural studies, critical theory, transatlantic studies, and more recently, ecocriticism. He has published articles and book chapters on Macedonio, Borges, Alfonso Reyes, and Octavio Paz, among others.

Todd S. Garth is professor of Spanish and Portuguese in the Languages and Cultures Department at the U.S. Naval Academy at Annapolis. His current research focuses on links between realist and post-realist narrative poetics, especially in Latin American and anglophone literature before 1950, with a particular interest in heroic conventions and their alternatives. His most recent book was *Pariah in the Desert: The Heroic and the Monstrous in Horacio Quiroga* (Bucknell University Press, 2015).

Horacio González (1944–2021) held a PhD in Social Science from Sao Pablo University. He was a former director of the National Argentinean Library and professor at several universities, among them the University of Rosario and the University of Buenos Aires. In addition to articles published in journals and books around the world, he published the books: *El filósofo cesante: gracia y desdicha en Macedonio Fernández* (Atuel, 1995), *Restos pampeanos: Ciencia, ensayo y política en la cultura argentina del siglo XX* (Puñaladas, 1999), *Historia crítica de la sociología argentina* (Colihue, 2000), *La crisálida* (Colihue, 2001), *Historia y pasion: La voluntad de pensarlo todo* (Plantea, 2011), and *Saberes de pasillo: Universidad y conocimiento libre* (Paradiso, 2018).

Sean Manning is a lecturer at the University of Texas at Austin in the Department of Spanish and Portuguese, where he received his PhD in Spanish and Latin

American literature. He teaches courses on language, literature, and writing. He is also a literary translator who has translated numerous books and essays including Ida Vitale's *Byobu's ABCs* (Charco Press, 2021), Azahara Palomeque's *American Poems* (Coolgrove Press, 2021), Carlos Pereda's *Lessons in Exile* (Brill, 2018), and Eduardo Lalo's *The Elements*. His translations have also appeared in *Asymptote, Exchanges*, and *aZonal*.

Luis Othoniel Rosa has published the novels *Otra vez me alejo* (Entropía, 2012; Isla Negra, 2013) and *Caja de fractales* (Entropía, 2017; La Secta de los Perros, 2018), which the poet Noel Black translated as *Down with Gargamel!* (Argos Books, 2020). His research on Macedonio is reunited in *Comienzos para una estética anarquista: Borges con Macedonio* (Cuarto Propio, 2016; 2nd edition by Ediciones Corregidor, 2020). He studied at the Universidad de Puerto Rico (Río Piedras) and holds a PhD in Latin American Literature from Princeton University. Currently, he is a professor at the University of Nebraska, Lincoln.

Julio Prieto is professor of Latin American literature at the University of Potsdam. He has published several books of poetry and essays on literary theory, art, and cultural criticism. His recent publications include the poetry book *Marruecos* (Amargord, 2018), the collective volume *Poéticas del presente: perspectivas críticas sobre poesía hispánica contemporánea* (Iberoamericana-Vervuert, 2016; co-edited with Ottmar Ette), and the essay book *La escritura errante: ilegibilidad y políticas del estilo en Latinoamérica* (Iberoamericana-Vervuert, 2016; LASA Iberoamerican Prize 2017).

Ricardo Piglia (1940–2017) was one of the most important contemporary Argentinean writers, a Professor Emeritus at Princeton University, and a scholar whose work has been fundamental to articulating the genealogy of writers in which Macedonio and Borges are inscribed. He published numerous novels including *Respiración artificial* (*Artificial Respiration*) (Pomaire, 1980; Duke University Press, 1994), *Ciudad ausente* (*The Absent City*) (Sudamericana, 1993; Duke University Press, 2000), which is inspired by fundamental tropes in Macedonio's literature, and *Blanco nocturno* (*Target in the Night*) (Anagrama, 2010; Deep Vellum Publishing, 2015). His scholarly work led him to publish several articles and books, and his research on Macedonio, and on other authors, can be found in his books *Teoria del complot* (Mate, 2007) and *Crítica y ficción* (Seix Barral, 2000).

Diego Vecchio is a Professor of Latin American literature and creative writing at the Paris 8 University, a writer, translator and essayist. He has published *Historia calamitatum* (Paradiso, 2000), *Microbios* (Beatriz Viterbo, 2006), and *Osos* (Beatriz Viterbo, 2010). In his book, *Egocidios: Macedonio Fernández y la liquidación del yo* (Beatriz Viterbo, 2003), he develops an exhaustive investigation of Macedonio's philosophy and metaphysics. His last novel *La extinción de las especies* (Anagrama, 2017) was a finalist in the 35th edition of the Herralde Prize for the novel.

Liliana Weinberg holds several prominent positions: professor in the Literature Department at the National Autonomous University of Mexico, a scholar in the Research Center on Latin America and the Caribbean (CIALC), and a member of the committee for the Miguel de Cervantes Prize, among several others. She is one of the most important scholars in the genre of essay and in Latin American history of ideas. She has published several books, among them, *Pensar el ensayo* (Siglo XXI, 2007) and *El ensayo en busca del sentido* (Iberoamericana, 2014). The Mexican Academy of the Spanish Language has recently appointed her as a new member, which is one of the most important distinctions for writers and scholars in Mexico.

Bibliography

Aimino, D. *Apertura y clausura de la metafísica en el pensamiento de Macedonio Fernández (con un apéndice de textos inéditos)*. Córdoba: Alción, 2010.

Abós, A. *Macedonio Fernández: la biografía imposible*. Buenos Aires: Plaza & Janés Editores, 2002.

Agamben, G. *The Coming Community*, Hardt, M. (transl.). Minneapolis: University of Minnesota Press, 1993.

Agamben, G. *Stanzas: Word and Phantasm in Western Culture*, Martinez, R. L. (transl.). Minneapolis: University of Minnesota Press, 1993.

Agamben, G. "O que é um dispositivo," in *Outra travessia* 5 (2005): 9–16.

Aguirre, G. "Filosofía política y política gnoseológica: el problema de enseñar Spinoza a la luz del caso de 'Teoría del Estado,'" *Revista de Filosofía del Derecho*, Año I, 2 (2012): 3–17.

Aristotle. *The Poetics of Aristotle*, Butcher, S. (transl.). London: Macmillan, 1922.

Arlt, R. *Los siete locos / Los lanzallamas*, Oberto, Goloboff, G. M. (ed.). Madrid: Allca XX, 2000.

Arpaly, N. *Unprincipled Virtue: An Inquiry into Moral Agency*. New York: Oxford University Press, 2003.

Attala, D. "Condiciones y sentido de la duda cartesiana," *Análisis filosófico* 12, no. 1 (1992): 1–26.

Attala, D. "De Macedonio a Borges. Un testamento lunático," *Variaciones Borges*, no. 11 (2001): 35–60.

Attala, D. "De la metafísica de la afección al personaje," in J. Premat ed., *Figures d'auteur/Figuras de autor. Cahiers de LI.RI.CO*, vol. 1107–122. Saint Denis: Université de Paris VIII, 2006.

Attala, D. "Naturaleza y anti-naturaleza o Macedonio contra Macedonio," in D. Attala ed., *Impensador mucho: Ensayos sobre Macedonio Fernández*, 237–76, Buenos Aires: Corregidor, 2007.

Attala, D., ed. *Impensador mucho: ensayos sobre Macedonio Fernández*. Buenos Aires: Corregidor, 2007.

Attala, D. "Macedonio y el orden: la aventura del escribir-pensando. O de cómo puede la literatura ser también filosofía," *Cahiers de LI.RI.CO*, 4(2008): 115–33.

Attala, D., ed. *Macedonio Fernández, lector del Quijote (con referencia constante a J. L. Borges)*. Buenos Aires: Paradiso, 2009.

Attala, D. "El amor secreto de Macedonio," *La Nación*, Febr. 2, 2010, Buenos Aires, www-lanacion-com-ar.proxy.lib.umich.edu/cultura/el-amor-secreto-de-macedonio-nid1236429/

Attala, D. *Macedonio Fernández, "précurseur" de Borges*. Rennes: Presses Universitaires de Rennes, 2014.

Bacon, F. *Novum Organum*. London: W. Pickering, 1850.

Badiou, A. *Breve tratado de ontología transitória*, Fernández A. and Eguibar, B. (transl.). Barcelona: Gedisa, 2002.

Balderston, D. "Rex Café, Buenos Aires, 1947: On the Spanish Translation of Gombrowicz's Ferdydurke," *The Polish Review*, 60, no. 2 (2015): 29–37.

Barthes, R. *The Rustle of Language*. New York: Hill and Wang, 1986.

Barthes, R. *Sade, Fourier, Loyola*, Millar, R. (transl.). Berkeley: University of California Press, 1989.

Barletta, L. *Boedo y Florida: una versión distinta*. Buenos Aires: Ediciones Metrópolis, 1967.

Bauman, Z. *Postmodern Ethics*. Malden, MA: Blackwell Publishing, 1993.

Benjamin, W. "The Work of Art in the Age of Mechanical Reproduction," in *Illuminations: Essays and Reflections*, 217–51, Zohn, H. (transl.). New York: Schocken Books, 2007.

Berardi, F. *The Soul at Work: From Alienation to Autonomy*, Cadel, F. and Mecchia, G. (transl.). Los Angeles: Semiotext(e), 2009.

Berlant, L. "Affect is the New Trauma," *The Minnesota Review* 71–72 (2009): 131–6.

Bioy Casares, A. *The Invention of Morel*, Jill Levine (transl.). New York: New York Review Books Classics, 2003.

Boglione, R. "Dardo vanguardista," *La diaria*, Uruguay, April 25, 2017. https://ladiaria.com.uy/articulo/2017/4/dardo-vanguardista/. Consulted September 17, 2020.

Borges, J. L. "Macedonio Fernández—El Recién venido—inédito aún," *Proa* 3(1923): 3–4.

Borges, J. L. "Después de las imágenes," *Proa*, 5 (1924, December): 22–3.

Borges, J. L. "Leyenda policial," *Martín Fierro* 4, no. 38 (1927): 4.

Borges, J. L. "Dos esquinas," in *El idioma de los argentinos*. Buenos Aires: M. Gleizer, 1928, 147–54.

Borges, J. L. [F. Bustos pseud.] "Hombres de la orilla," *Revista Multicolor de los Sábados*, September 10, 1933.

Borges, J. L *Notes. Red Avon Notebook*, Harry Ransom Humanities Research Center, University of Texas at Austin, 1952. Accessed March 2005.

Borges, J. L. "Macedonio Fernández (1874–1952)," *Sur* (1952), 209–10, March–April: 145–47.

Borges, J. L. ed. *Macedonio Fernández*. Buenos Aires: Ediciones Culturales Argentinas, 1961.

Borges, J. L. "Nuestro pobre individualismo," in *Otras inquisiciones. Obras Completas*, 51–53. Buenos Aires: Emecé, 1968.

Borges, J. L. *Obras completas 1923–1972*. Buenos Aires: Emecé, 1974.

Borges, J. L. "Diálogo sobre un diálogo," in *Obras completas 1923–1972*. Buenos Aires: Emecé, 1974.

Borges, J. L. "Testimonio de Borges," *La Opinión*, Transcribed by Martínez, T. E. Buenos Aires, 1974, 11.

Borges, J. L. "La noche de los dones," in *El libro de arena*. Buenos Aires: Emecé, 1975.

Borges, J. L. "Un criollismo conversador del Dios y del mundo," in *El libro de arena*. Buenos Aires: Emecé, 1975.

Borges, J. L. "Macedonio Fernández," in *Prólogos con un prólogo de prólogos*, 174. Buenos Aires: Torres Agüero, 1975.

Borges, J. L. *El aleph, Obras completas*. México: Emecé Editores, 1989.

Borges, J. L. "Pierre Menard, autor del *Quijote*," in *Ficciones, Obras completas*, vol. 1, 444–50. Buenos Aires: Emecé, 1989.

Borges, J. L. *Historia universal de la infamia*. Buenos Aires: Emece, 1991.

Borges, J. L. *Inquisiciones*. Buenos Aires: Seix Barral, 1994.

Borges, J. L. *El tamaño de mi esperanza*. Buenos Aires: Seix Barral, 1994.

Borges, J. L. "El Congreso," in *El libro de arena*, 27–52. Madrid: Alianza, 1997.

Borges, J. L. "Utopía de un hombre que está cansado," in *El libro de arena*, 96–106. Madrid: Alianza, 1997.

Borges, J. L. *Collected Fictions*, Hurley, A. (transl). New York: Viking, 1998.

Borges, J. L. "Tema del traidor y el héroe," in *Ficciones*, 145–52. Barcelona: Emecé, 1998.

Borges, J. L. "Macedonio Fernández (1874–1952)," in *Jorge Luis Borges en Sur, 1931–1980*, 305–07. Buenos Aires: Emecé Ediciones, 1999.

Borges, J. L, "Hombre de la Esquina Rosada," in *Historia universal de la infamia*, 89–103. Madrid: Alianza, 1999.

Borges, J. L. *Textos recobrados (1956–1986)*. Buenos Aires: Emecé, 2007.

Borges, J. L. "Tlön, Uqbar, Orbis Tertius," in *Obras completas*. vol. 1, 431–43. Buenos Aires: Emecé, 1989.

Borges, J. L. "El escritor argentino y la tradición," in *Discusión. Obras completas*. vol. 1, 267–74. Buenos Aires: Emecé, 1989.

Borges, J. L. "Kafka y sus precursores," in *Obras completas*, vol. 2, 107–9. Buenos Aires: Emecé Editores, 2007.

Borges, J. L. "Testimonio de Borges," in *Textos recobrados (1956–1986)*, 175. Transcribed by Tomás Eloy Martínez. Buenos Aires: Emecé, 2007.

Borges, J. L. Caraffa, B., and Güiraldes, R, "Cartas." *Proa*, 11 (1925, June): 47.

Borinsky, A. "Correspondencia de Macedonio Fernández a Gómez de La Serna," *Revista Iberoamericana* 36, no. 70 (1970): 101–23.

Borinsky, A. *Humoristica, novelística y obra abierta en Macedonia Fernandez*. Phil. diss., University of Pittsburgh, 1971 (1972).

Borinsky, A. "Macedonio: Su Proyecto novelístico," *Hispamérica*, vol. 1, no. 1 (1972): 31.

Borinsky, A. *Macedonio Fernández y la teoría crítica: una evaluación*. Buenos Aires: Corregidor, 1987.

Brennan, T. *The Transmission of Affect*. Ithaca: Cornell University Press, 2004.

Bueno, M. *Conversaciones imposibles con Macedonio Fernández. Primeras jornadas de homenaje*, Bueno, M. (ed.). Buenos Aires: Corregidor, 2001.

Bueno, M. *Macedonio Fernández, un escritor de fin de siglo: genealogía de un vanguardista*. Buenos Aires: Corregidor, 2000.

Cadús, R. *La obra de arte del pensar: metafísica y literatura en Macedonio Fernández*. Córdoba: Alción, 2007.

Carnap, R. *Der logische Aufbau der Welt*. Hamburg: Felix Meiner, 1998.

Camblong, A. *Ensayos macedonianos*. Buenos Aires: Corregidor, 2006.

Camblong, A. "Estudio preliminar," *Museo de la novela de la Eterna*, Edición crítica, Coleccion Archivos. Madrid: Fondo de Cultura Económico, 1993.

Camblong, A. "De Macedonio a Borges. Un testamento lunático," *Variaciones Borges*, Numb. 11 (2001): 35–60.

Camblong, A. *Macedonio. Retórica y política de los discursos paradójicos*. Buenos Aires: Eudeba, 2003.

Camblong, A. and Obieta, A. "Primera conversación: Adolfo de Obieta & Ana Camblong," in Bueno, M. (ed.), *Conversaciones imposibles con Macedonio Fernández. Primeras jornadas de homenaje*, 5–25. Buenos Aires: Corregidor, 2001.

Campbell, J. *The Hero with a Thousand Faces*. Princeton: Princeton University Press, 1968.

Carnap, R. "The Elimination of Metaphysics through Logical Analysis of Language," in *Logical Positivism*. Ayer, A. J. (ed.) and Pape, A. (transl.), 60–81. Glencoe: The Free Press, 1959.

Carlyle, T. *On Heroes, Hero Worship and the Heroic in History*, Goldberg, M. K. (notes and intro.). Berkeley: University of California Press, 1993.

Childers, W. "Baroque Quixote: New World Writing and the Collapse of the Heroic Idea," in Zamora, L. Parkinson, and Kaup, M. (eds), *Baroque New Worlds: Representation, Counterconquest*, 415–59. Durham, NC: Duke University Press, 2010.

Cívico-Lyons, I. "El humor de Macedonio Fernández según la teoría del humor basada en esquemas semánticos," *Hispania* 100, no. 3 (2017): 450–60. https://muse.jhu.edu/(accessed June 27, 2018).

Clough, P. and Halley, J., eds. *The Affective Turn: Theorizing the Social*. Durham, NC: Duke University Press, 2007.

Colson, D. *Little Philosophical Lexicon of Anarchism from Proudhon to Deleuze*, Cohn, J. (transl.), Colchester: Minor Compositions, 2019.

Comas de Guembe, D. "Jorge Luis Borges: El sentido heroico de la vida," *Revista de Literaturas Modernas* 29 (1999): 135–46 (accessed June 30, 2018).

Cortázar, J. *Rayuela*, Colección Archivos. Nanterre, France: ALLCA XXe, 1991.

Critchley, S. *Infinitely Demanding: Ethics of Commitment, Politics of Resistance*. London: Verso, 2013.

Croll, M. *Attic and Baroque Prose Style*. Princeton: Princeton University Press, 1969.

Cushman et al, eds. "The Princeton Encyclopedia of Poetry and Poetics." Princeton: Princeton University Press, 2012.

Damasio, A. *The Feeling of What Happens: Body and Emotion in the Making of Consciousness*. San Diego: Harcourt, 1999.

Derrida, J. *The Politics of Friendship*, Collins, G. (transl.). London: Verso, 1997.

Derrida, J. *Spinoza: Practical Philosophy*, Hurley, R. (transl.). San Franscico: City Lights, 2001.

Deleuze, G. and Guattari, F. *Anti-Oedipus Introduction to Schizoanalysis*, Holland, E. (intro.). New York: Routledge, 1999.

Deleuze, G. and Guattari, F. *A Thousand Plateaus: Capitalism and Schizophrenia*, Massumi, B. (transl.). Minneapolis: University of Minnesota Press, 2014.

Deleuze, G. and Guattari, F. *Mil mesetas, capitalismo y esquizofrenia*. Valencia: Pre-textos, 1994.

Deleuze, G. and Guattari, F. *What is Philosophy?* Tomlinson, H. and Burchell, G. (transl.). New York: Columbia University Press, 1994.

Descartes, R. *Discourse on the Method and Meditations on First Philosophy*. New Haven: Yale University Press, 1996.

Descartes, R. *A Discourse on Method. Meditations and Principles*, Veitch, J. (transl.). London: Orion Publishing Group, 2004.

Descartes, R. *Descartes*, Flórez M. C. (intro.). Madrid: Gredos, 2011.

Descartes, R. *Les Passions de l'âme*. InteLex: InteLex, 2001.

Emerson, R. W. "Society and Solitude" (1870), in *Emerson's Complete Works*, vol. 8, 181–210. Boston: Houghton, Mifflin and Company, 1899.

Emerson, R. W. *Representative Men: Seven Lectures*. Williams W. E. (intro. and notes), vol. 4 of *The Collected Works of Ralph Waldo Emerson*. Cambridge, MA: Belknap Press of Harvard University, 1987.

Elbert, M. "From Merlin to Faust: Emerson's Democratization of the 'Heroic Mind,'" in *Merlin Versus Faust: Contending Archetypes in Western Culture*, Spivack, C. (ed.), 113–37. Lewiston, NY: Edwin Mellen Press, 1992.

Engelbert, J. A. "El proyecto narrativo de Macedonio," in *Museo de la novela de la Eterna*, Camblong, A. and Obierta, A. (eds), 373–91. Madrid: Archivos, 1993.

Englebert, J. A. *Macedonio Fernandez and the Spanish American New Novel*. New York: New York University Press, 1978.

Faucher, K. X "The Decompression of Meta-Borges in "Borges and I," *Variaciones Borges*, 17 (2004): 160–85.

Fernández, M. "Desperezo en blanco," *Proa*, no. 1 (1922, August): 2–3.

Fernández, M. "El recien venido (fragmento)," *Proa*, no. 3 (1923): 3–4.

Fernández, M. "La Metafísica, Crítica del Conocimiento; La Mística, Crítica del Ser," *Proa*, no. 2 (1924, September): 30–4.

Fernández, M. "El capítulo siguiente," *Proa*, no. 14 (1925, December): 5–9.

Fernández, M. *No toda es vigilia la de los ojos abiertos: arreglo de papeles que dejó un personaje de novela creado por el arte, Deunamor, el No-Existente Caballero, el estudioso de su esperanza*. Buenos Aires: Gleizer, 1928.

Fernández, M. "Novela de la 'Eterna' y la Niña de dolor, la 'Dulce-Persona' de un amor que no fue sabido," *Libra*, Numb. 1 (1929): 34–46.

Fernández, M. *Papeles de Recienvenido. Cuadernos del Plata 3*. Buenos Aires: Editorial Proa, 1930.

Fernández, M. *Una novela que comienza*. Chile: Ediciones Ercilla, 1941.

Fernández, M. "Cirugía psíquica de extirpación," *Sur*, Numb. 84 (1941): 30–8.

Fernández, M. *Papeles de recienvenido: Continuación de la nada*. Buenos Aires: Losada, 1944.

Fernández, M. "El plagio y la literatura infinita," *Papeles de Buenos Aires*, 3 (1944): 5.

Fernández, M. *Cuadernos de todo y nada*. Buenos Aires: Corregidor, 1972.

Fernández, M. "Diario de vida e ideas," in *Teorías. Obras completas*, vol. 3, Obieta, A. de (ed.), 93–103. Buenos Aires: Corregidor, 1974.

Fernández, M. *Museo de la novela de la Eterna. Obras completas*, vol. 6, Obieta, A. de (ed.). Buenos Aires: Corregidor, 1975.

Fernández, M. *Epistolario. Obras completas*, vol. 2, Borinsky, A. (ed.). Buenos Aires: Corregidor, 1976.

Fernández, M. "Ensayo de una nueva teoría de la psiquis. Metafísica preliminar. Psicología psicológica," in *Papeles antiguos (1892–1907). Obras completas*, vol. 1, Obieta, A. de (ed.), 74–81. Buenos Aires: Corregidor, 1981.

Fernández, M. "Psicología atomística (Quasi-Fantasía)," in *Papeles antiguos (1892–1907), Obras completas*, vol 1, Obieta, A. de (ed.), 39–49. Buenos Aires: Corregidor, 1981.

Fernández, M. "Ensayo de una nueva teoría de la psiquis," in *Papeles antiguos (1892–1907), Obras completas*, vol. 1, Obieta, A. de (ed.), 74–81. Buenos Aires: Corregidor, 1981.

Fernández, M. "La idilio-tragedia," in *Papeles antiguos (1892–1907), Obras completas*, vol. 1, Obieta, A. de (ed.), 144–7. Buenos Aires: Corregidor, 1981.

Fernández, M. "La desherencia," in *Papeles antiguos (1892–1907). Obras completas*, vol. 1, Obieta, A. de (ed.), 65–66. Buenos Aires: Corregidor, 1981.

Fernández, M. "Psicología atomística (Quasi-Fantasía)," in *Papeles antiguos (1892–1907). Obras completas*, vol. 1, Obieta, A. de (ed.), 39–49. Buenos Aires: Corregidor, 1981.

Fernández, M., "La desherencia" (1897), in *La Montaña*, no. 3 (1987, May): 3.

Fernández, M. "Elena Bellamuerte," in *Relatos. Cuentos, poemas y misceláneas. Obras completas*, vol. 7, Obieta, A. de (ed.), 99–103. Buenos Aires: Corregidor, 1987 [1920].

Fernández, M. "Poema de trabajos de estudios de las estéticas de la siesta," in *Relatos. Cuentos, poemas y misceláneas. Obras completas*, vol. 7, Obieta, A. de (ed.), 133–7. Buenos Aires: Corregidor, 1987.

Fernández, M. "La siesta," in *Relatos. Cuentos, poemas y misceláneas. Obras completas*, vol. 7, Obieta, A. de (ed.), 95. Buenos Aires: Corregidor, 1987.

Fernández, M. "El zapallo que se hizo cosmos," in *Relato, cuentos, poemas y misceláneas. Obras completas*, vol. 7, Obieta, A. de (ed.), 51–4. Buenos Aires: Corregidor, 1987.

Fernández, M. "La Santa Cleptomanía," in *Relato, cuentos, poemas y miscelánea. Obras Completas*, vol. 7, Obieta, A. de (ed.), 82–84. Buenos Aires: Corregidor, 1987.

Fernández, M. *Adriana Buenos Aires: Ultima novela mala. Obras completas*, vol. 5, Obieta, A. de (ed). Buenos Aires: Corregidor, 1988.

Fernández, M. *No toda es vigilia la de los ojos abiertos. Obras completas*, vol. 8, Obieta, A. de (ed.). Buenos Aires: Corregidor, 1989.

Fernández, M. *Papeles de recienvenido y continuación de la nada, Obras completas*, vol. 4, Obieta, A. de (ed.). Buenos Aires: Corregidor, 1989.

Fernández, M. "Del Bobo de Buenos Aires," in *Papeles de Recienvenido y Continuación de la nada. Obras completas*, vol. 7, Obieta, A. de (ed.), 109–10. Buenos Aires: Corregidor, 1989.

Fernández, M. "Psicología atomística (Quasi-Fantasía)," in *No toda es vigilia la de los ojos abiertos. Obras completas*, vol. 8, Obieta, A. de (ed.), 23–7. Buenos Aires: Corregidor, 1990.

Fernández, M. "Ensayo de una nueva teoría de la psiquis. Metafísica preliminar. Psicología psicológica," in *No toda es vigilia la de los ojos abiertos. Obras completas*, vol. 8, Obieta, A. de (ed.), 33–40. Buenos Aires: Corregidor, 1990.

Fernández, M. "Bases en metafísica," in *No toda es vigilia la de los ojos abiertos. Obras completas*, vol. 8, Obieta, A. de (ed.), 43–62. Buenos Aires: Corregidor, 1990.

Fernández, M. "La metafísica," in *No toda es vigilia la de los ojos abiertos. Obras completas*, vol. 8, Obieta, A. de (ed.), 63–85. Buenos Aires: Corregidor, 1990.

Fernández, M. "Metafísica," in *No toda es vigilia la de los ojos abiertos. Obras completas*, vol. 8, Obieta, A. de (ed.), 163–77. Buenos Aires: Corregidor, 1990.

Fernández, M. "La metafísica, crítica del conocimiento. La mística, crítica del Ser," in *No toda es vigilia la de los ojos abiertos. Obras completas*, vol. 8, Obieta, A. de (ed.), 193–97. Buenos Aires: Corregidor, 1990.

Fernández, M. "Metafísica del amador," in *No toda es vigilia la de los ojos abiertos. Obras completas*, vol. 8, Obieta, A. de (ed.), 222–24. Buenos Aires: Corregidor, 1990.

Fernández, M. "El asombro de ser. Idealismo absoluto," in *No toda es vigilia la de los ojos abiertos. Obras completas*, vol. 8, Obieta, A. de (ed.), 243–6. Buenos Aires: Corregidor, 1990.

Fernández, M. "¿Sueño o realidad?" in *No toda es vigilia la de los ojos abiertos. Obras completas*, vol. 8, Obieta, A. de (ed.), 249–54. Buenos Aires: Corregidor, 1990.

Fernández, M. "El mundo es un almismo," in *No toda es vigilia la de los ojos abiertos. Obras completas*, vol. 8, Obieta, A. de (ed.), 255–6. Buenos Aires: Corregidor, 1990.

Fernández, M. "Ley de asociación," in *No toda es vigilia la de los ojos abiertos. Obras completas*, vol. 8, Obieta, A. de (ed.), 257–73. Buenos Aires: Corregidor, 1990.

Fernández, M. "Descripcio-Metafísica: el todo pensado como no-ser, como un 'todo' de 'no-ser,'" in *No toda es vigilia la de los ojos abiertos. Obras completas*, vol. 8, Obieta, A. de (ed.), 361–73. Buenos Aires: Corregidor, 1990.

Fernández, M. "Verdades pedantes frías y verdades calientes," in *No toda es vigilia la de los ojos abiertos. Obras completas*, vol. 8, Obieta, A. de (ed.), 375–80. Buenos Aires: Corregidor, 1990.

Fernández, M. "Una imposibilidad de creer," in *No toda es vigilia la de los ojos abiertos. Obras completas*, vol. 8, Obieta, A. de (ed.), 381–3. Buenos Aires: Corregidor, 1990.

Fernández, M. *Teorías. Obras completas*, vol. 3, Obieta, A. de (ed.). Buenos Aires: Corregidor, 1990.

Fernández, M. "Diario de vida e ideas," in *Teorías. Obras completas*, vol. 3, Obieta, A. de (ed.), 95–103. Buenos Aires: Corregidor, 1990.

Fernández, M. "Para una teoría del Estado," in *Teorías. Obras completas*, vol. 3, 115–95, Obieta, A. de (ed.). Buenos Aires: Corregidor, 1990.

Fernández, M. "Para una teoría del arte," in *Teorías. Obras completas*, vol. 3, Obieta, A. de (ed.), 235–51. Buenos Aires: Corregidor, 1990.

Fernández, M. "Para una teoría de la novela," in *Teorías. Obras completas*, vol. 3, Obieta, A. de (ed.), 252–8. Buenos Aires: Corregidor, 1990.

Fernández, M. "Para una teoría de la humorística," in *Teorías. Obras completas*, vol. 3, Obieta, A. de (ed.), 259–308. Buenos Aires: Corregidor, 1990.

Fernández, M. *Epistolario. Obras completas*, vol. 2, Borisnky, A. (ed.). Buenos Aires: Corregidor, 1991.

Fernández, M. *Museo de la novela de la Eterna*, Camblong, A. and Obieta, A de (eds). Madrid: Archivos, 1991.

Fernández, M. *Todo y nada. Obras completas*, vol. 9, Obieta, A. de (ed.). Buenos Aires: Corregidor, 1992.

Fernández, M. *Museo del romanzo della Eterna*, transl. F. Rodríguez Amaya. Genova: Il Nuovo Melangolo, 1992.

Fernández, M. *Museo de la Novela de la Eterna*, Camblong, A. and Obieta, A (eds). Nanterre: ALLCA XX, 1993.

Fernández, M. *Musée du roman de l'Éternelle*, Masson J-C. (transl). Paris: Gallimard, 1993.

Fernández, M. *No toda es vigilia la de los ojos abiertos. Otros escritos metafísicos. Obras completas*, vol. 8, Obieta, A. de (ed.). Buenos Aires: Corregidor, 1994.

Fernández, M. *Todo y nada. Obras completas*, vol. 9, Obieta, A. de (ed.). Buenos Aires: Corregidor, 1995.

Fernández, M. *Papeles de recienvenido y Continuación de la nada. Obras completas*, vol. 4, Obieta, A. de (ed.). Buenos Aires: Corregidor, 1996.

Fernández, M. *Museo de la Novela de la Eterna*, Camblong, A. and Obieta, A. de (eds), 2nd critical edition. Paris: ALLCA XX/Colección Archivos, 1996.

Fernández, M. *Relato, cuentos, poemas y misceláneas. Obras completa*, vol. 7, Obieta, A. de (ed.). Buenos Aires: Corregidor, 1997.

Fernández, M. "Para una teoría del valor," in *Teorías. Obras completas*, vol. 3, Obieta, A. de (ed.), 77–99. Buenos Aires: Corregidor, 1997.
Fernández, M. "Para una teoría del estado," in *Teorías. Obras completas*, vol. 3, Obieta, A. de (ed.), 113–95. Buenos Aires: Corregidor, 1997.
Fernández, M. "Para una teoría del arte," in *Teorías. Obras completas*, vol. 3, Obieta, A. de (ed.), 235–51. Buenos Aires: Corregidor, 1997.
Fernández, M. "Para un teoría de la humorística," in *Teorías, Obras completas*, vol. 3, Obieta, A. de (ed.), 259–308. Buenos Aires: Corregidor, 1997.
Fernández, M. "Bases en metafísica," in *No toda es vigilia la de los ojos abiertos. Obras completas*, vol. 8, Obieta, A. de (ed.), 43–62. Buenos Aires: Corregidor, 2001.
Fernández, M. "La metafísica," in *No toda es vigilia la de los ojos abiertos. Obras completas*, vol. 8, Obieta, A. de (ed.), 63–85. Buenos Aires: Corregidor, 2001.
Fernández, M. "Metafísica," in *No toda es vigilia la de los ojos abiertos. Obras completas*, vol. 8, Obieta, A. de (ed.), 199–214. Buenos Aires: Corregidor, 2001.
Fernández, M. "¿Sueño o realidad?" in *No toda es vigilia la de los ojos abiertos. Obras completas*, vol. 8, Obieta, A. de (ed.), 249–54. Buenos Aires: Corregidor, 2001.
Fernández, M. "Descripcio-Metafísica: el todo pensado como no-ser, como un 'todo' de 'no-ser'," in *No toda es vigilia la de los ojos abiertos. Obras completas*, vol. 8, Obieta, A. de (ed.), 361–73. Buenos Aires: Corregidor, 2001.
Fernández, M. "Brindis a Marinetti," in *Papeles de Recienvenido y continuación de la nada. Obras completas*, vol. 3, Obieta, A. de (ed.), 60–3. Buenos Aires: Corregidor, 2007.
Fernández, M. "Metafísica de 'estatua de Condillac' adicionada de 'asombro de ser'. Veinte comienzos para una Metafísica sin Principios," in Attala, D. (ed.), *Impensador Mucho. Ensayos sobre Macedonio Fernández*, 300–3. Buenos Aires: Corregidor, 2007.
Fernández, M. "Terminología," in Attala, D. (ed.), *Impensador Mucho. Ensayos sobre Macedonio Fernández*, 297–9. Buenos Aires: Corregidor, 2007.
Fernández, M. *The Museum of Eterna's Novel (The First Good Novel)*, Schwartz, M. (transl.). Rochester: Open Letter, 2010.
Fernández, M. *Museu do romance da eterna*, Andrade, G. (transl.). São Paulo: Cosac Naify, 2010.
Fernández, M. "Del Pensador Poco," in *Papeles de Buenos Aires. Edición facsimilar*, Obieta, A. (ed.), 64. Buenos Aires: Biblioteca Nacional, 2013.
Fernández, M. *Das Museum von Eternas Roman*, Petra Strien-Bourmer. Berlin: AB Die Andere Bibliothek, 2014.
Fernández, M. *Museo de la novela de la Eterna (Primera novela buena), Obras completas*, vol. 6, Obieta, A. de (ed.). Buenos Aires: Corregidor, 2015.
Fernández, M. *No toda es vigilia la de los ojos abiertos. Obras completas*, vol. 8. Buenos Aires: Corregidor, 2015.
Forster, E. M. *Aspects of the Novel*. New York:Harbourt, Brace & World, Inc., 1957.
Forster, E. M. *Aspectos de la novela*. Madrid: Debate, 1995.

Foucault, M. "What Is an Author?" in *Language, Counter-Memory, Practice: Selected Essays and Interviews by Michel Foucault*, Bouchard, D. (ed.), 113–38. Ithaca: Cornell University Press, 1989.
Foucault, M. *The Hermeneutics of the Subject. Lectures at the Collège de France 1981–1982*, Buchell, G. (transl.). New York: Palgrave Macmillan, 2004.
Gálvez, M. *Recuerdos de la vida literaria*, vol. 1. Buenos Aires: Hachette, 1961.
García, C., ed. *Correspondencia, 1922–1939: Crónica de una Amistad*. Buenos Aires: Corregidor, 2000.
García, C. "Borges y Macedonio, un incidente de 1928," *Cuadernos Hispanoamericanos*, núm. 585 (1999): 59–66.
García, C. "*Vigilia*: realia. La edición *príncipes* de No toda es vigilia la de los ojos abiertos (1928)," in D. Attala (ed.), *Impensador mucho: Ensayos sobre Macedonio Fernández*, 31–79. Buenos Aires: Corregidor, 2007.
García, C. "Arqueología de Papeles de Recienvenido (Macedonio entre Borges, Méndez y Reyes)," Academia.edu, 2016. García, C., (ed.), accessed August 22, 2020 www.academia.edu/26789448/Arqueolog%C3%ADa_de_Papeles_de_Recienvenido_1929_.
García, G. "Desvivirse de Macedonio Fernández," in Obieta, A. (ed.), *Hablan de Macedonio Fernández*. Buenos Aires: Atuel, 1969.
García, G. "Duelo imposible," in *Macedonio Fernández, la escritura en objeto*. Buenos Aires: Siglo Veintiuno Argentina Editores, 1975.
García, G. *Macedonio Fernández, la escritura en objeto*. Buenos Aires: Siglo Veintiuno Argentina Editores, 1975.
Garth, T. *The Self of the City: Macedonio Fernández, the Argentine Avant-Garde, and Modernity in Buenos Aires*. Lewisburg: Bucknell University Press, 2005.
Garth, T. "Confused Oratory: Borges, Macedonio and the Creation of the Mythological Author," in *MLN* 116, no. 2 (2001): 350–70. Accessed April 18, 2021. www.jstor.org/stable/3251624.
Garth, T. and Dubnick, H. "Uninvited Inversions: Borges, Macedonio and the Genesis of 'Tlön, Uqbar, Orbis Tertius,'" *Variaciones Borges*, no. 26 (2008): 157–70.
Gilman, C. "Florida y Boedo: hostilidades y acuerdos," in D. Viñas (ed.), *Literatura Argentina Siglo XX*, 44–62. Buenos Aires: Fundación Crónica General, 2006.
Goldman, N. *Mariano Moreno: De reformista a insurgente*. Buenos Aires: Edhasa, 2016.
Gombrowicz, W. *Diario argentine*, Pitol, S. (transl.). Buenos Aires: Adriana Hidalgo Editora, 2006.
Gómez de la Serna, R. "Macedonio Fernández," in *Retratos contemporáneos*. 153–174. Buenos Aires, Sudamericana, 1941.
González, H. *La ética picaresca*. Montevideo: Altamira, 1992.
González, H. *El filósofo cesante: gracia y desdicha en Macedonio Fernández*. Buenos Aires: Atuel, 1995.
González, H. *Arlt. Política y locura*. Buenos Aires: Colihue, 1996.

González, H. *Restos pampeanos: Ciencia, ensayo y política en la cultura argentina del siglo XX*. Buenos Aires: Colihue, 1999.

González, H. *Filosofía de la conspiración: marxistas, peronistas y carbonarios*. Buenos Aires: Colihue, 2004.

Heidegger, M. *What Is a Thing?* Burton, W. B. (transl.). New Jersey: Gateway, 1967.

Hegel, G. W. F. *Hegel: The Phenomenology of Spirit*, Inwood, M. J. (transl.). Oxford: Oxford University Press, 2018.

Hernández, J. J. "Borges y la espada justiciera," *Cuadernos Hispanoamericanos* 585 (1999): 67–70, accessed June 30, 2018.

Hume, D. *A Treatise of Human Nature*. London, New York: J. M. Dent; Dutton, 1974.

Hobbes, T. *Leviathan or the Matter, Form, and Power of a Common-Wealth Ecclesiasticall and Civill*, U.K.: McMaster University Archive of the History of Economic Thought, 1998.

Hoggett, P. and Thompson, S. (eds.) *Politics and the Emotions: The Affective Turn in Contemporary Political Studies*. London: Bloomsbury, 2012.

James, W. *The Principles of Psychology*. New York: Henry Holt, 1890.

James, W. *A Pluralistic Universe*. Lincoln, NE: University of Nebraska, 1996.

James, W. "Lecture II: What Pragmatism Means," in *Pragmatism*, 40–81. New York: Longmans, Green, and Co., 1912.

James, W. *The Will to Believe*. New York: Longmans, Green, and Co., 1907.

Jitrik, N. *La novela futura de Macedonio Fernández: con un retrato discontinuo, una antología y una bibliografía*. Caracas: Ed. de la Biblioteca de la Universidad Central de Venezuela, 1973.

Jitrik, N. ed. *Historia crítica de la literatura Argentina, vol. 4*. Buenos Aires, Argentina: Emecé Editores, 1994.

Jitrik, N. ed. *Historia crítica de la literatura Argentina, vol. 8*. Buenos Aires, Argentina: Emecé Editores, 2007.

Kaminsky, G. *Spinoza: la política de las pasiones*. Buenos Aires: Gedisa, 1990.

Kant, I. *Prolegomena to Any Future Metaphysics*, Little Library of Liberal Arts. New York: Liberal Arts Press, 1950.

Kierkegaard, S. *Migajas filosóficas o un poco de filosofía*. Madrid: Trotta, 1997.

Kierkegaard, S. *From the Papers of One Still Living. Kierkegaard's Writings*, vol. 1, Watkin, J. (ed. and transl.). Princeton: Princeton University Press, 2009.

Kierkegaard, S. *Philosophical Fragments and a Bit of Philosophy*, Hong, E. H., and Hong, H. V (eds/transl). Princeton: Princeton University Press, 1985.

Kierkegaard, S. *Either/Or. A Fragment of Life*, Hong, E. H., and Hong, H. V (eds/transl). Princeton: Princeton University Press, 1988.

Kropotkin, P. A. "Anarchism: Its Philosophy and Ideal," in *Anarchism: A Collection of Revolutionary Writings*, 114–44. Mineola: Dover Publications, 2002.

Kropotkin, P. A. *Mutual Aid: A Factor of Evolution*. New York: New York University Press, 1972.

Labanyi, J. "Doing Things: Emotion, Affect and Materiality," *Journal of Spanish Cultural Studies*, 9 (2008): 223–33.

Libertella, H. *Pathografeia: los juegos desviados de la literatura*. Buenos Aires: Grupo Editor Latinoamericano, 1991.

Libertella, H. *Las sagradas escrituras*. Buenos Aires: Sudamericana, 1993.

Lindstrom, N. "Macedonio Fernandez: Strategies against Readerly Sloth," *Latin American Literary Review*, 6, no. 11 (1977): 81–8.

Lindstrom, N. *Macedonio Fernández*. Lincoln: Society of Spanish and Spanish-American Studies, 1981.

Lindstrom, N. "Macedonio Fernández y su reinvención del discurso metafísico," *Revista de crítica literaria latinoamericana*, 11, no. 21/22 (1985): 151–64.

Locke, J. *An Essay Concerning Human Understanding*, Yolton J. W. (ed.). London: Dent, 1993.

Mach, E. *Contributions to the Analysis of the Sensations*, Williams, C. M. (transl.). Chicago and London: The Open Court Publishing Company, 1897.

Mach, E. *The Analysis of Sensations and the Relation of the Physical to the Psychical*, Williams, C. M. (transl.). Chicago and London: The Open Court Publishing Company, 1914.

Marechal, L. *Adán Buenosayres*. Buenos Aires: Seix Barral, 2018.

Marx, K. "Fragment of Machines," in *The Grundrisse*, McLellan, D. (ed.), 690–710. New York: Harper & Row, 1972.

Masiello, Francine *Lenguaje e ideología: las escuelas argentinas de vanguardia*. Buenos Aires, Hachette, 1986.

Mason, P. *Postcapitalism: A Guide to Our Future*. London: Allen Lane, 2015.

Massumi, B. *Parables for the Virtual: Movement, Affect, Sensation*. Durham, NC: Duke University Press, 2002.

Mill, J. S. *A System of Logic, Ratiocinative and Inductive: Being a Connected View of the Principles of Evidence, and Methods of Scientific Investigation*. London: John W. Parker, West Strand, 1843.

Miraux, J-P. *El personaje en la novela*. Buenos Aires: Nueva Visión, 2005.

Monder, S. *Ficciones filosóficas: narrativa y discurso teórico en la obra de Jorge Luis Borges y Macedonio Fernández*. Buenos Aires: Corregidor, 2007.

Montaldo, G. "El origen de la historia," in *Literatura Argentina siglo XX*, Viñas, D. (ed.), 24–29. Buenos Aires: Fundación Crónica General, 2006.

Montaldo, G. "Un argumento contraborgiano en la literatura argentina de los años '80 (Sobre C. Aira, A. Laiseca y Copi)," *Hispamérica* 55 (1990): 105–12.

Montiveros de Mollo, P. "Origen, nacimiento e irradiación de un mito borgeano," in *Coloquio internacional de literatura comparada: El cuento. Homenaje a María Teresa Maiorana*, Montiveros de Mollo, M. (ed.), 138–146. Buenos Aires: Universidad Católica Argentina, 1995.

Morey, M. "Traducir los Pequeños Tratados," in *El Cuaderno. Cuaderno digital de cultura*, 2018. https://elcuadernodigital.com/2018/03/20/en-torno-a-pascal-quignard/ accessed July 16, 2020.

Muñoz, M. "Macedonio Fernández y las vanguardias estéticas," in *El pensamiento alternativo en la Argentina del siglo XX. Vol. I*, 329–37. Buenos Aires: Biblos, 2004.
Muñoz, M. "Macedonio Fernández: su tesis inédita 'De las personas,'" *Cuyo*, vol. 27 (2010): 131–61.
Muñoz, M. *Macedonio Fernández, filósofo: el sujeto, la experiencia y el amor*. Buenos Aires: Corregidor, 2013.
Murena, H. *Los penúltimos días*. Valencia: Pre-textos, 2012.
Musil, R. *The Man without Qualities*. New York: Capricorn Books, 1965.
Nancy, J-L. *A la escucha*. Madrid: Amorrortu, 2007.
Negri, A. *Savage Anomaly: The Power of Spinoza's Metaphysics and Politics*, Hardt, M. (transl.). Minneapolis: University of Minnesota Press, 1999.
Nietzsche, F. *Beyond Good and Evil*, Zimmern, H. (transl.). New York: The Macmillan Company, 2007.
Nietzsche, F. "How the 'Real World' At Last Became A Myth," in *Twilight of the Idols and The Anti-Christ*, Hollingdale, R. J. (transl.), 50–1. London: Penguin Books, 1990.
Nietzsche, F. *Más allá del bien y del mal*. Madrid: Alianza, 2003.
Nietzsche, F. *Humano, demasiado humano*, vol. 1. Madrid: Akal, 2007.
Nietzsche, F. *The Birth of Tragedy*. New York: Dover Publications, 2012.
Nietzsche, F. *Human, All Too Human: A Book for Free Spirits*, Harvey, A. (transl.). Aukland: The Floating Press, 2013.
Obieta, A. de "Inéditos de Macedonio," *Hispamérica, Revista de literatura*, 1–5 (1972): 49–59.
Obieta, A. de "Introduction," in *Museo de la novela de la Eterna*, Camblong, A. and Obieta, A. Madrid: Archivos, 1993.
Obieta, A. de, ed. *Hablan de Macedonio Fernández*. Buenos Aires: Atuel, 1999.
Obieta, A. de, ed. *Macedonio: Memorias errantes*. Buenos Aires: Corregidor, 1999.
Ortega y Gasset, J. *José Ortega y Gasset*, James Maharg (ed.). Madrid: Cultura Hispánica, 1992.
Othoniel, L. Rosa *Comienzos para una estética anarquista: Borges con Macedonio*. Santiago: Editorial Cuarto Propio, 2016.
Pérez Melgosa, A. "Macedonio Fernández's Narrative Pharmakon: The Shared Project of 'Adriana Buenos Aires' and 'Museo de la novela de la Eterna,'" *Latin American Literary Review* 35, no. 70 (2007): 5–30.
Piglia, R. "¿Existe la novela Argentina? Borges y Gombrowicz," *Espacios de crítica y producción*, num. 6 (1987): 13–15.
Piglia, R. *Crítica y ficción*. Buenos Aires: Ediciones Siglo Veinte, 1990.
Piglia, R. *La ciudad ausente*. Buenos Aires: Editorial Sudamericana, 1992.
Piglia, R. *The Absent City*, Waisman, S. (transl.). Durham, NC: Duke University Press, 2000.
Piglia, R. "Notas sobre Macedonio en un diario," *Formas breves*. Barcelona: Anagrama, 2000, 14–28.

Piglia, R. *Teoría del complot*. Buenos Aires: Mate, 2007,

Piglia, R. and Guerra, B. eds. *Diccionario de La novela de Macedonio Fernández*. Buenos Aires: Fondo de Cultura Económica de Argentina, 2000.

Prieto, J. *Desencuadernados: vanguardias ex-céntricas en el Río de la Plata (Macedonio Fernández y Felisberto Hernández)*. Rosario: B. Viterbo Editora, 2002.

Prieto, J. "'Viajeras razones': metafísica y fantasía, o el extraño caso de Macedonio y Borges," *Variaciones Borges* 20 (2005): 197–213.

Prieto, J. "La inquietante extrañeza de la autoría: contrapunto, fugas y espectros del origen en Macedonio y Borges," in Noé Jitrik and Roberto Ferro (eds), *Historia crítica de la literatura argentina*, vol. 8, 475–504. Buenos Aires: Emecé, 2007.

Prieto, J. "Pro cosmética (diálogos con posos de café)," in D. Attala (ed.), *Macedonio Fernández, lector del Quijote (con referencia constante a J. L. Borges)*. Buenos Aires: Paradiso, 2009.

Prieto, J. "(Con)fines de la filosofía," in *De la sombrología: seis comienzos en busca de Macedonio Fernández*, 37–60. Madrid: Iberoamericana, 2010.

Prieto, J. *De la sombrología: seis comienzos en busca de Macedonio Fernández*. Madrid: Iberoamericana Editorial Vervuert, 2010.

Prieto, J. *La escritura errante: ilegibilidad y políticas del estilo en Latinoamérica*. Madrid: Iberoamericana, 2016.

Proa. Revista de Renovación Literaria, Buenos Aires, 1922–1923, Archivo Histórico de Revistas Argentinas (*AHIRA*), https://ahira.com.ar/revistas/proa-revista-de-renovacion-literaria/.

Proa. Buenos Aires, 1924–1926, Archivo Histórico de Revistas Argentinas (AHIRA), https://ahira.com.ar/revistas/proa/.

Proa. Buenos Aires, 1924–1926 Facsimile Edition. Corral, R. and Stanton, A. (eds). Buenos Aires: Biblioteca Nacional Argentina-Fundación Internacional Jorge Luis Borges, 2012.

Proudhon, P. J. *What Is Property?* [s.l.]: Generic NL Freebook Publisher, 1996. https://search.ebscohost.com/direct.asp?db=ifh&jid=2DCH&scope=site (accessed May, 2020).

Ramos Otero, M. *El cuento de la mujer del mar*. Puerto Rico: Ediciones Huracán, 1979.

Ramos Otero, M. *Pagina en blanco y staccato*, Biblioteca de Autores de Puerto Rico. Madrid: Playor, 1988.

Reyes, A. "Carta," *Proa*, no. 11 (1925, June): 51.

Rancière, J. *The Politics of Aesthetics: The Distribution of the Sensible*, Rockhill, G. (transl.). New York: Continuum, 2004.

Ribot, T. *The Psychology of the Emotions*. London: W. Scott Publishing, 1903.

Russell, B. *A History of Western Philosophy*. New York. Simon & Schuster, 1945.

Sada, G. *Macedonio Fernández. Confrontaciones filosóficas*. Buenos Aires: De los Cuatro Vientos, 2011.

Salguero Dela-Hanty, D. "Caricatura de Macedonio Fernández." *Proa*, no. 2 (1924, September): 29.

Salvador, N. "Cronología," *Museo de la novela de la Eterna*, 341–8, Critical ed., Coleccion Archivos. Madrid: Fondo de Cultura Economico, 1993.

Sarlo, B. "Vanguardia y criollismo: la aventura de Martín Fierro," in *Ensayos argentinos: de Sarmiento a la vanguardia*, Altamirano C. and Sarlo B. (eds), 39–69. Buenos Aires: Centro Editor de América Latina, 1983.

Sarlo, B. *Borges, un escritor en las orillas*. Buenos Aires: Ariel, 1995.

Sarlo, B. *Borges, A Writer on the Edge*, King, J. (transl.) London: Verso, 2007.

Schopenhauer, A. *The World as Will and Representation*, Payne, E. F. J. (transl.) New York: Dover Publications, 1969.

Scalabrini Ortiz, R. *El hombre que está solo y espera*. Buenos Aires: Gleizer, 1931.

Scalabrini Ortiz, R. *El hombre que está solo y espera*. Buenos Aires: Plus Ultra, 1964.

Scavino, D. "El autor y su musa," *Figures d'auteur/Figuras de autor*, in Premat J. (ed.), *Cahiers de LI.RI.CO*, vol. 1 (2006): 13–31.

Sedgwick, E. K. *Touching Feeling: Affect, Pedagogy, Performativity*. Durham, NC: Duke University Press, 2003.

Spencer, H. *The Principles of Psychology*, vol. 1. London: Williams and Norgate, 1870.

Spencer, H. *The Principles of Ethics*, vol. 1. London: Williams and Norgate, 1892.

Spinoza, B. *Ethica ordine geometrico demonstrata*. Amsterdam: Rieuwertsz, 1677.

Spinoza, B. *A Theologico-Political Treatise and A Political Treatise*. New York: Dover, 1951.

Spinoza, B. *Ética demostrada según el orden geométrico*, Peña García, V. (transl. and ed.). Madrid: Orbis, 1980.

Spinoza, B. *Tratado teológico-político y Tratado politico*. Madrid: Tecnos, 1996.

Spinoza, B. *Ethics Demonstrated in Geometrical Order*, Bennett, J. (transl.). Early Modern Texts, 2004, www.earlymoderntexts.com/assets/pdfs/spinoza1665.pdf, accessed 1 May 2020.

Spinoza, B. *Ética, demostrada según el orden geométrico*. Madrid: Trotta, 2009.

Thrift, N. *Non-Representational Theory: Space, Politics, Affect*. New York: Routledge, 2007.

Valdés, M. (ed.) *Cien años de filosofía en Hispanoamérica (1910–2010)*. México: Fondo de Cultura Económica, 2016.

Vecchio, D. *Egocidios: Macedonio Fernández y la liquidación del yo*. Rosario: Beatriz Viterbo, 2003.

Virno, P. *A Grammar of the Multitude: For an Analysis of Contemporary Forms of Life*, Isabella B., Cascaito, J. and Casson, A. (transl.). New York: Semiotext(e), 2004.

Visca, A. "Del epistolario de Horacio Quiroga," *Revista de la Biblioteca Nacional*, 5, no. 01 (1972): 45–59.

Weinberg, L. *El ensayo, entre el paraíso y el infierno*. Mexico: Fondo de Cultura Económica, 2001.

Weinberg, L. *Literatura Latinoamericana: Descolonizar la imaginación*. Ciudad de México: Universidad Nacional Autónoma de México, 2004.
Weinberg, L. *El ensayo en busca del sentido*. Madrid: Iberoamericana, 2014.
Wells, R. "Macedonio Fernández At the Front of the Rearguard," *Política Común*, 6, no. 20200129 (2015): 1. doi:10.3998/pc.12322227.0006.010.
Zéraffa, M. *Personne et personnage: le romanesque des années 1920 aux années 1950*. Paris: Klincksieck, 1991.

Index

absolute idealism 62–5. *See also* idealism
aesthetic emotion 170
affects 14, 104, 121–4, 132–3, 137, 151, 176; affective 56, 165–7; affective relations 57; affection(s) 76, 84–5, 87, 97, 148, 150, 152, 165–7, 174, 177; states of affection/affective state 63, 86, 166, 169; philosophy of *afección* (affection) 16, 158, 160; metaphysics of affect 126, 129, 171–4
Agamben, Giorgio 27 n10, 58–9
almismo ayoico (selfless soul/selfless soulism) 33, 44, 63, 83, 88, 94, 110, 124, 138, 147. *See also* selfless soul/selfless soulism
altruística (altruistics) 63–4, 66, 74, 112, 132, 174
anarchism 89, 153, 154–5; anarchist 8, 43, 14–6; anarcho-metaphysics 136; anarchist philosophy 150; anarchist aesthetics 152
anonimia (theory of anonymity) 167, 173, 177
Aristotle 28, 161
Arpaly, Nomy 12, 44, 52, 57
artística de la palabra (artistry of the word) 90. *See also* metafísica artística
Apercepciones (apperceptions) 14–5, 82–86, 90–3, 95, 104–5, 167–8, 170, 175, 203
Attala, Daniel 33, 35, 44
awake, awakened, wakefulness 85, 91, 106, 170, 174

Bacon, Francis 163 n14
Barthes, Roland 28–9, 32
baroque 33, 61, 67, 73, 127–8, 183, 187
Bauman, Zygmunt 12, 46–7, 51, 55–57
Belarte 81, 85–6, 90–1, 96–7, 147
Benjamin, Walter 15, 131, 141–3, 147, 152
Bergson, Henri 121, 167
Berkeley, George 145, 168, 175

Bioy Casares, Adolfo 36
Boglione, Ricardo 197
Borges, Jorge L. 2–6, 23–25, 29, 31–41, 44–48, 50–2, 58–59, 123–5, 129–30, 135, 141–42, 144–5, 154, 158, 165, 186, 195–99, 203
Bosch, Consuelo 13, 61, 68
Borinsky, Alicia 11
Brummel, George 58–9

Camblong, Ana 11, 38, 131
Campbell, J. 29, 30
Carlyle, Thomas 44–54, 46–7, 49–50
Carnap, Rudolf 125
Castañeda, Father 184
conciencia (consciousness) 14, 43, 51–52, 65, 102, 104, 112–3, 124, 136, 148, 164–178; *estado de conciencia* (state of consciousness) 160
contemplation 54, 95, 108, 114
Cortázar, Julio 118, 141
Critchley, Simon 147
crítica del dolor (critique of pain) 126, 133
Croll, Morris 127
culinaria del sentimiento (culinary of feelings) 84–6, 90, 92–3

de Obieta, Elena 4, 171
de Cervantes, Miguel 50, 130
de Obieta, Adolfo 4, 10–11, 27, 69, 145
de la Serna Gómez, Ramón 11, 199, 202
de Torre, Guillermo 6 n18, 202
de Condillac, Étienne Bonnot 168, 171
dreams 106, 108–9, 111, 174, 194; dreaming 58, 85, 110–11, 185, 199; daydream 127
Deleuze, Gilles 95, 122, 128, 143, 145, 150–2, 154
Derrida, Jacques 23, 122, 143
Descartes, René 14, 105, 107–8, 117, 119, 125, 158, 169, 170, 172; cartesian cogito 107, 118, 143, 145, 169

Del Mazo, Gabriel 19
Del Mazo, Angela 35
direct action 144, 147, 151–2, 155–6
Discépolo, Enrique S. 187
Don Quijote (Don Quixote) 36, 116, 129, 143, 155
dudarte (the art of doubting) 102

Emerson, Ralph Waldo 44–5, 47, 49, 51, 58, 161, 173
empiricism 61, 160; empirical 28, 82–3, 97, 163; empiricist 103, 108; radical empiricist 111; empirical theory 163
emoción (emotion) 165–6, 169; pure emotion 170, 172, 174
Engelbert, Jo Ann 11
ethics 12, 43–4, 45–7, 62–4, 81, 132–3, 135, 137, 170, 178
eudemonology 133, 139
experiencia mística (mystical experience) 137, 167–8, 178, 194

Fechner, Gustav 168
Ferro, Roberto 11
fractal 152–4
Foucault, Michel 34, 131
Forster, Edward M. 28
Freud, Sigmund 104, 131, 143

Gálvez, M. 23, 185
García, Carlos 198
Gödel, Kurt 199
Goethe, Johann Wolfgang von 50, 174
González, Horacio 128
Gombrowicz, Witold 10, 185–6
Guattari, Félix 95, 122, 128, 143, 145, 150–2, 154

Habermas, Jürgen 46
hedonismo (hedonism) 172, 176–8
Heidegger, Martin 121, 125
Hernández, Felisberto 111
Hernández, José 184
Hegel, Georg Wilhelm Friedrich 156
Hobbes, Thomas 44, 85–7, 109–10, 153
Hume, David 108, 120, 145, 161

humor 62, 77–8, 122, 168–9, 196; *humorística* (humoristics) 89–90, 92, 102, 117, 150; *humorística conceptual* (conceptual humor) 78, 109, 126; theory of humor 133–4

idealism 54, 111, 167–8, 170–73. *See also* absolute idealism
pure immanence 132, 138; "plane of immanence" 128
imagen (image) 63, 85–7, 104, 136, 165, 171, 176
impression 108, 170, 172
immateriality 119
impure perceptions 14, 105
inmortalidad (immortality) 171
inverse paramnesia 91–3, 96

James, William 17–8, 121, 127, 145, 167, 173, 193–4, 198
Jitrik, Noé 11, 29
Joyce, James 10, 46, 127, 187

Kant, Emmanuel 14, 46–7, 51–2, 61, 104, 128–9, 132, 161, 170, 174, 176, 182
Kierkegaard, Søren 14, 67, 121–5, 136, 158
Kropotkin, Pyotr 153–4

Lagerlöf, Selma 183
lector salteado 30–2, 90. *See also* reader who skips around
lector seguido 90. *See also* orderly reader
Lévinas, Emmanuel 47, 55, 57, 143
Lindstrom, Noemi 11
Libertella, Héctor 123, 134
Locke, John 162
longevismo (longevitism) 168, 175, 177
Lotze, Hermann 168
Lukacs, Georg 142–3
Lugones, Leopoldo 5, 24

Mandelbrot, Benoit 154
Mach, Ernst 168, 168 n27, 171
Marechal, Leopoldo 6 n18
Marx, Karl 121, 131, 145; marxism 131; marxist 152

Massumi, Brian 124–5
materia (matter) 165, 175; material 89, 104, 107, 109, 111, 113, 173
McIntyre, Alastair 46
metafísica de la afección (metaphysics of affection) 121, 126, 171–2
metafísica artística (artistic metaphysics) 173–4, 166
Miraux, Jean-Philippe 28
mysticism 41, 165, 193, 165, 193, 200; mystic 97, 137; mystical state 64, 86, 97, 103, 108–9, 111, 137, 176–8; mystical form of believing 192; mystical union 172; mystical experience 137, 167–8, 178, 194. See also *experiencia mística*
Moreno, Mariano 2
Murena, Héctor A 95
Musil, Robert 186

newcomer 9, 12, 27, 48, 86, 88, 94–5, 196–202. See also *recienvenido*
Nietzsche, Friedrich 52, 62, 83, 95, 120, 122–3, 125, 130, 142
nominalism 121, 137
novelística (novelistics) 89, 90–3, 102

orderly reader 31, 90–1, 94–5. See also *lector seguido*
Ortega y Gasset, José 202
Othoniel Rosa, Luis 44

Pascal, Blaise 127
pathografeia 123
Paul, Apostole 174
Passion 40, 43, 56–57, 61–71, 74, 76–79, 97, 111–3, 121–3, 126, 131–3, 136, 169–72, 174. See also *altruística* (altruistics) and *traslación* (transferal)
pragmatism 194; pragmatists 44, 121; pragmatic consideration 13; pragmatic criterion 173; pragmatic thought 43
philosophies of feeling 122; philosophy of love 174
percepción (perception) 175–6. See also apperception
perfect vision 173

phainomenon 104
Piglia, Ricardo 141, 143, 151
placer-dolor (pleasure-pain) 63, 165
plagiarism 3, 142, 145, 147, 155–6, 158, 184; the poetics of plagiarism 16
Plato 104, 161, 177
plenoamor (total love) 65, 68
Poe, Edgar A. 172
poemática (poematics) 102
Proudhon 145–6, 153
psiquis (psyche) 8, 92, 104, 110–13, 160, 165–7, 175–6, 193
psychology 160–1
pure perception (also see pure vision, pure sensitivity) 33, 83–4, 88, 96–7, 104

Ramos Otero, Manuel 141
reader who skips around 30–1, 90. See also *lector salteado*
realism 115–116
recienvenido 9, 12, 27, 48, 86, 88, 94–5, 196–202. See also newcomer
representación (representation) 2, 28, 32, 52, 63, 83, 87, 91, 94, 109, 131–2, 145, 148, 150–2, 161, 163, 166–7, 172–4, 176, 200
Renzi, Emilio 184
Reyes, Alfonso 203
rhizome 151
Ribot, Théodule-Armand 160, 166, 176
Russell, Bertrand 121

Salguero Dela-Hanty, Dardo 17, 197
Sarmiento, Domingo F. 32
Sarlo, Beatriz 130
Scalabrini Ortiz, Raúl 103
Schopenhauer, Arthur 7, 83, 92, 101, 109, 121, 129, 160–2, 165, 166–70, 172–4, 176–7, 185, 198; Schopenhauer's denial of the Will 170
selfless-soul/selfless soulness 8 33, 44, 63, 71, 79, 83, 88, 97, 110–1, 124, 127, 137–8, 147, 152, 155. See also *almismo ayoico*
sensación (sensation) 31, 75, 85–6, 90, 104–5, 160, 165–71, 175–7

Solar, Xul 200, 202–3
Spencer, Herbert 145, 159–61, 166, 177; spencerian 145
Spinoza, Baruch 14, 52, 62, 87, 121, 133, 135–9, 166
stream of consciousness 127
Stuart Mill, John 162

Tarde, Gabriel 150
theory of humor 78
theory of passion 112–3, 132
theory of the novel 11, 29, 134
theory of the state 89, 134
todo-amador (total-lover) 112
todo-conocibilidad (all-knowingness) 125

traslación (transferal) 112, 174
transvalue 84, 86, 89, 97

unidad místico-práctica (mystical–practical unity) 177

Vaz Ferreira, Carlos 121
verbalismo (verbalism) 163
vision pura (pure vision) 14, 83–4, 103–5, 108, 125
Voltaire 82, 183

Wittgenstein, Ludwig 122, 125, 163, 173

Yrigoyen, Hipólito 187–8